PERSONAL FAITH
AND
INSTITUTIONAL
COMMITMENTS:

ROMAN CATHOLIC
MODERNIST
AND
ANTI-MODERNIST
AUTOBIOGRAPHY

PERSONAL FAITH
AND
INSTITUTIONAL
COMMITMENTS:

ROMAN CATHOLIC MODERNIST
AND
ANTI-MODERNIST AUTOBIOGRAPHY

Edited By:

Lawrence Barmann
Harvey Hill

SCRANTON: The University of Scranton Press

Library of Congress Cataloging-in-Publication Data

Personal faith and institutional commitments : Roman Catholic modernist and
anti-modernist autobiography / [edited] by Lawrence Barmann, Harvey Hill.
   p. cm.
   Includes bibliographical references and index.
   ISBN 1-58966-001-3 (pbk.) 1-58966-020-X (hc)
   1. Modernism (Christian theology)--Catholic Church--History. 2.
Autobiography--Religious aspects--Catholic Church. 3. Catholics--Biography--
History and criticism. I. Barmann, Lawrence F. II. Hill, Harvey, 1965-

BX1396 .P47 2002
273'.9--dc21   2001034672

Distribution:

University of Scranton Press
Chicago Distribution Center
11030 S. Langley
Chicago IL 60628

CONTENTS

FOREWORD

We have been fortunate indeed in the amount and quality of help that we have received on this project, and we would like to acknowledge, however inadequately, some of those who have contributed. First, of course, we would like to thank the authors of the various chapters for their work and for their collegiality. They all responded to editorial requests thoughtfully, promptly, and with good humor. We would especially like to thank C. J. T. Talar, who first conceived of this project and did much to sustain it during the years we worked together on it. We would also like to thank those who formally responded to the chapters when they were presented as working papers at the Seminar on Roman Catholic Modernism at the annual meetings of the American Academy of Religion. The respondents, all of whom offered helpful suggestions, were: John Barbour; Ronald Burke; Michael Fahey, S.J.; Michael Kerlin; John Root; Jeffrey van Arx. The other members of the seminar strengthened the project during the discussions that followed the more formal presentations, as well as with informal advice throughout the year. Thanks particularly to George Gilmore, who handled the logistics for the seminar. Finally, we are grateful to Katie Fellows for her help with the index and to Richard Rousseau, S. J., and the staff at the University of Scranton Press for their interest in this project and the professionalism with which they have brought it to completion.

Lawrence Barmann
Saint Louis University

Harvey Hill
Berry College

INTRODUCTION

John Barbour

This collection of essays should appeal not only to scholars of Roman Catholic modernism,[1] but also to readers interested in autobiography and in problems of Christian belief in the modern world. The book addresses a broader audience through its insights into the roles of autobiography in religious controversy and its exploration of conscience in relation to religious authority, which continues to be a vital and contested issue not only for Roman Catholics but for those from other religious traditions. This introduction suggests several ways in which these essays have larger implications, especially for understanding religious dimensions of autobiography.

The modernists came to doubt or dissent from official positions of the Roman Catholic Church on such matters as biblical criticism, the history of the Church, Thomistic neo-scholastic theology, the Vatican's authoritarian reaction to controversy, or the Church's policies on political issues such as its role in education or Church-State relations. For the individuals studied in this book, autobiographical writing involves documenting their beliefs, doubts, and dissent. Sorting out what they believed, rejected, and wanted to transform at different points in their lives preoccupies them. Albert Houtin, Joseph Turmel, and John R. Slattery eventually left the Church and abandoned Christian faith. When Alfred Loisy was excommunicated, he was relieved. The autobiographies by these individuals offer intriguing views of deconversion, which involves four primary features: intellectual doubt about the truth of a belief system, moral criticism of a way of life, emotional suffering, and disaffiliation from a community.[2] Loss of faith may involve all of these things, but it may also focus on certain aspects of a religious worldview and way of life. Deconversion usually requires a lengthy period of time and may provide the basic plot of a work such as Houtin's *Une vie de prêtre*. The author may delineate the stages of loss of faith and mark ritual moments, as former priests record when they performed their last mass, took off clerical dress, or received the proclamation that made them lose hope for a reconciliation with Rome.

1

Many modernists, however, did not lose their faith. Maude Petre had views that challenged the dominant ideas of the Vatican, but she remained a faithful Christian, probably believing that the Church was not yet ready for her ideas. For someone who did not reject Christianity, autobiographical writing was a defense against the charge of deconversion and a response to those who saw her as undermining the faith of others. Petre explains her actions and motives in the controversy and suggests her understanding of what was essential to Christian faith, what needed criticism, and what needed to be reinterpreted for a new age. Either the reality or the accusation of deconversion thus provides the background for the autobiographical writings of the five authors in this study linked to modernism. (The sixth figure, Luis Martin, is rather different from the others not only in his anti-modernism but in the nature of his personal writing.)

The personal narratives by the modernists are apologias: defenses and moral justifications of the authors' conduct. A person who has lost faith or one accused of apostasy faces moral criticism when he has held a position as priest or teacher. When such a person articulates doubts, he may appear to have been dissembling or hiding his ideas up to that point. How can the reader trust the writer's truthfulness in either the past or the present? Addressing these questions engages the writer in what can be called "the ethics of disbelief," which concerns the considerations that guide both what an individual can believe in good conscience and how he or she informs other people of changing beliefs and doubts.[3] Intellectual issues intertwine with moral scruples in this situation. The demands of critical thought, intellectual honesty, and moral integrity may conflict with commitments to religious creeds and vows.

The writers discussed in this volume defend their veracity and integrity at every stage of their religious development. There is not much confession of sin in these works—or even acknowledgment of mixed motives. I think John Henry Newman's *Apologia Pro Vita Sua* strongly influenced the modernists' conception of what they were doing in writing autobiographically. Newman's work is the paradigmatic example of an autobiography that scrupulously examines the morality of expressing doubt and assent about particular Christian doctrines. Newman went through a form of deconversion as he slowly lost faith in Anglicanism as a "via media" between Catholicism and Protestantism. Although his journey was finally to a new form of faith, Newman was an important role model even for those like Houtin who lost their faith, in that the *Apologia* demonstrated compellingly how one could defend one's integrity to a broad audience.[4] Newman's work is formulated in terms of his efforts to practice certain virtues that are broadly and publicly embraced by those of differing religious views. Newman was widely perceived to have triumphed in his public controversy with Charles Kingsley in spite of prejudice against Catholics in Great Britain. He did not have to convert his audience to his beliefs in order to vindicate his name and ideas. Rather, he had to convince them of his practice of certain virtues. He began his *Apologia Pro Vita Sua* with an appeal to his readers to judge this: "There are virtues indeed, which the world is not fitted to judge of or to uphold, such as faith, hope, and charity: but it can judge about Truthfulness; it can judge about the natural virtues, and Truthfulness is one of them. . . . Mankind has the right to judge of Truthfulness in a Catholic, as in the case of a Protestant, of an Italian, or of a Chinese."[5] As much as an effort to convince others of the substantive truth of his beliefs, Newman's work attempts to vindicate his name by demonstrating his practice of the virtue of truthfulness over the course of his career.

The modernist writers discussed here use similar rhetorical strategies to address a diverse audience composed of Catholics of various theological positions, other Christians, and nonbelievers. The rhetoric of public virtue—of integrity, honesty, and commitment to truth—unites even bitter antagonists about particular Christian doctrines. Such appeals are mixed with specifically Christian arguments and, in scholars like Loisy, Turmel, and Houtin, with new ideals of dispassionate objectivity and scientific rigor. These texts offer insights into the varieties of moral rhetoric, shaping that form of autobiographical writing known as the apologia, and into the ways religious concerns are articulated in a public context.

Again and again, these writers engage in defenses against and accusations of the charge of hypocrisy. Hypocrisy means assuming a false appearance of virtue and hiding one's real character. The issue of hypocrisy inevitably arises in a religious tradition where leaders make vows and public commitments to uphold official positions. For public profession and private belief are not always in harmony. According to *The Oxford English Dictionary*, the term *hypocrisy* originally meant acting a part on the stage. Charles Talar offers an intriguing perspective on the issue of hypocrisy by using Erving Goffman's dramaturgical approach to sociology to describe the ways in which authors respond to disparities between "front stage" official roles and "backstage" realities in the Church, or assert that their own conduct has involved no such disparity. This approach seems helpful in understanding most of these autobiographies. Accusations of hypocrisy and deception flew in both directions. Critics of the Church condemned the facade that its institutions, especially the seminary, presented to aspiring priests, while concealing important matters such as divergent intellectual perspectives or troubling historical facts. Houtin, Turmel, Loisy, and Slattery not only defend their own conduct by explaining their motives, but characterize others as duplicitous or dishonest. Their defense of their own integrity seems to require as a foil the hypocrisy of others. At the same time, the anti-modernists saw the modernists as wolves in sheep's clothing, as hypocrites pretending to profess Christian faith while secretly working to undermine the Church from within. The case of Joseph Turmel's pseudonymous writings was taken as damning evidence of the covertly destructive aims of modernism. Notice how the authors of these six essays see first-person writing in relation to "back-stage" and "front stage" realities. For William Portier and David Schultenover, unpublished first-person documents reveal the person behind the role, the hidden motives that illuminate the public actions of former priest John Slattery, Bishop Denis J. O'Connell, and Luis Martin, the superior general of the Society of Jesus. C.J.T. Talar and Harvey Hill, in contrast, view the formal autobiographies published by Houtin, Turmel, and Loisy as public performances and analyze their works in terms of the unstated agendas and unacknowledged motives that shaped their polemical and apologetic strategies.

The intensity of the conflicts associated with Roman Catholic modernism is illuminated as these autobiographies reveal how intellectual disagreements and differences of faith were entangled in personal relationships. The conflict reflects, too, the participants' common dismay at the acrimony in the institution that functioned as their second home and family. Talar describes how the process of socialization of seminarians deeply affected even those who were essentially loners, such as Houtin and Turmel. This background helps explain the bitterness of those who felt that they had been betrayed or abandoned by old friends or, when the papacy tried to stifle liberal views, by Holy Mother Church. On the anti-modernist side, David Schultenover explores how Luis Martin's family of origin and Spanish understanding of honor and shame influenced his attitude to those whom he saw threatening the unity of the Church. Feelings of resentment, desire for revenge, and aspirations to vindicate one's honor and to shame one's antagonist had deep roots in complex human relationships and cultural values, complicating disagreements over the substantive theological issues confronting the Church. Without reducing the history of ideas to a mere clash of personalities or institutional roles, these essays describe a

complex interplay between intellectual argument and personal relationships, the ways individuals were influenced by many years of socialization in the Church, and the human dramas that unfolded during the
controversy.

The question of the historical value of autobiographical documents
is answered in contrasting ways by the five authors of this collection of
essays, reflecting their recognition of different genres of first-person
writing. Harvey Hill and C.J.T. Talar speak of autobiography as a
performance that may obscure hidden agendas or crucial motivations.
Yet, critically interpreted, their personal narratives are crucial for understanding Loisy, Houtin, and Turmel. William Portier takes J.R.
Slattery's letters and unpublished autobiographical manuscript as
important documentary evidence of the connection between modernism
and the currents of thought that came to be known as Americanism. For
David Schultenover, Martin's *Memorias* reveals his "mythic tale," the
way he understood himself, as well as the sources of his character in
family trauma, struggles with sexuality, and Spanish cultural values.

The scholars approach their texts with diverse theoretical lenses.
Talar's work builds on autobiographical theory and is especially
interesting in its use of sociology. He takes Goffman's ideas about the
presentation of self in social roles to illuminate the reactions of Houtin
and Turmel to discrepancies between the "front stage" public face of the
Church and the true state of affairs "backstage." Anthony Giddens'
conception of social practices helps Talar interpret tensions between the
role of priest and the skills and orientation of a new scholarly breed, the
disinterested academic historian. Ellen Leonard tests Maude Petre's
autobiography against generalizations about women's autobiographies
postulated by literary theorists such as Carolyn Heilbrun, focusing on
the ways women tell their own stories in relation to the stories of the
men in their lives. Harvey Hill's work is primarily a contribution to our
understanding of the most influential modernist, Alfred Loisy, interpreting motives that Loisy does not acknowledge. Since almost no one
has written specifically on Loisy's autobiographies, Hill's essay fills an
important gap in the scholarship on modernism. William Portier dis-
cusses J. R. Slattery in relation to recent historiography dealing with
American Catholicism, exploring the links between modernism and
Americanism. David Schultenover's rich essay creatively integrates
Spanish and Jesuit history, autobiographical theory, Arthur Kleinman's
work on illness narratives, psychological studies of human development,
and cultural anthropology on Mediterranean concepts of honor and
shame. These scholars do not simply use autobiographical texts as

illustrations of a preformulated thesis, but sometimes challenge, complicate, or qualify theoretical orientations, offering new under-standing of both a personal narrative and the limits of generalization, method, or theory.

One of the most intriguing ideas implicit in these essays is that there are similarities between each autobiographer's construction of his or her life and the construal of modernism. Let me offer a hypothesis: Versions of self and versions of modernism may be correlated in terms of various elements of narrative that authors use to describe both personal experience and religious controversy. When they describe the events associated with Roman Catholic modernism, the narrators of these historical accounts see their own stories writ large. It is not just that they tell the larger story from a particular point of view, but that elements of narrative form—the essential plot, the human motivations of pro-tagonists, the narrator's stance, and the significance of events—resemble their own life stories. For example, Maude Petre saw both her own life and the fate of modernism in terms of "martyrdom to the truth," and the genre of a saint's life shaped the way she conceived of both matters. According to Harvey Hill, both Alfred Loisy's autobiographies and his scholarly works deliberately obscured his theological interests and ambitions, downplaying the deeper questions raised by biblical criticism and historical scholarship. In both kinds of writing, Loisy's stance as narrator is the dedicated and disinterested scholar who simply reports historical facts. Talar describes the "binary mentality" of Houtin and Turmel, their assumption that all of Catholic tradition must be either truth or lies. They take the same attitude toward autobiography, asserting their own truthfulness while denouncing the Vatican hierarchy and priests who took other positions. Houtin apparently believed that he could avoid ambiguity in interpretation, as well as self-deception, if he applied the methods of objective scholarship and documentary evidence to his own life and to the history of the Church. To us he seems naive about the difficulty of interpreting human experience without taking account of one's own perspective and values. Hermeneutical self-consciousness seems lacking in his autobiographical and scholarly writing alike. For Houtin and Turmel, the stories of their own lives and of the overall direction of history are conceived as a triumph of rationality over superstition and credulous belief, and the claim of truthfulness entails that other perspectives must be false.

A final correlation between personal history and Church history emerges in David Schultenover's analysis of Jesuit superior general Luis Martin. After detailed analysis of the personal and cultural conflicts that shaped Martin's life, Schultenover turns to Martin's 1900 warning to his order about the dangers of liberalism and "intellectual levity." Martin was concerned that these tendencies would arouse the imagination, distracting priests from religious matters and corrupting their moral purity. This worry reflects his own struggles with prohibited readings and sexual desire. The reasons he opposed liberalism, argues Schultenover, have autobiographical roots that are revealed in his massive *Memorias*. The case of anti-liberal Martin shows another way in which personal experience shaped perception of what was essentially at stake in the modernist controversy.[6] In all of these cases, then, there are analogies between the writer's conception of personal identity and his or her understanding of modernism.

Did certain intellectual tendencies in modernism give a distinctive shape to autobiographical writing? Talar suggests that modernist autobiography may be "homologous with efforts to secure autonomy in apologetics, biblical exegesis, and church history vis-a-vis ecclesiastical authority" (p. 24). Autobiography is indeed often a representation of, and sometimes a theoretical reflection on, a person's desire for autonomy in relation to communal commitments and loyalties. This tendency may explain some of autobiography's appeal to modernists. (According to Schultenover, the only known personal narrative by anti-modernists is Martin's *Memorias*, which stands somewhat apart from the other works considered here because of its form, content, and apparent motivation. Martin wrote his memoirs for himself and did not intend for it to be published.)

A distinctively religious idea, which may have played a role in shaping modernist autobiography, is development. The modernist thinkers were especially concerned to understand the implications of the Church's historical development. Newman's ideas in his *Essay on the Development of Christian Doctrine* about the Church's continuity throughout its history influenced several of these writers.[7] But in 1907 the papacy refused to allow further reflection on the theological significance of historical change and crushed modernist tendencies, disappointing those who hoped for new thinking along those lines. At this point, was the ideal of development displaced from the Church to the self, and to the larger scope of world history? For those who left the Church (Loisy, Houtin, Turmel, and Slattery), idealistic hopes were transferred to the world beyond the Church, and they saw their efforts as contributing to a secular but more ethical post-Christian world. They believed themselves to be working on the side of inexorable laws of history that would finally destroy superstition and usher in a more rational outlook. For those who remained hopeful that the Church would someday welcome historical consciousness, such as Petre, the harsh Vatican repression may have been a factor in redirecting their efforts toward interpreting their personal development. They retained their interest in continuity-in-change, seeking to understand it in the growth of their own mind and faith and suggesting their hopes for the long-term future of Christianity.

It would seem that an autobiographer would find theories of historical development useful in thinking about personal identity, as he or she sought to discern the persistence of a core sense of self and the ways that experience modified that identity. Yet this hypothesis must be qualified by recognition that the concept of individuality, of a unique identity developing and realizing itself in the particularities of historical experience, is not specifically Catholic or Christian, and informs most nineteenth century autobiographical writing.[8]

Is there anything distinctive about the influence on autobiography of specifically Catholic ideas about development? Are there other links between autobiography and modernist thought? These questions suggest an orientation to the essays that follow and a promising direction for further work. Modernist autobiographies, like other personal narratives, need to be understood in relation to conceptions of history, including Christian understandings of Providence and modern theories of development, cultural evolution, and "progress," the secular myth that human destiny is finally subject to human control and that changes are basically for the better.

Is it true that "pour tout comprendre, c'est tout pardonner?" Does understanding more about the lives of these individuals make us more inclined not only to sympathize with them, but to excuse or forgive their morally questionable actions and motives? Does immersion in the subjective worlds of these autobiographers persuade us to adopt their own inevitably favorable view of their actions? What is the appropriate place for moral judgment in scholarship on Roman Catholic modernism? Contrasting responses to these ethical questions are implied by these six essays. Talar finds it necessary to supplement sociological and literary analysis with moral assessment of Houtin's and Turmel's self-representations, for instance, challenging the way that Houtin's skeptical and critical perspective does not apply to the difficult task of self-knowledge. Ellen Leonard's essay not only elucidates Maude Petre's self-understanding, but affirms that Petre successfully "fulfilled her ambition to become a philosopher, a saint, and especially a martyr"(p. 14). Portier's study of John Slattery's writings discloses two sides of

Bishop O'Connell: a scheming ecclesiastical careerist who tailored his views to conform to the official Vatican position, and "Gilpin," the sly fox whom Slattery also knew as traveling and dinner companion, intellectual conversation-partner, and friend. Not only Slattery, but Portier, as well, seem torn between wanting to judge O'Connell negatively as a dishonest opportunist and a more accepting view based on recognition of his personal qualities and the pressures of ecclesiastical politics. Finally, although Luis Martin can be criticized for his part in the harsh repressive measures the papacy used to crush alternative views within the Church, Schultenover's study leads him to a more sympathetic and forgiving judgment: "His personal struggles humanized him and converted a pathological perfectionist into a compassionate and holy man. When, for the sake of unity and fidelity to his office, he felt constrained to come down on men like Tyrrell, he did so only with the greatest care and at the greatest personal cost" (p. 55). While Martin had many character defects, he also knew himself as "first and foremost a loved sinner," and this self-understanding somewhat moderated his disciplining of the modernists. If we are persuaded by Schultenover's reading, access to Martin's *Memorias* enables us to judge him more accurately and more mercifully than we would without the diary's inside view of his life.

In these diverse ways the authors of these essays seek to integrate their primary concern with historical understanding of the autobiographers with normative evaluations of these individuals as Christians, writers about the self, and fallible human beings attempting to live according to their professed ideals and such virtues as courage, honesty, and truthfulness. How does autobiography constitute evidence for a more informed and nuanced moral assessment? Answering this question in contrasting ways, these essays together address a crucial issue for the humanities: the place of ethical judgment in scholarship. They offer, as well, insight into a crucial historical episode with implications for the Roman Catholic Church today. These essays should interest not only Roman Catholics, but anyone who wants to understand how tension between loyalty to religious tradition and the need for creative thinking can engender intellectual controversy and a struggle for moral integrity.[9]

Notes

[1] "Modernism" was a social construct created by Vatican officials and theologians, and formalized in Pope Pius X's encyclical *Pascendi dominici gregis* in 1908, in order to marginalize those Catholic theologians, philosophers, biblical critics, political theorists,

and social activists who were attempting to reconcile the intellectual and social insights of their era with the dogmas of Roman Catholicism as traditionally formulated. The pope's encyclical claimed that the "modernists" were an organized group of subversives, bent on undermining the Catholic faith of millions, and operating from the most demeaning of motives. The encyclical also claimed to have discovered a coherent and destructive philosophico-theological system in the writings of this very heterogeneous group of scholars working in a multitude of different fields. In fact, the modernists were never an organized opposition group; they were merely men and women who came to recognize one another as mutual pilgrims in the struggle toward religious truth. As such they sometimes worked together, but mostly they worked solitarily and supported one another only from a distance and spasmodically. Nonetheless, Rome's absolute and authoritarian crackdown on all Catholics who deviated ever so slightly from the official line led to the excommunication of many of those designated as modernists and the silencing of the rest. Some of these wrote autobiographies to vindicate themselves and to shed light on their perspectives on the crisis. But a serious and scholarly and objective historiography of the Catholic modernist crisis by Roman Catholics themselves was made impossible by Rome's threatening control for more than fifty years. Only since about 1970 has modernist scholarship flourished. The essays in this book, which studies modernist and anti-modernist autobiography, are themselves a product of this scholarly resurgence, having developed from the Roman Catholic Modernism Seminar of the American Academy of Religion. The Seminar's first meeting was held at the 1976 Annual Conference of the American Academy of Religion in St. Louis, MO. It was organized and chaired by Ronald Burke of the University of Nebraska at Omaha. It has been meeting at the same annual conference ever since.

[2] John D. Barbour, *Versions of Deconversion: Autobiography and the Loss of Faith* (Charlottesville, Va: University Press of Virginia, 1994), chapter 2.

[3] *Ibid.*, chapter 6.

[4] Another form of Newman's influence may be that Houtin tries to present Roman Catholic modernism in a way analogous to Newman's version of Anglicanism, as a "via media" that proves ultimately untenable. Slowly and painfully Houtin realizes, as did Newman, that his ideal of intellectual reconciliation finally collapses into two stark alternatives. Newman's choice was between Protestantism and Roman Catholicism. Houtin decides that there is finally no halfway house between traditional Catholic belief and skeptical atheism. Like Newman, he discredits the mediating intellectual position that he had himself occupied for many years. A basic strategy in each autobiography is to dramatize the pathos of a would-be believer in a via media who reluctantly follows his conscience and, condemning mediating positions as hopelessly muddled, confronts the reader with the necessity for the same radical either-or choice.

[5] John Henry Newman, *Apologia Pro Vita Sua*, ed. David DeLaura (New York: Norton, 1968), 8.

[6] To be precise, Schultenover holds that although Martin was not an anti-modernist (for he died in 1904), Martin's anti-liberalism reveals patterns of thought and attitude in the Church that explain the Vatican's harsh reaction to modernism.

[7] See Bernard M.G. Reardon, "Roman Catholic Modernism," in *Nineteenth Century Religious Thought in the West*, volume II, ed. Ninian Smart (Cambridge: Cambridge University Press, 1985), 147: "That Catholic Christianity had not remained the same over the ages did not imply corruption of the 'purity' of the original deposit but rather the natural expression of a vital spiritual impulse. In Newman's own words, 'a power of development is a proof of life, not only in its essay, but in its success . . . A living

idea becomes many, but remains one.' To Loisy the English divine seemed 'the most open-minded theologian the Church had had since Origen.'"

[8] On the emergence of the concept of individuality, which he sees fully manifested in the works of Rousseau and Goethe, see Karl Weintraub, *The Value of the Individual: Self and Circumstance in Autobiography* (Chicago: University of Chicago Press, 1978).

[9] For helpful suggestions, I thank Harvey Hill and Lawrence Barmann, who contributed the description of modernism in the first footnote.

1

More Than A Biblical Critic: Loisy's Reform Agenda in Light of His Autobiographies

Harvey Hill

Alfred Loisy (1857–1940) looms large in any study of modernist autobiography. Over the course of his career, Loisy showed an almost obsessive interest in publicizing his version of his story, particularly the part of his story relating to his career as a Catholic modernist. He first commissioned a confidant, Albert Houtin, to write his biography in 1907, the year that Pope Pius X pronounced the condemnation of modernism and the year before Loisy's excommunication. Shortly thereafter, Loisy decided to undertake the task of telling his story himself, and he published *Choses passées* as a series of articles in *L'Union pour la Vérité* in 1912 which were then published integrally the next year. Loisy returned to this task in 1930 and 1931, when he released his three volume *Mémoires pour servir à l'histoire religieuse de notre temps*, again in 1937 with "From Credence to Faith" (published in English translation), and yet again in 1939 with *Un mythe apologétique*. To these might be added a volume of letters that he published in 1908 and autobiographical sections in other works such as the introduction to *Autour d'un petit livre*, released in 1903. Even apart from this additional material, Loisy's autobiographical output totaled well over 2,000 pages and covered the most significant periods of his Catholic career in exhaustive (and exhausting!) detail. The quality of his autobiographies makes them an exceptionally valuable resource for students of Loisy's role in Roman Catholic modernism, and their quantity makes them an important, arguably the most important, example of modernist autobiography.

In his autobiographical writings, Loisy offered his readers a careful representation of himself and of his religious and intellectual evolution that has served as the starting point for all subsequent interpretations of his work.[1] Loisy presented himself as a disinterested student of history and biblical criticism. Pursuing his research with intellectual integrity and courage led him to the realization that many of the foundational claims of the Catholic Church of his day had little or no grounding in historical fact. This realization troubled him, but he continued to put his historical and biblical scholarship at the service of the Church. Unfortunately, an intransigent and short-sighted hierarchy, blinded by its theological blinkers and/or its ambition for dominance, resisted his efforts and finally drove him from the Church, thus proving Catholicism unable to adapt to modern scholarship. This was the version of his story that Loisy sought to propagate.

There was certainly an element of truth in Loisy's self-presentation and his interpretation of the events that culminated with his excommunication in 1908. But Loisy's version of these complex events was also one-sided, even apart from his picture of the Church hierarchy. Loisy emphasized his disinterested biblical and historical scholarship, but careful analysis of his two most important autobiographical writings, *Choses passées* and the *Mémoires*, shows that Loisy was more than a biblical critic. Despite his own claims to the contrary, formulating a distinctively modern theology, including addressing the contemporary political situation, also played a large role in Loisy's intellectual life.

Personal Apologetics

Before we examine Loisy's stated reasons for writing, we should first note what he claimed *not* to be doing—in both *Choses passées* and the *Mémoires*, Loisy insisted that he was not writing an "apologia." He claimed that he "passes no final judgment upon himself, and [that] he inclines to question the right of others to sit in judgment upon him. He is aware of no need for self-defense." He "scorn[ed] certain defamatory estimations that he will [only] signal briefly in their place."[2] Loisy did not, it seems, seek to write a defense of himself or of his beliefs.

At the same time, Loisy stated that both of his autobiographies sought to set the record straight against those who misrepresented his motivations or those of the modernists more generally. In the preface to *Choses passées*, Loisy claimed to "testify" only to ensure that "our past is not to be placed in a radically wrong light."[3] He made a similar claim in the *Mémoires*, although he put it in broader terms. *Choses passées*, he explained, "was entirely personal . . . ; it aimed rather to report the evolution of a religious thought and conscience than to situate this evolution in the history of the time." The *Mémoires* took up where *Choses passées* left off—it told Loisy's story as part of the larger drama of Roman Catholic modernism. Here too, however, Loisy tried to rebut various misunderstandings of the recent religious past. "Books of ecclesiastical history and biographies of important personages" were too often "not of a scrupulous truth nor of a serene impartiality toward those whom the Church has judged it good to treat as enemies." Once again, Loisy sought "to furnish to readers of good faith a documentation more sure and not tendentious."[4]

Those who placed Loisy's past "in a radically wrong light" tended to err in either of two directions. First, many critics accused Loisy of teaching heresy and leading others astray. These critics, said Loisy, "have already consigned him to the despicable class to which he belongs—that of Judas, forsooth!"[5] In a letter written at the same time that Loisy wrote *Choses passées*, he indicated whom he had in mind. "Mgr Baudrillart," he explained, "has published a *Vie de Mgr d'Hulst*" which, although "materially exact," gave a false "general impression" about Loisy's interactions with d'Hulst.[6] Loisy did not specify which ecclesiastical history or biography inspired him to take up his autobiographical pen again in the late 1920s, but the *Mémoires* gave strong hints. Maurice Clément had published his *Vie du Cardinal Richard* in 1924, and Jean Rivière released *Le modernisme dans l'Église* in 1929.[7] Like Baudrillart, both Clément and Rivière described Loisy as an unfaithful Catholic, and the *Mémoires* rebutted the accounts of both. Loisy explicitly referred to Clément twenty times, ten of them refuting Clément's description of the negotiations with Cardinal Richard that led to Loisy's submission in 1904. Loisy was even more critical of Rivière, whom he mentioned twenty-nine times. Their works seem to have been the biography and the ecclesiastical history whose lack of scrupulous truth and serene impartiality Loisy sought to correct.

At the same time, Loisy faced attacks from his other flank. "Frank unbelievers," he said in *Choses passées*, criticized his "want of insight or of candor" for remaining a Catholic so long and then for not opposing the Church more vigorously.[8] In the *Mémoires*, too, Loisy complained that "The modernists have been incriminated by the Church as if they had wanted cunningly to destroy it; they have become very suspect to others for having had the intention of saving it or for not having decided to combat it after having been rejected by it."[9] Loisy's 1912 letter to von Hügel and his subsequent comments shed light on his opponent to the left in both works. The letter mentioned Albert Houtin's forthcoming history of modernism, although in 1912 Loisy worried more about Baudrillart's biography of d'Hulst. By the time of the *Mémoires*, however, Loisy appeared more interested in Houtin than in Baudrillart. In his comments on his 1912 letter in the *Mémoires*, Loisy ignored Baudrillart altogether to criticize Houtin, and he quoted a letter from Paul Desjardins offering additional criticisms.[10] The likely reason for this increased concern with Houtin in the *Mémoires* was Loisy's realization in 1926, the year before he began work on the *Mémoires*, that Houtin's *Vie d'Alfred Loisy* still existed and that Félix Sartiaux intended to publish it. Loisy presumed (correctly) that Houtin's biography would attack the sincerity of his religious convictions during his years as a Catholic. Loisy could not refute Houtin's biography itself, which did not appear in print until 1960, but he spent nearly five pages in the *Mémoires* undermining Houtin's credibility as a biographer and historian.[11]

Noting the authors to whom Loisy's autobiographies responded suggests the degree to which *Choses passées* and the *Mémoires* shared a polemical agenda, as well as the subtle ways in which they differed. Both sought simultaneously to defend Loisy's integrity and to refute hostile accounts by critics on the left and the right.[12] At this level, the autobiographies told the same story in much the same way. But *Choses passées* focused more on Catholic critics like Baudrillart, with the result that Loisy stressed his *religious* integrity, his sincere (if misguided) commitment to the Church. The *Mémoires*, by contrast, concentrated on rationalist criticisms more than did *Choses passées* and therefore placed more emphasis on Loisy's *intellectual* integrity, his commitment to academic freedom. Both engaged opponents, and essentially the same opponents, but with subtle differences in emphasis that will become clear as we go through the two works in more detail.

However, the first step in refuting competing interpretations of his Catholic career was common to both of Loisy's autobiographies: he sought to discredit their objectivity by emphasizing their dogmatism. In *Choses passées*, he criticized "absolute believers of one or the other category [Catholic or skeptic]" as "intransigents of the right and the left," and he rejoiced that "the dogmatisms, always proud and grandiloquent, were exhausting themselves by their own excesses."[13] And in the *Mémoires*, Loisy expressed his belief and hope that "these fantasies of extremists [in both camps] will fall of themselves with time." He added that these fantasies would fall "provided they do not remain the sole witness to that to which they testify."[14] Loisy's autobiographies—his effort to ensure that such biased presentations did not remain the sole witnesses—did not go unchallenged.

In contrast to his biased opponents, Loisy promised to offer an objective account of the events of his life. His critics, he said, were so blinded by their own prejudices that they could not appreciate the facts in their true significance. He claimed to answer with a simple exposition of the facts. He said, particularly in the *Mémoires*, that he, unlike his critics, would "report impartially towards others as towards himself," and he added that he possessed relevant documents that no one else had. He based his *Mémoires* significantly on these documents, which he described as "personal notes having the character of an intimate journal [and] . . . diverse correspondence preserved by the author." Where "the reference [to his private papers] presented a documentary interest," he promised to cite it, and he promised always "to verify his sources before using them."[15] That is, Loisy would approach his own life as a true historian. Unlike his prejudiced opponents, he would report the facts in an unbiased way based on a critical assessment of the textual evidence. He addressed this report to "those who want simply to know the truth, and who have not made up their minds in advance to a verdict of condemnation," and he asked these "honest readers to examine his witness without prejudice."[16] They would, he assumed, see the superior accuracy of his account.

We can now return to Loisy's denial that either *Choses passées* or the *Mémoires* was an "apologia" and his claim "to scorn certain defamatory estimations that he will [only] signal briefly in their place." The defamations that Loisy claimed to scorn inspired both autobiographies, and both autobiographies were certainly polemical and apologetic in the sense that they attacked opponents and defended Loisy from what he insisted were false accusations. Loisy did not forgo polemics or apologetics—quite the contrary. But to acknowledge that his autobiographies were apologetic would undermine his efforts to portray himself as an unbiased reporter and interpreter of events and thus undermine both his credibility and the persona that he sought to create. Despite his denials, then, his autobiographies were works of personal apology,[17] and their strong emphasis on scientific history rather than personal apologetics was itself part of their polemical and apologetic strategy.

Loisy the Scientific Historian and Critic

The content of Loisy's self-presentation in his autobiographies was consistent with his pose of historical detachment; he portrayed himself as a disinterested biblical critic and historian beset by prejudiced opponents. He claimed that he simply followed the "normal evolution of his thought" which resulted from "studies loyally and disinterestedly pursued" and which he published in works "in no way designed to promote heresy or schism." He sought merely to clarify "the actual incidence of certain historical, theological and ecclesiastical problems." Unfortunately, the Catholic hierarchy reacted by "impressively, even sensationally expelling [him] from the Roman Communion."[18] He was, he conceded, perhaps naïve, at least at the start of his ecclesiastical career, but he was not disloyal or biased in his research. Rather he was a scholar victimized by Catholic intransigence and bigotry.

1. Loisy's 1893 dismissal: Rather than trace Loisy's career as a whole, we will focus on two crucial and contested moments in it in order to illustrate how his polemical and apologetic agenda shaped this self-representation as a disinterested historian and biblical critic. First, we will examine his dismissal from the Institut catholique de Paris in 1893. In that year, Maurice d'Hulst, the rector of the Institut, published an article on "La question biblique" which unleashed a storm of protest, forcing d'Hulst to defend his own orthodoxy and the orthodox reputation of his school. As part of these efforts, he demoted Loisy and then asked for his resignation.[19]

Loisy wrote *Choses passées* in part to correct the impression that Baudrillart's biography of d'Hulst gave of these events. Baudrillart portrayed d'Hulst as the hero of the story, but, in Loisy's view, d'Hulst was quite the opposite; faced with ecclesiastical censure, he sacrificed Loisy to protect his own political interests. As Loisy told the story, d'Hulst's political motivations initially appeared in his decision to demote Loisy. When d'Hulst returned from a trip to Rome to avert a potential condemnation of his article, he visited Loisy to report what had happened. "For the first time," Loisy said, "he seemed to think that my opponents were not altogether in the wrong." D'Hulst even "cited the case of . . . a student of rare ability [the *Mémoires* identified Baudrillart as this student] . . . whom my comments on the Synoptic Gospels had troubled quite recently." D'Hulst said that he therefore felt obliged to confine Loisy to the teaching of languages. Loisy commented that d'Hulst "did not tell me the true reasons, at base entirely political, of his determination."[20]

Loisy's fortunes continued to decline, and he continued to blame d'Hulst's politicking in *Choses passées*. Loisy insisted that "It was understood that . . . my scientific activities should be in no wise curtailed by the change in my situation as a professor," and he reminded his readers that "the revolution in my affairs was not brought about by any published indiscretions of my own, but by the imbroglio provoked by the article which the Rector himself [d'Hulst] had printed on the Biblical Question."[21] Accordingly, Loisy felt free to publish an article distancing himself from the most controversial of d'Hulst's claims. Loisy still wanted to believe, he said in a passage omitted from the *Mémoires*, that "the simple evidence of my principal assertions" and "the merit of my sincerity" would protect him.[22] However, d'Hulst immediately confronted Loisy with his imprudence. Why, he asked, did Loisy not at least postpone publication until after a meeting of the bishop-protectors of the Institut? Loisy responded that he had considered doing so, but that his article was "an act of sincerity" that no one could reasonably fault. Apparently d'Hulst was comforted, and he left Loisy with the promise that "I at least will not carry your case to the Cardinal." Loisy continued the story: "Yet he himself took my article to Cardinal Richard, knowing full well what must be the consequence"—Loisy would be forced to resign from the Institut catholique altogether.[23] In reporting this outcome to Loisy, d'Hulst told him, "You threw yourself before a moving locomotive" by publishing the article. Loisy commented, in a passage omitted from the *Mémoires*, that it was d'Hulst who threw him before the moving locomotive, and added that "to his dying day," d'Hulst "felt the need of explaining his conduct on this occasion. He could not have acted otherwise, he would say. No doubt he would have been glad to be more assured of this than he actually was."

The *Mémoires* told much the same story, often in the same words, with omissions that I have already noted and with additional commentary that, taken together, shifted the blame somewhat. This is not to say that the *Mémoires* exonerated d'Hulst,[24] but the true guilt now lay with the authoritarian structure of the Church itself. "The great culprit," Loisy explained, "is the institution of spiritual tyranny and inquisitorial delation which succeeds in terrorizing, in turning against themselves, souls as noble as that of Maurice d'Hulst, and which induces them to acts contrary to their nature, odious to their conscience, disturbing to their reason." D'Hulst, too, was a victim of the Church, although in a different way than Loisy. "If Maurice d'Hulst died young, it is because . . . he suffered much in his interior, and suffered atrociously, without succeeding in finding in his high piety an entire peace of soul."[25] Almost nowhere else in Loisy's writings did he refer to d'Hulst by his first name, but doing so twice here gave d'Hulst additional humanity, adding pathos to Loisy's final assessment of his life. D'Hulst did victimize Loisy, according to the *Mémoires*, but d'Hulst himself was the greater victim because he allowed ecclesiastical tyranny to rob him of his integrity and ultimately to shorten his life. D'Hulst thus served as a counter-example to Loisy, both illustrating and justifying Loisy's resistance to ecclesiastical authoritarianism by contrast.

Because Baudrillart's biography of d'Hulst conflicted with this presentation of the events surrounding Loisy's dismissal from the Institut catholique, Loisy sought to undermine it. In *Choses passées*, he did not actually cite Baudrillart's biography of d'Hulst in his narration of these events (although he did cite Baudrillart's work as the source for several of the documents that he included in the appendix). Loisy left the differences in their two versions implicit. In the *Mémoires*, on the other hand, Loisy made his differences with Baudrillart explicit. Baudrillart, he began by saying, "had been irreproachable. It was wrong to represent him as having been my denouncer to Mgr d'Hulst." "It is true," Loisy immediately added, "that [Baudrillart] himself had almost suggested the hypothesis," and Loisy gave as evidence a quotation from Baudrillart's biography of d'Hulst. Loisy went on to say that d'Hulst probably did find out what Loisy said in classes from Baudrillart and that Baudrillart "was already in some distrust of my opinions." Finally, Loisy explained that "P. Baudrillart was astonished and pained at the use that had been made against [Loisy] by [Baudrillart's] confidences [to d'Hulst]," thus simultaneously absolving Baudrillart of malicious intent and indicting him for, in fact if not in intent, denouncing Loisy to d'Hulst.[26] The picture of Baudrillart that emerges is one who early opposed Loisy, although not openly or even intentionally. Despite Loisy's comment that Baudrillart had been irreproachable, his witness about Loisy's dismissal becomes suspect.

Loisy continued to undermine Baudrillart's credibility in subsequent passages of the *Mémoires*. Baudrillart heard Loisy deliver the lecture that, when published, led to Loisy's dismissal. Loisy commented, "Mgr Baudrillart, who criticized this study quite severely, without, however, taking the trouble to analyze it, forgot to say that P. Baudrillart heard the lecture, attentive like all the others and moved by the conclusion like the others and more than the others, as it seemed to me."[27] Loisy did not speculate at this point in his narrative on the motives for Baudrillart's change of heart. When Loisy discussed his article itself, he quoted Baudrillart's description of it as a "sovereign imprudence" and a "positive failure of engagements made."[28] Loisy responded, "Nothing was more natural than this publication. One will remark that Mgr Baudrillart placed himself solely at the point of view of opportunity. . . . And as for the 'positive failure of engagements made,' it is a pure fiction." Loisy concluded, "Let us leave Mgr Baudrillart and his administrative opportunism. In order to understand it, we have only to recall that, in the Catholic Church, superiors are never wrong."[29] Baudrillart's "administrative opportunism" and his institutional loyalties, Loisy implied, governed his assessment and description of the article, and, by extension, of events more generally, to the point that his biography was, in places, "pure fiction."

Having called Baudrillart's credibility as an historian into question, Loisy exploited this credibility gap in his narrative of the final events leading to his dismissal. Baudrillart, he noted, published the minutes of the episcopal assembly that resolved to ask for Loisy's resignation, "it seems as an apology for Mgr d'Hulst." After describing d'Hulst's characterization of Loisy's article in the minutes as "laughable," he turned to Baudrillart's comment. "'Mgr d'Hulst,' said Mgr Baudrillart, 'was profoundly saddened at this inevitable denouement' of which 'he had been, not certainly the cause but the occasion.'" But only "if all human actions are determined by fate," added Loisy, was "the denouement inevitable. Otherwise, not."[30] The bitter sarcasm in these lines suggests that this was the heart of Loisy's disagreement with Baudrillart's account. Baudrillart blamed Loisy's dismissal on his imprudence. In response, Loisy insisted that his "imprudence" was an act of intellectual honesty that neither d'Hulst nor Baudrillart could appreciate or understand.

Loisy said less about Maurice Clément's *Vie du Cardinal Richard* in his account of these events, but he viewed it as unfavorably as Baudrillart's *Vie de Mgr d'Hulst*. In the midst of describing his final resignation from the Institut catholique, which occurred in November 1893, Loisy noted that "[Richard's] biographer reported that I submitted my resignation in December under the benevolent counsel of His Eminence." This, he commented, was "an inexplicable blunder on the part of an author who had at his disposal the *Vie de Mgr d'Hulst* and the documents of the archbishopric: Mgr Clément has misinterpreted, as reporting this fictitious resignation, one or two letters that I wrote to the Cardinal about the cessation of *l'Enseignement biblique*."[31] In a footnote, Loisy added that "The whole affair is presented [in Clément's work] under a false light." Demonstrating his own greater regard for documentation and accuracy, Loisy then quoted his actual resignation letter, and he included the date of both composition and posting. As in the case of Baudrillart, so here, the contrast with a Catholic biography highlighted the "scientific" character, and hence greater credibility, of Loisy's work.

Given the contrast that Loisy drew between his sincerity and d'Hulst's politicking, and between the scientific character of his autobiographies and the distortions of Catholic biographies, Loisy had to avoid the appearance that political or theological considerations shaped his own behavior. He did so by emphasizing, particularly in the *Mémoires*, the *clarity* with which he articulated his *scientific* views to his ecclesiastical superiors. Both points were important. He had always, he said, refused to conceal his opinions in an effort to curry favor. For example, although he had, he conceded, edited the controversial lecture that, when published, led to his dismissal, he insisted that this editing did not dilute the lecture's essential message. The published version was still "forceful, frightening in its clarity for people who did not want to see."[32] He did not share d'Hulst's or Baudrillart's "administrative opportunism." Furthermore, theological considerations had not affected the scientific character of the lecture or article. In his survey of the article, he included the potentially embarrassing quotation that "the critic thus offers an apology for the Church against the sects founded on the sole authority of the Bible."[33] Such a statement implied that his critical work had an apologetic or theological agenda, which could undermine its scientific credibility. Loisy commented that "One will allege that the critic does not offer an apology of theological dogmatism," and added, "It is true, and my article itself said enough to be understood [on this point]. But this is another issue. To each day its own task; to each article as well its own object. Mine already contained, it seemed to me, enough of substance."[34] In other words, his critical work was not an apology for the Church in its present form; the article did not mean what it appeared to say. Unlike his opponents in the Catholic hierarchy or the biographies written to defend them, Loisy did not adulterate his history with apologetics. Such, at least, was his apologetic claim, an apologetic claim that was reinforced by and in turn reinforced his polemic against those who, in Loisy's view, misrepresented him.

2. The condemnation of Loisy's works: Both *Choses passées* and the *Mémoires* continued the same apologetic strategy in recounting Loisy's ongoing struggles with the Church hierarchy. In his description of the events surrounding the release and then condemnation of *L'Évangile et l'Église* in 1902 and 1903, Loisy again took great pains to emphasize that he was a critical historian. His book, he said in *Choses passées*, "paved the way, discreetly yet definitely, for an essential reform in Biblical exegesis, the whole of theology, and even in Catholicism generally."[35] And yet he claimed that he simply "set forth facts, from which it seemed to me that certain consequences must follow. I drew the

attention of persons of good faith, as well as that of the Church, to the existing state of the texts and of the evidences. . . . My attitude was perfectly loyal."[36] Despite the reform agenda of L'Évangile et l'Église, Loisy thus continued to insist in Choses passées that he was an historian and nothing more.

As Choses passées continued the story, it established an implicit contrast between Loisy and those who quickly voiced their theological opposition to the views expressed in L'Évangile et l'Église. After a short time, these "zealots for orthodoxy" attacked. Loisy offered the abbé Gayraud as a typical example of a theological critic of his book. Gayraud, Loisy commented, "knew nothing at all about [biblical] criticism, but he wielded a trenchant pen, and he was not even abashed when it was proved to him that he had taken citations of Harnack for the expression of my own views, and had refuted them in that capacity!" Such critics, said Loisy, did not merit a reading, much less a response, and he therefore refused to answer anyone.[37] The general picture that emerges from this account is Loisy the loyal historical critic stoically enduring the ignorant attacks of those who could not understand or appreciate his critical analyses.

When Loisy retold this story in the Mémoires, he stressed his intellectual integrity more than he did in Choses passées by again laying greater emphasis on the clarity with which he articulated his views. Following several sentences that quoted Choses passées exactly, the Mémoires added that the precautions of language in L'Évangile et l'Église "did not tend to dissimulate my opinions, but to remove their aggressive character. Affair of moral honesty rather than political cleverness."[38] Loisy did not deign to conceal his historical opinions. To have done so would have compromised his "moral honesty" by conceding too much to "political cleverness," precisely the accusation Houtin made against Loisy and that Loisy made against d'Hulst.

At the same time, and again paralleling the shift from Choses passées to the Mémoires in his treatment of d'Hulst, Loisy placed greater weight on his opposition to the institutional Church. The reforms that he "discretely insinuated" were no longer in "Biblical exegesis, the whole of theology, and even in Catholicism generally," as in Choses passées. They were now in "the received exegesis, the official theology, and ecclesiastical government in general." And between two paragraphs that came straight from Choses passées, he inserted a new paragraph criticizing "Catholic publicists, official theologians, and the Roman congregations" for their failure to appreciate his "scientific loyalty" and "human sincerity."[39] The contrast between the official representatives of the Church and Loisy the sincere scholar could not be clearer.

The Catholic hierarchy soon voiced its disapproval of Loisy's work, forcing him to engage in extensive negotiations in an effort to find a formula of submission to the judgments against him without compromising his intellectual or moral integrity.[40] Nonetheless, the fact that he submitted at all apparently embarrassed him, and he consistently downplayed the significance of his various "submissions." For example, after quoting his first letter to Cardinal Richard (even before Rome's condemnation), Loisy commented that "This was not going very far, still it went much too far."[41] Richard invited Loisy to come for an audience, but Loisy refused with another letter which, he insisted, "restored to its rightful proportion—that is, to naught—the foregoing 'submission.'"[42] When the Holy Office placed five of his writings, including *L'Évangile et l'Église*, on the Index of Forbidden Books, Loisy again "resolved to perform an act of respectful submission with," he added, "the express reservations which sincerity dictated."[43] Even, he said, his final submission, in which he "condemn[ed] the errors which the Holy Office has already condemned in my writings" without making express reservations, meant little in light of his other letters and an earlier conversation with Cardinal Richard. "Fortunately for myself," he added, "Rome understood quite clearly that my new statement belonged in the same category with the former ones, and signified nothing beyond my wish to remain in the Church, as in my letter to the Pope, and without any disavowal of my opinions as a historian, as in my two letters to Cardinal Merry del Val."[44] Respectful though he was, Loisy said, he remained firm even in his most sweeping submission.

Yet Loisy expressed regret in *Choses passées* at the extent to which he did submit. He followed his second letter to Cardinal Merry del Val with the comment that his letter "was not merely superfluous; it further accentuated the equivocation in which I found myself entangled in my relations with the Church."[45] His language after his final letter was considerably stronger: "I wish that it lay in my power to expunge that note from the record!" Although Loisy had told Richard in a conversation earlier in the day that he did not mean to make an unqualified submission, even in this conversation "there was not wanting a certain equivocation . . . ; and moreover, my declaration would have to be forwarded to Rome, of course unaccompanied by any oral exposition."[46] Although Loisy insisted that he had preserved his integrity in his extended negotiations with the Vatican, he conceded that his "submissions" could be interpreted more broadly than he intended them to be.

The *Mémoires* were more apologetic. In them, Loisy downplayed the degree to which his "submissions" could reasonably be misunderstood, and he insisted more forcefully that his position was always perfectly clear to the Catholic hierarchy. For example, in his considerably expanded commentary on his second letter to Merry del Val, he first attributed his concessions to the advice of two friends. More tellingly, he added that his concluding statement of faith "did not prevent my letter from being superfluous, just as insufficient, as empty, as the first, with regard to Rome, since it made, in terms more moderate but more clear, perhaps, and, one could suspect, with some irony, the same reserves on the article of the submission."[47] He went on to mention his equivocation in terms drawn from *Choses passées*, but cut short his discussion at this point. Similarly after his final concession, Loisy substituted for his expressions of regret the claim that

> in light of the conversation that I had had that morning with Cardinal Richard, this was not an artificial formula and susceptible of being misunderstood. . . . My little letter was a monument of ineptitude, which testified to the extreme fatigue of my mind during those days, rather than an equivocal act and a political subterfuge. . . . If the Holy Office and I had based an equivocal contract on this vague text, it was I who had been duped in it. . . . Cardinal Richard, the Pope, and the Holy Office did not attach any importance to a sheet of paper which signified, for me, nothing.[48]

None of this language appeared in *Choses passées*. There Loisy expressed regret at his submission. Here he insisted that everyone knew exactly what his submission meant: nothing. Insofar as it was an act of equivocation at all, the Holy Office shared fully in the responsibility for it and benefitted from it far more than did Loisy. And in sofaras Loisy had any responsibility at all for the equivocal submission, he blamed his poor health.

The hardening of Loisy's position as presented in the *Mémoires* also appeared in his comments on his intended response to his anticipated excommunication. Before making his final submission, Loisy resolved to wait for excommunication and then to write a last letter to the pope explaining his actions and offering personal sacrifices. He would, he planned to say, renounce his teaching at the Sorbonne and withhold his current publishing projects. In *Choses passées*, he added, "His Holiness could judge whether or not to maintain in its rigor the censure that had been brought against me."[49] The *Mémoires* followed *Choses passées* until this sentence, and then substituted "I did not flatter myself that I might obtain, by this means, my reconciliation; to tell the truth, I am not sure that I wanted it."[50] On the advice of friends, Loisy decided not to wait for his excommunication before informing the pope of the sacrifices he was willing to make. But the important point, for our purposes, is the way in which he altered the tone of his plan by changing the final sentence. Loisy portrayed himself as more intransigent vis-à-vis Roman demands in the *Mémoires* than in *Choses passées*. Presumably he did so because he had a different antagonist in mind. In *Choses passées* he was more concerned to vindicate the integrity of his religious convictions against Catholic critics like Baudrillart. In the *Mémoires*, he was more concerned to vindicate his moral and intellectual integrity against skeptical critics like Houtin.

Further highlighting Loisy's intellectual integrity was the contrast that he drew in the *Mémoires* between his own (apparently) disinterested recounting of the facts and Clément's tendentious biography of Cardinal Richard. According to Loisy, Clément selectively omitted relevant information in order to present Loisy's difficulties with Cardinal Richard in a false light. Clément "amputated" Loisy's first letter to Merry del Val and omitted altogether Merry del Val's response in favor of a brief summary. Loisy quoted this summary and commented, "It is almost touching; but the complete text would have given an entirely different impression."[51] After noting more omissions, Loisy added, "The two omissions, which could not have been made in the interest of truth, were made, I believe, in the interest of edification."[52] The contrast between edification which depended on a falsehood and truth was, Loisy implied, the difference between Clément's hagiography and the kind of critical history that Loisy himself did both as a scholar and as an autobiographer. Loisy continued to accuse Clément of misrepresenting him and his negotiations in an effort to make the Catholic hierarchy look more humane, and Loisy continued to try to correct this biased and untrue view.[53] Clément thus served as a foil for Loisy's presentation of these events, just as Baudrillart had served as a foil for Loisy's presentation of the events surrounding his dismissal from the Institut catholique. Once again, his polemic reinforced his apology.

Complementing his efforts to defend his own integrity and to demonstrate the superiority of his account to the accounts of writers like Clément, Loisy continued to emphasize his professional identity as a pure historian and biblical critic. His scientific works, he said, took precedence over theological polemics, at least in his own mind. For example, faced with Richard's initial censure of *L'Évangile et l'Église*,

Loisy claimed that he defended his intellectual liberty by continuing "to work without ceasing and to produce studies of critical exegesis as independent as the progress of my thought allowed."[54] Following the publication of *Autour d'un petit livre* shortly thereafter, Loisy commented, "I received many blows without giving any. I had, as always, works to continue."[55] And at the beginning of his account of his negotiations with the Vatican, Loisy said,

> In place of declaring plainly, as I did in 1908, that such a requirement [of submission] was stupid and that I was not obliged to make myself stupid in conformity to it, I was going to enter into confused and useless negotiations in order to make the Holy Office recognize . . . that it did not have either the power or the right to impose on anyone historical or scientific opinions or any opinions at all.[56]

His negotiations had as their purpose not the prevention of his excommunication but the education of the Holy Office—Loisy negotiated in order to defend critical history from the Church's illegitimate pretensions to govern it. Thus, throughout his "duel with the Vatican" in the early years of the twentieth century, Loisy portrayed himself as a simple historian who did his historical work with little regard for the theological polemics that it caused and who engaged in theological and/or political debate only for the cause of critical history itself. Ironically, this self-representation as a disinterested historian was the key to his polemical and apologetic strategy, the key to the very interested interpretation that Loisy offered of his own life.

Loisy's Larger Agenda

Given that Loisy sought to portray himself as a disinterested scholar beset by opponents who did not appreciate scientific objectivity, he necessarily downplayed any polemical and apologetic agenda in his work. I have suggested, however, that Loisy's autobiographies were polemical and apologetic—he wrote to discredit opponents and to defend himself—and that his self-representation as a disinterested scholar was actually part of a polemical and apologetic strategy.[57] This equivocation on the apologetic goals of his work dated back at least to 1902 and *L'Évangile et l'Église*. Despite Loisy's claims in that book, scholars are appropriately skeptical that it was exclusively an historical refutation of Harnack and have noted that his true target seems to have been Catholic theology.[58] Might we ask the same kind of question about his autobiographies and the claims they made for his critical work more generally? Was he as focused on critical exegesis as his autobiographies suggested? Put differently, if Loisy placed his biblical criticism on what C.J.T. Talar, following Erving Goffman, calls the "frontstage" in the interests of his polemical and apologetic strategy, what can we say about the "backstage," those aspects of his intellectual and religious agenda that he deemphasized for the same reason?[59] The rest of this chapter will argue that at least three backstage issues were important to Loisy: his academic reputation; modern(ist) theology; and French politics.

1. His academic reputation: Although Loisy said little about his academic reputation in his autobiographies, his concern about it seems to have influenced his behavior in his negotiations with the Vatican. Beginning in 1900, Loisy taught courses at the Sorbonne as an adjunct professor, and he was willing to use his position there as political leverage with representatives of the Church.[60] However, he soon had to defend his career at the Sorbonne against threats posed to his academic reputation by the requirements of the Catholic hierarchy. "Concerned by my adhesion to the censure of Cardinal Richard [on *L'Évangile et l'Église*]," he reported in the *Mémoires*, "the section of the Religious Sciences at the École des Hautes Études seemed disposed not to renew my course for the year 1903–1904."[61] In a letter written at this time and marked "confidential," Loisy identified two possible responses:

> My adhesion to the sentence of the Cardinal has compromised my situation at the Sorbonne and it is a question of suppressing my course next year. If, therefore, the condemnation of Rome comes, I will be obliged to publish an act establishing that I reserve my full liberty as a scholar or else quit the Sorbonne without waiting to be chased out.

Given these options, Loisy's choice was easy. "I will publish the act, a letter to M. Réville, which is already written. And I have the intention of publishing soon an explanation of the little book [*L'Évangile et l'Église*]. They will quickly condemn it if they want; but my situation will be clear with the scholarly world."[62] In another letter a few months later, Loisy again mentioned the publication of "the little apologetic volume" and a commentary on the fourth gospel. "My scientific situation will," he commented, "be well-established and the censures, if they come, will mean nothing."[63] In yet another letter, he reported that Cardinal Richard had announced Loisy's submission in two newspapers. Albert Réville, the head of the section of the Religious Sciences at the École, had previously informed Loisy, he continued, that "a retraction in the sense that Cardinal Richard understands it would hurt me in public opinion and would render impossible the continuation of my course even for the present year. I immediately rectified, in two papers, the communiqué of the archbishopric."[64] These letters suggest that Loisy's negotiations with Cardinal Richard and the Vatican over the proper form of his submission had another audience in addition to the Catholic authorities. He also had to maintain his reputation in the academic world by defending the freedom of his scholarly opinions. In fact, these letters suggest, Loisy's responses to the demands made on him by various members of the hierarchy were significantly determined by his concern for maintaining his academic reputation. He was, at this stage, apparently less concerned with the judgment of the hierarchy than with the judgment of his academic colleagues.

However, Loisy's difficulties at the Sorbonne continued to mount, encouraging him to make greater concessions in his ongoing negotiations with the Catholic hierarchy. When Loisy adhered to the decision of the Holy Office condemning five of his works, Albert Réville warned him that he needed to make public his express reservations as an historian to guarantee his academic reputation. Loisy reassured Réville but remained concerned about the attitude of administrators in the Sorbonne. In a letter dated two days after Reville's letter, he said, "This morning I feel for our scholarly world a sentiment other than admiration." He went on to mention "objections to the renewal of authorization for my class" and concluded that "between inquisitors of the right and inquisitors of the left there is a great resemblance of spirit."[65] Distressed by the attitude of the administration and under pressure from Rome, Loisy decided to renounce his teaching with the comment,

> I still had some illusions to lose on the subject of Roman intransigence. For the other part,—and the thing is worthy of remark,—the experience that I had just had at the École des Hautes Études had not demonstrated to me that I had the least useful future outside the Church. I quitted the section of Religious Sciences without regret.[66]

Discouragement about his future at the Sorbonne thus seems to have contributed to Loisy's decision to abandon his teaching as a concession to the Vatican.

Loisy's description of his problems at the École took little space in his autobiographies. *Choses passées* almost entirely ignored both Loisy's experiences at the École and his concern for his academic reputation. The *Mémoires* included only a few isolated comments in more than one hundred pages, and most of them occurred in letters that Loisy quoted for other reasons. This reticence is easy to understand. Loisy could not emphasize his more practical reasons for making reservations in his first letters of adhesion to the Catholic hierarchy. Neither could he stress the role that his disappointment with the administration at the École played in his decision to renounce his teaching there and then to submit to the judgment of the pope without express reservations. After all, these motivations could call into question the sincerity of Loisy's religious and academic convictions by suggesting that the shifting tone of his letters was dictated by self-interest and professional opportunism. Still, concerns about his academic career clearly played a role in Loisy's decision-making process, and presumably in his subsequent self-characterization as a critical historian as well, even if they remained on the backstage.

2. Theology: Loisy's concern with his reputation as a scientific historian and biblical critic seems to have surfaced, at least as a major issue, only in the first years of the twentieth century, during the period when he experienced problems with the Catholic hierarchy. A much earlier backstage element of his intellectual life was theological reform. Here, too, Loisy downplayed his interest. He frequently claimed to be an historian rather than a theologian and to deplore the ways in which theologians found theological errors in his historical books, particularly after 1900. And yet he displayed a consistent interest in the reform of Church teaching from the very beginning of his Catholic career. While serving as a parish priest in the late 1870s, before he encountered critical history, Loisy "dreamed, for the first time, of undertaking an exposé of Catholic doctrine in relation with the needs of modern times."[67] Having learned the rudiments of historical criticism, he drafted a thesis reinterpreting the doctrine of biblical inspiration in 1884.[68] The following year, he tried yet another "outline of the compromise between the Catholic tradition and scientific progress without profound damage to the substance of dogmatic theology."[69] To this point in his career, Loisy had published nothing, but he had undertaken several efforts to modernize Church teaching. As he learned historical criticism, he used it to give shape and authority to these efforts at theological reform, but historical criticism and the response of the hierarchy to it did not initiate his reform agenda.

Even when Loisy turned to technical questions of historical criticism in the next several years, his theological agenda was not absent. In notes from 1884, after the rejection of his thesis on biblical inspiration, he wrote that "it was too soon to produce my conclusions.

It would be much better to begin with works of detail; the conclusions will then come of themselves. The terrain is not ready."[70] This passage is absolutely crucial in understanding Loisy's scholarly activity over the next several years. He did not abandon the kinds of theological questions that he had addressed in his earlier works of theological reform. Rather, as a strategic move, he shifted his attention to more narrowly critical questions in an effort to prepare the terrain for the theological reforms that he sought.

After his dismissal from the Institut catholique in 1893, Loisy turned back to more explicit work on theological reform, an effort that culminated with the "Essais d'histoire et de philosophie religieuses," an immense manuscript that he finished in the late 1890s and never published integrally. In the preface to the "Essais," Loisy described his agenda for the work. He sought "to interpret the witness that historical science renders to religion . . . [and] to show not only the permanent solution that Catholicism furnishes to the religious problem but the [reform] program which is imposed on it in order that it realize [this solution]."[71] The structure of the "Essais" reflected this agenda. Two chapters of introduction in which Loisy addressed the philosophy of religion and the nature of revelation were followed by five historical chapters. Then "The Intellectual Regime of the Catholic Church" "served as a transition from the historical chapters to these later chapters of theoretical discussion, in which reformatory suggestions prevailed over considerations of apologetics."[72] In these last 441 typed double-spaced pages, Loisy addressed questions about the relation of "Dogma and Science," of "Reason and Faith," and of "Religion and Life," before concluding with a chapter on "The Past and the Future." These chapters represented the climax of the book, the place where Loisy explicitly addressed the program that the Church needed to adopt in order to resolve the religious problem. Historical considerations dropped out of sight except insofar as they contributed to clarifying the reforms in Church teaching that Loisy advocated.

The reform agenda of the "Essais" resurfaced in more subtle form in Loisy's modernist works. The Firmin articles, L'Évangile et l'Église and Autour d'un petit livre, all derived, in different degrees, from the "Essais,"[73] but the way in which the "Essais" can clarify Loisy's program of theological reform appeared most clearly in the case of L'Évangile et l'Église. Loisy acknowledged that L'Évangile et l'Église was distorted by being separated from the more critical, reforming chapters at the end of the "Essais,"[74] and L'Évangile et l'Église itself ended with a reference to these final chapters. After mentioning "a great religious crisis" due to "the evolution, political, intellectual, economic, of the modern world," Loisy glanced ahead to further treatment of questions about the proper relation "of dogma and science, reason and faith, the Church and society."[75] These were the topics of the last three chapters of the "Essais." *L'Évangile et l'Église* did not stand alone, but rather was one step in the program of theological reform that Loisy developed at much greater length in the "Essais."

Even in his last years as a Catholic, Loisy continued to reflect on the question of Church reform, although with less and less expectation of its realization. In 1906, apparently after he lost any real attachment to the Church, he began to revise the final section of the "Essais" for publication as "Le regime intellectuel de la catholicisme et les fondements de la foi," a work that he called "a sort of testament."[76] Loisy never finished the work, but he said at least as late as 1913 that he regretted "not having published my chapter on 'The Intellectual Regime' in a small volume while I was still inside the Church. This criticism might at that time have been extremely useful."[77] Henceforth, Loisy naturally renounced his efforts at theological reform within the Catholic Church, but he continued to address "theological" questions in such later works as *Guerre et Religion, Mors et Vita, La Paix des Nations et la Religion de la Avenir, De la discipline intellectuelle, La Morale humaine, L'Église et la France, Religion et la Humanité*, and *La Crise morale du témps présent et l'éducation humaine*. Such works and Loisy's self-chosen epitaph, "Prêtre," "Priest," have led one scholar to suggest that Loisy always saw himself as a priest because he continued to seek to mediate religious truths to the reading public through his academic work.[78] That is, Loisy remained vitally interested in what may be broadly described as "theology" even long after he left the Church despite his insistence that he was simply an historian and biblical critic.

3. Politics: Loisy's views on the need for theological reform stemmed in part from a somewhat idiosyncratic view of the task of theology. In a lecture delivered in 1892 and subsequently published, he defined theology as the "adaptation of revealed doctrine to the different states of culture that humanity has traversed." The historical study of the Bible, he continued, "teaches us to conceive and to present [religious] truth under the form which best suits the contemporary spirit."[79] Theologians had always adapted traditional views of religious truth to the contemporary spirit. Loisy simply wanted theologians to continue this work at the turn of the twentieth century.

This view of theology helps to explain another element of Loisy's backstage intellectual life: politics.[80] As with theology more generally, so with politics, Loisy downplayed his interest. As a youth of thirteen, he had cheered a train carrying Napoleon III. "It was," he commented, "the only occasion of my life in which I made a political cry."[81] Nevertheless, Loisy did, in fact, comment extensively on politics. As early as 1883, he expressed concern about the "political teaching" of the Church, particularly its anachronistic "pretensions to privileges which, according to it, are absolute rights." The Church, continued Loisy, affirmed these pretensions "in formulas which are scarcely more current today than the coins of Henry IV or rather those of good St. Louis."[82] Theologians therefore badly needed to revise the political teaching of the Church to make it better suit the contemporary spirit. The next decade only increased his interest in politics. In the mid-1890s, he wrote a "Dialogue des morts sur la question religieuse dans le temps présent." After Renan, Jules Ferry, a prominent anticlerical politician in the 1870s and 1880s, appeared more than any other character to share his views on "the Church in France" generally and more specifically on "The Secular Laws" on public education.[83]

Loisy continued to reflect on the political situation in his modernist works. In the "Essais," he devoted the chapter on "Religion and Life" (over one-hundred typed double-spaced pages) to political questions, including the battles over religious education, the *Ralliement*, and the proper relation of Church and State. He summarized this chapter, with extensive quotations, in both autobiographies.[84] Although less overtly political, *L'Évangile et l'Église* repeated his concern that the political evolution of the contemporary world was leaving the Church behind, and *Autour d'un petit livre* argued that "Catholicism must not be a party of reaction in either the political or the social order."

Furthermore, Loisy closely followed and commented on the political battle between the French government and the Vatican as it escalated in the early years of the twentieth century, the same time that his own struggles with the Vatican reached a climax.[85] He wrote three anonymous articles for publication advocating the secularization of the State. These articles are the best reflection of his evolving attitude toward the Church between his final submission in 1904 and his excommunication in 1908. Loisy summarized them, with extensive quotations, in both his autobiographies, and he titled the two relevant chapters (over fifty pages) of the *Mémoires*, "Separation" and "Separation continued."[86] However the strongest indication of the importance that these political events had for Loisy was in *Choses passées*. "The pretensions of Pius X to interfere in political matters," he said,

seemed to me as illegitimate and as disturbing as his pretensions to
dominate in the realm of scholarship. Only, here the practical
consequences appeared immediately, and it was a vital interest of
France that was involved. . . . [Pius's actions] made me more
indignant, and irritated me more deeply, than the acts of ecclesiastical
power by which I myself had been oppressed in the past.[87]

Loisy compared Pius's political pretensions as revealed in the conflict
between Church and State to the scientific pretensions that were Loisy's
more frequent concern, and he said that the political pretensions were
even more disturbing.

Conclusion

That Loisy had a reform agenda has always been clear. However,
the emphasis on biblical criticism in his autobiographies has obscured
the centrality of this reform agenda to his sense of vocation. Given the
collapse of this agenda with the condemnation of modernism, the fact
that Loisy located his theological interests and ambitions "backstage" is
not surprising. Foregrounding his critical work, on the other hand,
served a variety of functions for him. It reinforced his assertions of
intellectual autonomy, highlighted his differences with the Catholic
hierarchy, and lent his autobiographies additional credibility, especially
as compared to those biographies and histories that he sought to refute.
Of course, Loisy valued modern biblical criticism for its own sake. He
was truly a biblical critic. But he was also more. His claims to be a
simple biblical critic who only addressed theological questions when
they were forced on his attention was part of an apologetic strategy more
than an accurate representation of his interests during the modernist
period. To discern the full range of his modernist program and his place
in modernism more generally, we need to recognize Loisy's theological
agenda, including his political interests, as one of the driving forces in
his work from the beginning of his Catholic career.

Notes

[1] Every student of Loisy's thought makes use of his autobiographies, but there is only
one study of his autobiographies themselves, "Autobiography and the Rhetoric of
History" in C.J.T. Talar, *(Re)reading, Reception, and Rhetoric* (New York: Peter Lang,
1999).

[2] Loisy, *Choses passées* (Paris: Émile Nourry, 1913), ix; ET (*My Duel with the Vatican*,
trans. Richard Wilson Boynton, New York: Greenwood Press, 1968), viii; *Mémoires
pour servir à l'histoire religieuse de notre temps* (3 vols. Paris: Émile Nourry,
1930–1931), 1:7. Unless otherwise noted, all translations are my own.

[3] Loisy, *Choses passées*, v; ET, v.

[4] Loisy, *Mémoires*, 1:5–6.

[5] Loisy, *Choses passées*, vi, ET, vi.

[6] Loisy to von Hügel, May 16, 1912, quoted in *Mémoires* 3:242.

[7] Maurice Clément, *Vie du Cardinal Richard* (Paris: De Gigord, 1924); Jean Rivière, *Le modernisme dans L'Église* (Paris: Letouzey et ané, 1929).

[8] Loisy, *Choses passées*, vi–vii; ET, vi. See also Émile Poulat, "Critique historique et theologie dans la crise moderniste" (*Recherches de science religieuse* 58 [1970]): 540w 543.

[9] Loisy, *Mémoires*, 1:6.

[10] *Ibid.*, 3:242–243. Cf. Houtin, *Histoire du modernisme catholique* (Paris: chez l'auteur, 1913).

[11] *Ibid.*, 3:502–506, especially 502–503. Cf. Albert Houtin, *La vie d'Alfred Loisy*. In *Alfred Loisy: Sa Vie—Son Œuvre*, edited by Émile Poulat. Paris: Centre national de la recherche scientifique, 1960.

[12] See John Barbour's discussion of the "ethics of disbelief" in narratives of "deconversion" (*Versions of Deconversion*, Charlottesville and London: University Press of Virginia, 1994: 106–121). However, Barbour does not deal specifically with Loisy.

[13] Loisy, *Choses passées*, vii, viii, ix; ET, vii, viii, my translation.

[14] Loisy, *Mémoires*, 1:6.

[15] *Ibid.*, 1:6.

[16] Loisy, *Choses passées*, v; ET, v; *Mémoires*, 1:7.

[17] Literary critics have suggested that this is true of autobiography in general. See, for example, Georges Gusdorf, "Conditions and Limits of Autobiography," trans. James Olney, in James Olney, ed., *Autobiography: Essays Theoretical and Critical* (Princeton: Princeton University Press, 1980): 39–40.

[18] Loisy, *Choses passées*, ix–x; ET, viii.

[19] See Maurice le Sage d'Hauteroche d'Hulst, "La question biblique" (*Le Correspondant* n.s. 134 [1893]): 201–251; Alfred Baudrillart, *Vie de Mgr d'Hulst* (2d ed. 2 vols. Paris: Poussielgue, 1912–1914): 1:480–487 and 2:145–170; Dietmar Bader, *Der Weg Loisys zur Erforschung der Christlichen Wahrheit* (Freiburg: Herder, 1974): 23–64; Valentine Moran, "Loisy's Theological Development" (*Theological Studies* 40 [1979]): 414–415; Marvin O'Connell, *Critics on Trial: An Introduction to the Catholic Modernist Crisis* (Washington, D.C.: The Catholic University of America Press, 1994): 114–131; Freidrich Heiler, *Alfred Loisy: Der Vater des katholischen Modernismus* (Munich: Erasmus-Verlag, 1947): 34–38.

[20] Loisy, *Choses passées*, 134; ET, 144, partly my translation.

[21] *Ibid.*, 135–136; ET, 146.

[22] *Ibid.*, 137; ET, 147, my translation.

[23] For this and what follows, see *ibid.*, 143–48; ET, 151–155.

[24] In fact, they added material that made d'Hulst's responsibility for the whole affair even clearer in some ways. See, for example, Loisy, *Mémoires*, 1:247, 250–251.

[25] *Ibid.*, 1:269

[26] *Ibid.*, 1:248.

[27] *Ibid.*, 1:250.

[28] Baudrillart, 1:486, quoted in Loisy, *Mémoires*, 1:264.

[29] Loisy, *Mémoires*, 1:264–265.

[30] *Ibid.*, 1:269–271; Baudrillart, 1:487.

[31] *Ibid.*, 1:272. See also Clément, 233.

[32] *Ibid.*, 1:261.

[33] Loisy, "La question biblique et l'inspiration des Écritures," in *Études bibliques*, 167, quoted in *Mémoires*, 1:263.

[34] Loisy, *Mémoires*, 1:264.

[35] Loisy, *Choses passées*, 245–246; ET, 227–228.

[36] *Ibid.*, 247; ET, 228.

[37] *Ibid.*, 248–249; ET, 229. See also C.J.T. Talar, *Metaphor and Modernist: The Polarization of Alfred Loisy and his Neo-Thomist Critics* (Lanham, MD: University Press of America, 1987); Émile Poulat, *Histoire, dogme et critique dans la crise moderniste* (Paris: Casterman, 1962): 125–160, 190–243; Gabriel Daly, *Transcendence and Immanence: A Study in Catholic Modernism and Integralism* (Oxford: Clarendon Press, 1980): 167–216.

[38] Loisy, *Mémoires*, 2:169.

[39] *Ibid.*, 2:168–169, my emphasis.

[40] See Poulat, *Histoire, dogme et critique*, 244–263; Francesco Turvasi, *The Condemnation of Alfred Loisy and the Historical Method* (Rome: Edizioni Di Storia e Letteratura, 1979): 121–159; O'Connell, 252–271.

[41] Loisy, *Choses passées*, 252; ET, 232.

[42] *Ibid.*, 254; ET, 234.

[43] *Ibid.*, 276; ET, 250.

[44] *Ibid.*, 301–302; ET, 268–270.

[45] *Ibid.*, 283–284; ET, 256.

[46] *Ibid.*, 299–300; ET, 268–269.

[47] Loisy, *Mémoires*, 2:322.

[48] *Ibid.*, 2:367–368.

[49] Loisy, *Choses passées*, 290; ET, 261.

[50] Loisy, *Mémoires*, 2:349.

[51] *Ibid.*, 2:314, 316–317. Cf. Clément, 403–404.

[52] *Ibid.*, 2:325.

[53] See *ibid.*, 2:332, 333, 334, 357.

[54] *Ibid.*, 2:246.

[55] *Ibid.*, 2:267.

[56] *Ibid.*, 2:304.

[57] I might add that, in my view, Loisy was sincere in his equivocation—he wrote in the assumption that a disinterested presentation of the facts would discredit his opponents and vindicate him.

[58] Several commentators have discussed the dangers of taking Loisy's words too literally. See, for example, Daly, 55–58; Poulat, *Histoire, dogme et critique,* 90–92; Stephen Sykes, *The Identity of Christianity* (London: SPCK, 1984): 137–138; Talar, "A Reading of the Gospel (and the Church) According to Alfred Loisy," *Thought* 67 (1992): 302–316.

[59] See Talar, "Identity Formation, Identity Reconstruction, and Identity Transformation: Albert Houtin," 38–39, 41–42.

[60] See, for example, Loisy to Mathieu, October 27, 1902, quoted and summarized in *Choses passées*, 235–236; ET, 219–221; *Mémoires*, 2:146

[61] Loisy, *Mémoires*, 2:233.

[62] Loisy to von Hügel, March 20, 1903, quoted in *ibid.*, 2:237. The book to which he referred was *Autour d'un petit livre*, and Rome did indeed condemn it.

[63] Loisy to von Hügel, June 30, 1903, quoted in *ibid.*, 2:246.

[64] Loisy to von Hügel, January 10, 1904, quoted in *ibid.*, 2:308

[65] Loisy to Desjardins, January 8, 1904, quoted in *ibid.*, 2:329.

[66] *Ibid.*, 2:352–353.

[67] *Ibid.*, 1:80.

[68] *Ibid.*, 1:130–131.

[69] *Ibid.*, 1:148–149.

[70] Loisy, Notes, 1884, quoted in *ibid.*, 1:136 and in Houtin, *La vie d'Alfred Loisy*, 38. On the way that Loisy sought to put his historical scholarship at the service of modern(ist) theology, see also my "La science catholique: Alfred Loisy's Program of Historical Theology," *Zeitschrift für neuere Theologiegeschichte/ Journal for the History of Modern Theology* 3 (1996): 39–59.

[71] Loisy, "Essais d'histoire et de philosophie religieuses" (Volumes 3–5 of the Papiers Loisy. Bibliothèque nationale de France, Department of Manuscripts, NAF 15636–15638): 3:9/10, quoted in *Mémoires*, 1:446.

[72] Loisy, *Choses passées*, 181; ET, 178.

[73] See *ibid.*, 174, 177, 180–181; ET, 173, 175, 177–178. See also Normand Provencher, "Un inédit d'Alfred Loisy" (*Église et Théologie* 4 [1973]): 394–395.

[74] Loisy, *Mémoires*, 1:445–446.

[75] Loisy, *L'Évangile et l'Église* (3d ed. Bellevue: chez l'auteur, 1904): 227–278; ET (*The Gospel and the Church*, trans. by Christopher Home, Philadelphia: Fortress Press, 1976): 276–277.

[76] Loisy, Notes, March 17, 1906, quoted in *Mémoires*, 2:513.

[77] Loisy, *Choses passées*, 181; ET, 178–179.

[78] Ron Burke, "Loisy's Persona: The Priest" (paper presented at the annual meeting of the American Academy of Religion, Orlando, FL, 1998).

[79] Loisy, *Études bibliques* (3d ed. Paris: Alphonse Picard et Fils): 120–121; cf. *L'Évangile et l'Église*, 209–210; ET, 217.

[80] See my "The Politics of Moral Education" in Darrell Jodock, ed., *Catholicism Contending with Modernity: Roman Catholic Modernism and Anti-Modernism* (Cambridge: Cambridge University Press, 2000).

[81] Loisy, *Mémoires*, 1:21.

[82] Loisy, Notes, July 7, 1883, quoted in *ibid.*, 1:119.

[83] See *ibid.*, 1:425–426. See also Loisy, "Dialogue des morts sur la question religieuse dans le temps présent," Volume 9 of the Papiers Loisy, Bibliothèque nationale de France, Department of Manuscripts, NAF 15642: 7–35.

[84] Loisy, *Choses passées*, 193–202; ET, 187–193; *Mémoires*, 1:474–476.

[85] See my "French Politics and Alfred Loisy's Modernism," *Church History* 67 (1998): 521–536.

[86] Loisy, *Choses passées*, 323–333; ET, 286–293; *Mémoires*, 2:441–444, 478–484.

[87] *Ibid.*, 323–333; ET, 291.

.

2

Identity Formation, Reconstruction, and Transformation:
The Autobiographical Trajectory of
Albert Houtin

C.J.T. Talar

He alone is sure of never speaking an untruth to his fellows who in the silence of scientific meditation has felt the impossibility of being untrue to himself.

Léon Brunschvicg[1]

I n his history of French Catholic biblical exegesis in the nineteenth century, Albert Houtin (1867–1926) adopted as his epigraph an admonition of Leo XIII: "The first law of history is not to venture to lie; the second not to be afraid to tell the truth; in addition to which the historian should not lend himself either to suspicion, flattery, or animosity."[2] Though Houtin was capable of subtle irony, the epigraph was meant straightforwardly and taken seriously. When he later came to write the history of the modernist movement, he cited George Tyrrell's characterization of the modernist as "a churchman [sic], of any sort, who believes in the possibility of a synthesis between the essential truth of his religion and the essential truth of modernity."[3] It is quite likely that the double repetition of the word "truth" appealed strongly to Houtin. He prided himself as an historian on his unflinching commitment to portraying "the facts" and ruthlessly exposing "pious fraud." But, as Slavoj Zizek reminds us, "'Let the facts speak for themselves' is perhaps the arch-statement of ideology—the point being, precisely, that facts *never* 'speak for themselves' but are always *made to speak* by a network of discursive devices."[4] In Houtin's histories of the biblical question, the pursuit of historical truth carries heavy ideological baggage.

Less than surprisingly, the characteristics of Houtin the historian reappear in Houtin the biographer. For example, commenting on Houtin's interpretation of Alfred Loisy, one scholar notes that "Houtin had no 'finesse,' did not understand nuance, judged things according to narrow categories, and simplified positions despite their irreducible complexity and subtlety."[5] Houtin's temperament, then, cannot be discounted as a factor when weighing his assessments of modernist contemporaries. It is of potential significance in attempting to appreciate him as historian of the origins of French dioceses, of the biblical question, or of the modernist movement itself. Certainly it will be reflected in Houtin's autobiographical writings[6] as well as constitutive of the self displayed in them.

At the core of autobiography is self-perception. A sociological translation of such perceptions is captured in the notion of "identity" —the self-image generated by performance of a role. Identities are created and re-created in the course of face-to-face interaction, but are also subject to the influences of institutional contexts. In what follows, Houtin's *Une vie de prêtre* and *Ma vie laïque* are explored under three rubrics: identity formation, identity reconstruction, and identity transformation. The first of these focuses on his formative years in seminary, on his characterization of the "Sulpician mould" and his active cooperation in fitting himself into it.[7] Despite his best efforts, this fit was a somewhat uneasy one. After ordination, Houtin's appointment to his diocesan seminary as professor of ecclesiastical history subjected him to the role strain between the priest committed to the intellectual formation of seminarians and the historian committed to the scientific study of history. His larger ideal—that of reconciling Catholicism with modern thought—entailed considerable renegotiation of the formation he had received in seminary. The acquisition, largely self-taught, of critical methods of doing history required a reconstruction of his identity to accommodate the revisionist historian who remained a priest.

One of the most sensitive analysts of social interaction and the construction and maintenance of the self has been Erving Goffman. His dramaturgical approach to sociological analysis will be drawn on to open up aspects of these first two rubrics.[8] Goffman is concerned in part with the disparity that can occur between "official selves"—those put on display "front stage" for public consumption—and selves that emerge "backstage," seemingly safe from prying eyes. Part of Houtin's concern in his retrospective look at his seminary formation is the disparity between the "official Church" that is presented to the seminarian—and to the faithful more largely—and the true state of affairs, the true facts that are routinely concealed or avoided. In the latter case, the dramatic metaphor is applied in a somewhat extended sense. But Goffman's analysis of cooperative efforts by teams to promulgate and preserve acceptable impressions, or of means to penetrate behind such official facades, provides more direct links to Houtin's narrative. Part of our concern with Houtin's retrospective look at the period in which he worked to propagate his ideal of Catholic renewal is with the disparity between what he could safely promulgate as a cleric and the full extent of his private convictions. A dramaturgical perspective will prove useful in exploring this as well.

But Goffman's approach also has its limitations. He has been criticized for a view of behavior that concedes too much to its governance by rules and to rational calculation, at the expense of individual creativity and imagination.[9] While the highly structured environment of the post-Tridentine seminary is congenial to Goffman's emphases, the reconstruction of identity accents individual creativity more heavily. Hence, Goffman will be supplemented by conceptualization generated by Anthony Giddens to address the latter dimension.

The final rubric, identity transformation, tracks Houtin's movement from Catholic modernist through Christian theist and ultimately to unbeliever. John D. Barbour's work on deconversion guides this portion of the study.[10]

Identity Formation

I have been formed by the Church; I owe her all that I am, and I shall never forget it. The Church has cut me off from the profane world, and I am thankful for it.

Ernest Renan[11]

Houtin's route to priesthood was not at all untypical for the time. His parents were of modest means; his upbringing, influenced by his mother's family, "very devout."[12] His health as a child was rather fragile, and he portrays himself as something of a loner. Early on, he conceived the desire to be a priest, and his education was confided to the local abbé, for whom, at the time he wrote his autobiography, Houtin still cherished a "deep affection." His tutor emerges as one who was staunchly monarchist in politics and staunchly credulous in religion. "He delighted in the most improbable stories, provided they were pious."[13] The only book at Houtin's disposal in his parents' house, on the lives of the saints, reinforced this same tendency in him. The years spent at the minor seminary of Angers (1880–1886) in no way disturbed this sort of faith. Though possessed of "a curious mind, an eager desire to learn," Houtin was not stimulated by a seminary regime which stressed "the cultivation of memory at the expense of intelligence, the exaltation of authority at the expense of reason, of obedience at the expense of a sense of responsibility."[14]

The chief impact of these initial years in seminary appears to have been to deepen Houtin's idealism, directing him toward the monastic life. Following his year of philosophical studies at the Angers seminary, he tested his vocation with the Benedictines at Solesmes (1887–1888). Houtin's experience at Solesmes proved somewhat shocking. Far from his anticipated angelic ideal, he found a community engaged in an all too human power struggle. Of greater importance, however, than a discrepancy between religious ideal and institutional reality was Houtin's growing unease with another form of discrepancy. He notes the stirrings of a consciousness of inconsistencies between the traditional version of ecclesiastical events and a more critical reading of the historical record.

> Certain mystical works were attributed to St. Denys the Aeropagite, first Bishop of Paris; but it seemed to me impossible to maintain the authenticity of these books or to identify their author. I laid my misgivings before Dom Fromage. He replied with a pitiful smile: "If you wish to doubt, then you can doubt anything." This did not reassure me. If one could doubt anything, then could one not just as well believe anything one wished to?[15]

Dissatisfied, Houtin returned to the diocesan seminary, under the direction of the Society of St. Sulpice, to do the three years' study of theology. Although individual Sulpicians may strike a fond chord in Houtin's memory, his opinion of the society as a whole was far from flattering. "The community's most persistent feature is credulity." Interest in secular disciplines was actively discouraged, while ecclesiastical subjects were often poorly taught by ill-prepared professors. Scripture and ecclesiastical history functioned more as adjuncts to apologetics than as serious studies in their own right.[16]

In looking back upon his years in the theologate, Houtin voices the usual complaints regarding the poverty of the manuals, the lack of library access (the seminary library existed for the faculty's benefit, not the students'), the stress on docile memorization, and the low level of expectation which fostered an intellectual mediocrity. But what really seems to have disturbed him is not so much what was put forth as what was withheld. The highly controlled access to information inflated the force of traditional arguments by representing opposing positions only at second hand—or by failing to discuss them at all. Embarrassing episodes, "such as the Church's complicity in the Massacre of St. Bartholomew," were given a highly selective presentation. Or, as was the case with "certain questions such as the condemnation of Galileo and the history of the Inquisition," simply avoided. From the vantage point of several decades later, this appeared to be a conscious and culpable duplicity: "they concealed from us not merely the conflict between traditional theology and modern discovery, but things we had the right to know before we could contract an engagement with the full knowledge of what we were doing."[17]

While primarily responsible for forming priests, the seminary was busily engaged in maintaining a representation of the Church. Furthermore, it is apparent that, to Houtin's mind, the former's success depended upon a certain duplicity regarding the latter. Goffman's dramaturgical analysis can provide insight into both processes: the maintenance of institutional image and the formation of clerical self-image.

The dramaturgical metaphor appears most prominently in Goffman's early work. There it serves as a sort of root metaphor,[18] generative of a series of analogies between the theatre and everyday life. One of the analogies central to Goffman's analyses is the regionalization of performances into front and back stages. In contrast to the front stage, where a carefully crafted display is put on for audiences, the backstage is "where the suppressed facts make an appearance."[19] Performers seeking to maintain the desired public impression have a stake in closing off audience access to this region. To sustain the desired definition of a situation, they will seek to exercise information control: by overcommunicating some facts, undercommunicating others, by maintaining silence or even misrepresenting. Facts which are incompatible with the desired image are termed "dark secrets," which are in effect "double secrets": "one is the crucial fact that is hidden and another is the fact that crucial facts have not been openly admitted."[20] In this connection one need not belabor the implications of the geographical segregation of seminarians, their intellectual segregation via seminary textbooks, the relegation of such potentially disruptive areas of the curriculum as scripture and church history to the status of "minor studies," or an instructional approach that emphasized memorization and required virtually nothing in the way of research, while encouraging docility and clearly sanctioning "argumentativeness."

Goffman's framework takes us further in his examination of the maintenance of front-stage performances by teams. The sustaining of a performance often requires the intimate cooperation of a number of individuals. The character and extent of the cooperation necessary are likely to be concealed.[21] Among the mechanisms that contribute to successful operation are dramaturgical loyalty, discipline, and circumspection. The first of these is of primary interest here. The functioning of the seminary system depended, after all, on the active cooperation of the faculty. Sulpician directives prescribed adherence to the manuals by the instructors. This compensated for the poorer student's deficiencies while it restricted the originality of the more gifted. By conscious design it served an analogous function for instructors, ensuring that the content communicated remained within strict boundaries. Those boundaries were set by the paramount importance accorded faith.[22]

Nonetheless, there were countervailing tendencies, however modest. The social distance that obtained between seminarians and priest faculty was mitigated by the regular contact between them, particularly in the case of the seminarian's director. Goffman observes,

> Perhaps the key problem in maintaining the loyalty of team members (and apparently with members of other types of collectivities, too) is to prevent the performers from becoming so sympathetically attached to the audience that the performers disclose to them the consequences for them of the impression they are being given, or in other ways make the team as a whole pay for this attachment.[23]

While Houtin's narrative at this stage does not evidence any instances of outright performance disruption by a faculty member, it does indicate several occasions where alternative perspectives on the standard teaching were communicated. At one point, when particularly dissatisfied with the unconvincing exegesis put forward by the professor of scripture, Houtin consulted his director, M. Houbert. Knowledgeable in Hebrew, Houbert indicated the difficulties raised by the prophetic text, confessed his inability to resolve them, and made an act of faith. Houtin was obviously more impressed by this honest admission of exegetical problems than by repetitions of inadequate attempts at resolution repeated at increasing decibel levels![24] Houbert's successor, Georges Letourneau, proved instrumental in providing alternative intellectual fare to the theology manual, including works by Newman.[25] Nonetheless, one should not make too much of such exceptions. Even the faculty member who had studied at the Paris Institut catholique, and thus had imbibed liberal notions firsthand from Louis Duchesne, believed some matters too delicate to treat in class and some questions best deferred until seminary studies had been completed.[26]

Given the highly controlled nature of the seminary environment and the level of commitment of its "audience" of seminarians, the successful inculcation of a selective image of the Church is hardly surprising. In his interpretation of the dynamics of scientific revolutions, Thomas Kuhn observes that, as long as the dominant paradigm retains credibility, any failures in its application will be attributed to deficiencies in its practitioners, not in the paradigm itself.[27] *Mutatis mutandis*, this can serve as an apt characterization of Houtin's understanding at this stage of anomalies in the ecclesiastical tradition:

> I had difficulties, but not doubts. . . . The Church represented for me science, morals, art, truth, beauty, and goodness. Nothing prompted me to question either its infallibility or its holiness. The imperfections I perceived in the Church seemed to proceed merely from human frailty. I distinguished between popes and the indefectible chair in which they sit; I distinguished between popes and their surroundings; I was always distinguishing.[28]

Correlative with an image of Church is the self-image of the priest as its professional servant. As Goffman observes, a self "virtually awaits the individual entering a position."[29] Insofar as an individual occupies multiple positions, sociologically speaking he or she will possess multiple selves and be faced with the task of interrelating them. The formational system in effect sought to simplify the task by making the clerical role paramount. As Dumoulin observes, "The cleric belonged to the seminary as much as, if not more than, to his family."[30] In Goffman's terminology, the desired outcome is role embracement: "to disappear completely into the virtual self available in the situation, to be fully seen in terms of the image, and to confirm expressively one's acceptance of it. To embrace a role is to be embraced by it."[31] And to have successfully embraced a role is to exhibit the "demeanor" deemed proper to it. Through deportment, dress, and bearing one conveys the impression of possessing "the attributes popularly associated with character training or socialization, these being implanted when a neophyte of any kind is housebroken."[32] In the Sulpician mould the dominant demeanor trait is identified as "an outward gravity." Houtin notes the seminary's effectiveness in imparting this "mask of gravity so much appreciated by our teachers."[33] J. Brugerette has left a testimony of just how effective and durable this socialization process was on Houtin himself. "Even in lay attire this implacable enemy of all religion retained the ecclesiastical mark. His face reflected its serenity, his conversation retained the unction that is found with so many men of the Church."[34]

At the time of his ordination, much of the discrepancy between the images of Church and priesthood presented in seminary and embarrassing counterfactuals remained opaque to Houtin or were chalked up to human weakness. A great deal of this portion of his autobiography which reflects a different sensitivity is obviously written from the standpoint of his subsequent apostasy. Enough of the view that he possessed at the time of ordination does come through to sharpen the question of how he progressed beyond it. There are elements of role distance already evident in this period of formation. Houtin notes how his attraction to the monastic life introduced a degree of dissociation from identification with the Sulpician system during his year of philosophy. Yet he carried the effects of that formation into his time at Solesmes. As he was told by the abbot, "You are still in certain respects a stranger among us,"[35] a sensibility Houtin carried back into the diocesan seminary. He retained something of a monastic mindset and some of the habits of piety he had imbibed from the Benedictines, and so he remained something of a stranger there too. None of this, however, is sufficient to account for the changes that occurred in his sense of self over the decade following his ordination. It was Houtin's prolonged and intense encounter with the critical study of history that would virtually force him to reconstruct an identity along very different lines than had been accomplished in seminary.

Identity Reconstruction

Two things are certain: Catholicism cannot perish; Catholicism cannot remain as it now is. It is true that we cannot see how it can change. Hours in which every issue seems barred are the great hours for Providence.

Ernest Renan[36]

Following his ordination Houtin was appointed to the faculty of the diocesan minor seminary as professor of history in 1894. He found its intellectual climate notably improved over his own student days, which he attributed to the effects of the Instituts catholiques. The dynamic whose results he saw in the microcosm of seminary fueled his optimism for its influence in the universal Church. In the 1880s, there seemed reason to believe that a reconciliation between truth in both its Catholic and modern guises was attainable. "There existed in France at that time a kind of small idealist renaissance which was full of hope. . . . Every quarrel between the Church and the age seemed to me about to disappear. It was called the ralliement, the new spirit, the new apologetics."[37] The lines along which his own contribution to this process of renewal were to proceed were set down by his faculty appointment. The reading, research, and publication this led to, when combined with Houtin's basic temperament, were to have a decisive impact on his subsequent development.

At the time Houtin received this appointment, it was still the normal practice for priests to serve on seminary faculties without regard for any specialized training. The studies leading to ordination were considered sufficient foundation to expound the manuals or to acquire any additional learning that might be required.[38] To this rule Houtin was no exception. In the time-honored traditions of seminary teaching, he learned as he taught.

Houtin's historical research led to a revisionism that did not confine itself to a number of specific incidents or matters of detail. That research centered on local history, first on the history of the Angers minor seminary, then on the life of the Benedictine Dom Couturier, who had strong connections with the region. The reception accorded the latter work within the Benedictine community taught him something of the politics of historical representation. From some quarters his portrait was said to suffer from an excess of truth. As one monk put it, "Certain details might have been passed over in silence"—either because they were unflattering to the order, or to the subject of the biography who appeared with all his prejudices intact. Houtin emerged from the experience with a better sense of "the obstacles that *esprit de corps* may raise in the way of truth."[39] His next forays into the ancient history of the diocese showed him that political interests were not confined to matters of modern or contemporary history. *La controverse de l'apostolicité des Églises de France au XIXe siècle* (1900) and *Les origines de l'Église d'Angers: La légende de saint René* (1901) revealed the indefensible legendary basis on which arguments for the apostolic origins of French dioceses rested. Moreover, Houtin showed that this had been established earlier by the Bollandists in the eighteenth century and by some local historians at the outset of the nineteenth. In the course of the nineteenth century, however, in a sort of anti-critical regression the thesis of apostolic origins had found new defenders—a move judged by Houtin to be connected to revenues generated by pious societies and works connected with these legendary founders.

This set of experiences seems to have turned his quest for truth rather paradoxically into a determined search for fraud: he "began to collect forgeries by ecclesiastics, false miracles, false prophecies, pious frauds, devout impostures." The "patriotic frauds" that were coming to light in the course of the Dreyfus Affair apparently stiffened his intolerance of any temporizing with the truth.[40] The hostility he discovered in the Church toward those who would reveal the truth of things in the historical arena, coupled with the reaction toward those who would know the truth in the political arena, was hardly reassuring.

During the period of his professorship, Houtin indicates a renewed acquaintance with Newman's work as pivotal for his developing position. He had been introduced to Newman's writings while still in the midst of theological studies. A summer sojourn in England in 1897 provided the opportunity to read the cardinal's *oeuvre* both extensively and intensively. The impact made by Newman's book on miracles was especially noteworthy—what Anthony Giddens terms a "fateful moment."[41] "It is one of the books which have most powerfully influenced my life. It marks a date, a stage. . . . It entirely destroyed my faith in the great miracles of Christian antiquity."[42] At that point biblical miracles remained in a category apart, guaranteed as they were by the inspiration of the sacred text.

The readiness to concede large blocks of ecclesiastical tradition to "pious fraud" is rather striking. It is not unrelated to an underlying attitude that can be detected in Houtin. In a way, it is something of a mirror image of an attitude that can be discerned in his neo-scholastic opponents, expressed in a supernatural rationalism which Blondel labeled "extrinsicism." As Gabriel Daly has pointed out, this orientation was rationalist less in its substance than in its method. Although it derived its primary data from supernatural revelation, not autonomous reason, it approached those data as *facta externa* whose transcendent meaning was readily discernible to the observer of goodwill. Thus this mentality may also be fairly described as positivist insofar as historical facts are objective givens whose sole function is to constitute a sign and proof of supernatural dogma. The role accorded an interpretive element is minimal, given the phobia over "Kantian subjectivism."[43] The effect of this approach has been neatly summarized by Christoph Théobald: "Because it was believed possible to attribute the same value to dogma, to legend and to historical fact, that of an historically verifiable reality, the attempt to reconcile orthodoxy and history led necessarily to the suppression of history."[44]

Houtin's mentality emerges as both rationalist and positivist on its side, though deriving those more proximately from "scientific" history than from scholasticism.[45] For Houtin, historical criticism must verify the relationship between a document and reality. Basically, it comes down to a single alternative: if a text appears legendary, it is eliminated; if credible, the fact to which it testifies must be accepted as a reality. This applies equally to facts labeled "supernatural." And the effect ultimately is to preserve history at the price of orthodoxy. Théobald points out the symmetry between this epistemological position and that of extrinsicism. "Dogma and historical fact again appear on the same plane, in the sense that their reality or non-reality is considered scientifically verifiable." Supernatural dogma is "either as a whole in conformity with the historical facts and is accepted, or is legendary and must be rejected."[46] This orientation fits well with the impression of Houtin's temperament indicated earlier: a certain inflexibility, inability to handle nuance, a tendency to oversimplify.

Despite Houtin's circumspection in the classroom, allowing for the age and sensibilities of his students, there were instances in which his critical evaluation of the legendary found its way into his teaching. In light of Goffman's observations, noted earlier, on the maintenance of front-stage performances by teams, the following comment is worth remarking:

> Several professors in the upper school, who taught apologetics and Church history, had learnt nothing on these subjects since they had left the seminary. We contradicted one another sometimes. Two of my colleagues bore me a grudge for errors in which my pupils surprised them.[47]

From the narrative one receives the impression that, even more disconcerting for his fellow faculty than the occasional counterfactual raised by a student, was Houtin's overall approach to history and his methods of communicating it. He goes out of his way to emphasize that he did not rest content with mere memorization, but attempted to develop his students' critical abilities. He changed textbooks "used from time immemorial, abounding in apocryphal tales" in favor of those which gave access to the broad sweep of "intellectual and social evolution." In short, "I aroused in them thoughts which I wish had been aroused in me when I was their age."[48]

The institutional repercussions of Houtin's research and teaching placed him in an increasingly difficult position. Priests complained of his lectures; colleagues mobilized students against him, who in turn clashed with other students who were his partisans. Intellectual conflicts found expression in playground riots during recreation, leading Houtin to tender his resignation from the seminary faculty. If Houtin did not experience outright team performance disruption during his own formational years, the same obviously cannot be said of his students.

Houtin the autobiographer has attempted to provide an organized account of the conflicts he experienced between what he knew and what he could acceptably say. As he notes, his earliest work showed him that, "if it is difficult to know the truth, it is even more difficult to tell it."[49] His account also indicates some of the experiences that he saw as being particularly significant in contributing to this developing awareness. Newman's book on miracles is a case in point. Still, it is possible to press the narrative further, drawing on the rubric of identity reconstruction. To do so, Gidden's' refinement of Goffman's analysis of the self will prove useful.[50]

The notion of social practices plays a pivotal role in Gidden's theory. Social practices both embody structures and socialize actors. With respect to the process of agency, three levels can be distinguished: (1) the motivation of action, (2) the rationalization of action, and (3) the reflexive monitoring of action. By and large, these levels of agency correspond to three levels in the mind of the agent or actor: (1) unconscious motives and cognition, (2) practical consciousness, and (3) discursive consciousness.[51] Practical consciousness is a leading theme in Gidden's conceptual framework and is significant in this attempt to account for Houtin's reinvention of himself as a revisionist historian.

To the extent that behavior remains embedded in routine (a category underemphasized in Goffman's sociology), it remains closer to unconscious compliance with routine and the authority structure that lies behind it. Even in the course of the maintenance of routine, however, problems arise and actors draw upon practical knowledge for their solution. To the extent that the rationalization of action thus involved remains at a taken-for-granted, tacit level, it is appropriate to speak of "practical consciousness." Precisely because of the routine nature of so many social practices, agents can continuously monitor their ongoing behavior without necessarily having to bring such rationalization to the level of discursive awareness. In circumstances where an actor's conduct puzzles others and they press for reasons underlying such conduct, a reflexive level of awareness is called for. Rational accounts of action engage discursive consciousness. Though the "line between discursive and practical consciousness" is admittedly "fluctuating and permeable,"[52] the distinction is a useful one, which can shed some light on the process of acquiring a critical historical consciousness on Houtin's part.

Certainly the highly routinized nature of seminary life, which extended to its intellectual regime, fostered unconscious compliance.

Memorization in Latin rather than discursive formulation of independent research formed the cornerstone of the system. Intellectual habits acquired in seminary carried over into parish life, and even those who eventually taught in the system were expected simply to expound the manuals in their turn, replicating the seminary product. Against this background Houtin emerges as rather exceptional. How does one begin to account for his departure from accepted (and acceptable) practice?

The process of achieving mastery over a particular discipline is less a matter of assimilating "agreed-upon theoretical commitments" and more one of absorbing "exemplary ways of conceptualizing and intervening in particular empirical contexts." That is to say, it is "more like acquiring and applying a skill than like understanding and believing a statement." Or, to be more precise, it "involves multiple skills simultaneously."[53] Thus, part of learning to do critical history engages practical activity and is located at a pre-theoretical level. The academic not only possesses a consciously acquired knowledge in a given discipline, together with an understanding of its methodological rules, but a set of durable dispositions acquired in the course of learning a (sub)field and practicing research. In Gidden's terms, some of this knowledgeability tacitly resides in practical consciousness while much—given the nature of scholarly work, writing, and publication—is discursively formulated.

The largely self-acquired nature of Houtin's historical education makes these distinctions particularly relevant in his case. He prepared for the assumption of his history professorship by independent reading at the Solesmes library over summer vacations. Placed in charge of the seminary's library and archives, "which were in utter confusion," the work of classification put him in contact with the sources for his initial attempts at local history—undertakings which cost him "infinite labour," because he "had not been taught how to work."[54] For guidance he had as positive models the work of a very restricted number of Catholic scholars such as Duchesne, while a much larger number of "romantic historians like Ozanam and Montalembert, [and] ultramontane writers like Rohrbacher, Dom Guéranger, Mgr. Freppel, Cardinal Bourret" served as negative role models in their neglect or alteration of sources. A great deal of his historical expertise was thus acquired as the result of practical trial-and-error engagement with archival and published sources. That is not to say that more explicit guidance was entirely lacking. Among the handful of books highlighted in the autobiography as formative influences is the *Principes de la critique historique* by the Bollandist Charles de Smedt. It was this book that taught Houtin to consult sources and reinforced his "sorrow" and "indignation" over Catholic authors whose work lacked "serious research and historical honesty."[55] *La controverse de l'apostolicité des Églises de France au XIXe siècle* strongly reflected de Smedt's influence. The practice of historical research and the reflexive application of methods represented in the works of critical historians gradually weaned Houtin from his earlier admiration for the romantic and ultramontane authors noted. Still, if by the time he resigned from his faculty position the sphere occupied by the legendary in ecclesiastical history had grown significantly in Houtin's perception, it had not yet intruded upon biblical terrain. A commitment to biblical inspiration set ideological limits to the discursive awareness of critical methods and their application.

Giddens advances a constellation of terms that help to position Houtin's reconstruction of identity as he sought to accommodate cleric to scientific historian. Giddens stresses tradition's orientation to the past, a past that is made to exercise a heavy influence over the present. The established practices of tradition correlate with a "formulaic notion of truth," which "renders central aspects of tradition 'untouchable'" and "to which only certain persons have full access." The latter, as "guardians" of tradition, hold their right to authoritative interpretation based more on their status in the traditional order than on the "competence" characteristic of the "expert."[56] Houtin's summary of his bishop's arguments in favor of maintaining the traditional version of the diocese's origins, including the miraculous events surrounding St. René, are illustrative of the orientation Giddens describes. The bishop invoked the authority of legends in the breviary (*lex orandi, lex credendi*); Rome's careful scrutiny of the smallest details of the liturgical observances of the various dioceses; the soundness of the principle of accepting authority in matters of diocesan origins, as well as in other controverted subjects; and the illusions of individual authors coupled with the arbitrariness of criticism.[57] The connection with ritual and devotional matters, and the failure to engage seriously the arguments advanced by critical historians, recapitulate the emphases made by Giddens. In contrast to traditional authority stands the "indefinite pluralism of expertise" with its commitment to rational inquiry. Such expertise "is tied not to formulaic truth but to a belief in the corrigibility of knowledge, a belief that depends upon a methodical skepticism."[58] Houtin's commitment to rational inquiry led him to positions at variance with official views on a number of matters in which legend yielded to critical scrutiny. He drew up a first inventory of his beliefs and took stock of his options. To teach what he no longer believed would be "immoral"; to teach what his research had uncovered would but arouse further protest.[59] He tendered his resignation from the seminary's faculty.

Identity Transformation

Man belongs neither to his language nor to his race; he belongs to himself alone; for he is a free being—that is, a moral being.

Ernest Renan[60]

Houtin secured his bishop's permission to leave not just the seminary faculty but the diocese as well. He joined his parents, who were then living in Paris and eked out a marginal living by tutoring, and secured through the offices of his former seminary rector, Georges Letourneau, an appointment as assistant priest at Saint-Sulpice. Letourneau is credited for catalyzing—rather backhandedly— Houtin's decision to research the history of the biblical question.[61] Less than surprisingly, Loisy proved more encouraging, though hardly blind to the risks involved in venturing onto such sensitive terrain. What Houtin, at least, had not anticipated was the effect such study would have on himself:

> What was my surprise, therefore, when I came to take stock, to find on every hand withdrawals and capitulations! Even on points which were not yielded the only defense set up was borrowed from Protestants. . . . The totaling up of the results of this controversy on matters of dogma shocked the prejudices which my education had inculcated upon me. In my opinion, there can hardly be anything in the world more sad than the moment when a priest perceives his dogmatic theories to be refuted by a few clearly established facts.[62]

Houtin's *La Question biblique chez les catholiques de France au XIXe siècle* appeared in March 1902.The positivist mindset sketched earlier reappears in Houtin's characterization of his book:

> It set forth no system of interpretation, not even on any particular point; it carefully left on one side all dogmatic questions, and confined itself to relating incontrovertible facts. It was, therefore, no book of theology nor of exegesis, but of history; and to lay stress on this, so that there should be no possibility of mistake, I had taken as an epigraph for the book [an] extract from Leo XIII's letter on history. . . .[63]

In general, reviewers favorable to Houtin's position tended to take him at his word,[64] but not everyone was quite so willing to award Houtin the palm of impartial historian. There were those who, while admitting the justice of some of his claims, noted—and deplored—their tone.[65] For others, clearly hostile to Houtin's position, the ideological character of the representation was apparent. Rather than being a faithful recital of the facts, it too often degenerated into "caricature." In the words of one reviewer, far from being "the complete and impartial history of the biblical question in France during the nineteenth century," it was in reality "a manifesto of a school," its author more pamphleteer than historian.[66]

In Goffman's terms, Houtin's book on the biblical question constituted an instance of performance disruption. It moved "backstage" matters squarely into the front-stage limelight and adopted a tone toward ecclesiastical authority deemed thoroughly inappropriate for public consumption. Goffman's observation that "Renegades often take a moral stand, saying that it is better to be true to the ideals of the role than to the performers who falsely present themselves in it"[67] sums up a great deal of the stance adopted in the autobiography.

La Question biblique chez les catholiques de France au XIXe siècle further strained Houtin's relations with his bishop, escalated his difficulties as his work came to the attention—and sanction—of Roman authorities, and brought into sharp relief his growing divergence from his former religious beliefs. Early in 1903, the book evoked the condemnation of several French bishops. By the end of that year, it had been placed on the Index, along with Mes difficultés avec mon évêque and five of Loisy's works. Unlike Loisy's case, no personal demand for a submission was ever communicated to Houtin by Rome. But, in any event, a retraction would not have been forthcoming. Convinced of the factual nature of his history of the question, he viewed it as "beyond all recantation."[68]

That was certainly not the case with the tenets of his dogmatic faith. Over the first several months of 1904, he undertook a second inventory of his beliefs.[69] The upshot of this exercise in discursive awareness reveals a commitment to belief in God, in free will, and in the immortality of the soul, founded on reason rather than on any revelation. The authority of maternal piety, of the priests who had instructed him, of seminary manuals, of liberal apologetics and its partisans—all had been dissolved in the cold light of historical research. He retained a role for religion, but for religion purified of the mythology which concealed more than it revealed of the philosophic and moral truths that were of genuine worth to humanity. At this point, Houtin characterized himself as a "theist with Catholic tendencies" with an emotional rather than dogmatic Christianity, "venerating Christ as a master, though no longer worshiping him as a God."[70] Convinced that neither people nor nations could live without religion, and also convinced that much of traditional Christianity was based on "pious fraud," he put his hopes in the possibility of evolving a purified Christianity. Its content would be reflective of Unitarianism; its life would be drawn from Catholicism. To this ideal he devoted the next several years of his life.

In 1904, Houtin could invoke the words of Renan, which stand as epigraph for the section in this study on Identity Reconstruction.[71] By 1912, his position had evolved to the point where Renan's comments that begin this section were more apt. In a third inventory Houtin recorded his loss of faith in any possibility of modernizing Christianity; theism had dissolved into unbelief, religion into sheer mystification.

> And when I reconsidered the interpretations to which Modernists had resorted in order to replace outworn myths and to reinterpret their formulae, I asked myself whether Frazer was not right when he wrote: "The history of religion is one long effort to reconcile an ancient custom with a new idea, to find a reasonable theory to explain an absurd practice."[72]

Houtin therefore finally discarded "the old uniform of idealism," the cassock, that his opinions no longer permitted him to wear.[73] His life subsequent to that decision is set forth in *Ma vie laïque*. This includes a fourth inventory, which reflects his enduring commitment to unbelief. Houtin advised his reader, "Be *unbelieving*. Do not be taken in."[74]

The Ethics of Disbelief

> [A]utobiography's narrative form is especially suited for exploring the ethical dilemma arising when a person has begun to doubt a belief and must decide when and how to inform others, especially those who are part of the rejected religious community.[75]

The avowedly "intellectual" and "literary" quality of Houtin's faith meant that issues of fundamental theology and critical historiography would loom large in his autobiographical account of deconversion. As he says, the moral counterexamples provided by fellow clergy, while frequently a factor in undermining the faith of "young, uneducated priests," played but little role in his own case.[76] *Un vie de prêtre* is clearly no exercise in clerical scandal mongering. One of the rare instances in which he does refer to notable moral lapse is, however, telling. After the publication of *La Question biblique chez les catholiques de France au XIXe siècle*, Letourneau requested of the archbishop that Houtin be moved to another parish. Instead, Houtin was dismissed absolutely and told that he would never receive another post in the Paris archdiocese. Houtin contrasts the treatment accorded him for his intellectual deviance with that given to two priests convicted, one of concubinage, the other of sodomy. To the first, the archepiscopal council shut its eyes, while the second priest was simply moved to another, and quite "comfortable" position.[77] Although the moral shortcomings of others remain on the whole recessive, Houtin does highlight his own moral rectitude. What Barbour calls "the ethics of disbelief" engages "the moral considerations that guide what an individual can believe in good conscience and the scruples that guide how one informs other people of beliefs and doubts."[78]

Before examining intellectual honesty at greater length, two further characteristics of deconversion raised by Barbour will receive attention. Intellectual doubt and moral criticism (or justification) are frequently accompanied by emotional suffering and disaffiliation from a community.[79] In his autobiography, Houtin occasionally lets the reader backstage, revealing some of the personal cost his own evolution exacted.

> As I have never dwelt on the emotional side of the crisis I had passed through, nor expressed my great sorrow in any book, I have often been represented as a pure intellectual, happy in being delivered from mythology. The truth is quite different. My emancipation was very painful.[80]

Although Houtin does not belabor his suffering in his autobiographical narratives, and explicit allusions to it remain rather exceptional, it is never very far below the surface.

Both intellectual commitments and emotional ties have their institutional components. Detachment from religious beliefs with attendant emotional upheaval were intertwined with detachment from vocation and the Church. The term "role exit" has been applied to the process of disengagement from a role that has been central to one's self-definition and the reestablishment of a new identity in a subsequent role that takes account of the ex-role.[81] The literature emphasizes that this is indeed a process, and Helen Rose Fuchs Ebaugh develops a four-stage model. Without going into the details of each stage, one might simply note that the initial phase, "first doubts," is already apparent in Houtin's experience of seminary formation. However, it was not until after ordination, in the course of his teaching and research in history, that such doubts became acute enough to motivate entry into a second stage, "seeking alternatives." In Houtin's narrative, this corresponds to his attempted transposition of the traditional theological framework via evolutionary categories. In Ebaugh's model, a third stage, "the turning point," is identified with the point at which "the individual makes a firm and definitive decision to exit."[82]

For Houtin, this phase, as well as the final one—"creating the ex-role" were both gradual and complex. Although his separation from seminary faculty was obviously an important event in his life, its greater significance perhaps lies in the events it set in motion. It propelled him toward Paris, initiation of contact with Loisy, research into the biblical question, and, following the publication of that research, his bishop's refusal to renew his authorization to say mass. The last is one of those exceptional instances where Houtin explicitly registers the emotional impact of some event on him, but its importance transcends that. In light of what has been said earlier regarding the legitimating impact of routine, the intellectual and institutional repercussions of this cessation of priestly routine are worth noting. In the nine months following it, Houtin remarked "how much clearer my ideas became." Institutionally, "a priest deprived of the power of saying mass loses caste"—with severe consequences for opportunities of earning a livelihood, not to mention self-definition.[83] This is not to minimize the impact of larger events, such as the series of controversies unleashed by Loisy's "little red books," to which Houtin's contribution on the biblical question was assimilated. Nor of the fallout resulting from the Separation of Church and State—a decisive event for Loisy's detachment—and one in which Houtin was actively involved through his journalistic contributions.[84] Certainly he did not have to wait for the Roman condemnations of modernism in 1907 to realize that his youthful dreams for the modernization of Catholicism were unrealizable.

But it is clear that his ceasing to say Mass was catalytic. At the time that authorization was refused (March 1903), Houtin counted himself "still orthodox": "I believed in the whole body of Catholic dogma—not merely in the divinity of Jesus Christ, but in transubstantiation and in my priestly office."[85] By the following year, his second inventory of beliefs reveals a very different set of commitments, more "Unitarian" than Catholic—themselves to undergo further evolution until his assumption of lay attire symbolically proclaimed his arrival at unbelief. This drawn-out process of reconfiguring beliefs has its counterpart in an equally drawn-out process of creating an ex-role. If by 1907 he had given up on

Catholicism but still retained some hope for a theistic version of Christianity, by 1912 he had come to the conclusions expressed in the third inventory that religion would "soon be as out of date as magic."[86] Houtin's final and enduring attitude toward religion may be encapsulated in Max Scheler's notion of *ressentiment*, a theory that for Barbour "explains some of the dynamics at work in many versions of deconversion and seems especially relevant in those accounts that are unrelievedly hostile to their former faith."[87]

More still needs be said regarding the moral dimension of deconversion narratives. To this point, while not completely ignoring the moral ramifications of Houtin's research and conclusions, their cognitive side has received the major emphasis. But it is clear from his narrative that the intellectual and the moral are closely intertwined on a number of levels. Houtin's very positioning of his work is cast in moral terms. In its undeviating pursuit of truth; it exposed both "pious fraud" and pious frauds—those Catholic authors whose writings failed the test of "historical honesty." To the elements of cognitive incommensurability between the official history and Houtin's exposure of the "true facts," and those of normative incommensurability between his critical historiography and the methodological practices of his opponents, there is added a dimension of moral incommensurability. This moral element has implications for the conceptual analysis drawn from Goffman and Giddens. It indicates that learning to be an historian is more than a matter of assimilating a body of knowledge, or certain methodological norms, more than acquiring a set of skills and dispositions. The "practice" of history not only fosters determinate intellectual habits, but in addition requires courage and moral rectitude. Likewise, taking into account the moral dimension of the historian's role surfaces some of the limitations of Goffman's dramaturgical perspective. Goffman himself came to realize the limits of the metaphor and in his later work shifted to others. A significant problem, detected by himself and frequently repeated by his critics, is that it can lead to a cynical perception of the actor as a manipulative performer, acting out of purely strategic motives to put that performance across.[88] The dramaturgical perspective does provide sensitizing concepts that are helpful in framing cognitive elements which are paramount in the narrative. It highlights elements of the socialization undergone in seminary and the role conflict experienced in the process of resocialization into the practice of critical history. However, the perspective cannot be pushed too far analytically, as it does less than justice to the very real moral concerns that are prominent in Houtin's account. In short, Goffman's perspective is illuminating; but it should be treated as he himself did, "as an interesting stepping-stone to another analysis: a step on the way rather than the final destination."[89]

The moral dimension poses some additional problems which need to be resolved in the autobiographical account itself. To adopt a tone of moral criticism toward the deceptions practiced by an institution and its leadership is to lay oneself open to the same charge, especially if one has had an active role in socializing members of that institution. Portraying oneself as someone who increasingly came to have doubts does not solve the problem: "At whatever point one articulates one's doubts, one may appear to have been dissembling or hiding one's ideas, raising questions about one's truthfulness in both the past and the present."[90]

In the course of depicting his formational years, Houtin stresses at more than one point the idealism and moral soundness of seminarians. When combined with selective exposure to learning, these qualities help to explain how young men actively cooperated to fit the Sulpician mould. Given such idealism and motivation, it is hardly surprising that there would be added to the deception involved in the official portrayal of Church and priesthood an element of self-deception on the part of aspirants.[91] As in Houtin's own case, doubts could be handled by taking refuge in a distinction between institution and incumbent, between office and unworthy occupant.

The sincerity of seminarians depends upon a high degree of insulation, and ordination changes that.[92] Exposure to a world of less than ideal peers and institutional structures can be a shattering experience, in some cases leading to a loss of faith. The newly ordained gains a heightened sense of the discrepancy between seminary ideal and ecclesiastical reality. It follows that those who administer the seminary system are not innocent of deception.[93] And this of course creates something of a dilemma for Houtin. After all, he served for a number of years on a seminary faculty. Part of his strategy in the narrative is to distance himself from faculty colleagues, with respect to his acquisition of further learning in some cases, or his willingness to disseminate it in others. As noted earlier, he aroused in his students thoughts which he wished had been aroused in him at their age. His "scientific honesty" as an historian is linked to aspirations for reform. In short, he seeks not to perpetuate the problem but to participate in the solution. His voluntary resignation from faculty, when he perceives that his attempts to communicate the results of his research receive opposition from his bishop, alienate colleagues, and have a disruptive effect on students, once again shows Houtin to advantage. He will simply find another way to contribute to the movement for renewal.

The delegitimating tactics indulged in by theological opponents appear at a number of points in the narrative. The strategy once again is one of contrast. Houtin's scrupulous regard for the facts extends to his conduct of controversy,[94] as opposed to the distortions and deceptions resorted to by some critics. Even the small detail of referring to the *soutane* as "the old uniform of idealism" defangs charges of hypocrisy in continuing to wear clerical garb after years of no longer saying mass, remaining unsubmissive to the Index, and holding quite un-Catholic beliefs.

The moral overtones that pervade Houtin's description of his intellectual development provide an element of continuity in his life, despite the transformations that are evident. His commitment to seeking out the truth, his courage in speaking and writing it once found, run like a thread from initial seminary experience through his *vie laïque*, persisting through those various changes. Underlying the transformation of beliefs and identities are these consistent character traits.

Conclusion

The autobiographical act and the rejection of one's religious community alike represent an attempt to choose personal identity rather than being defined by a social authority.

John Barbour[95]

Barbour's observation points to a consideration of modernist autobiography as homologous with efforts to secure autonomy in apologetics, biblical exegesis, and church history vis-à-vis ecclesiastical authority. The autobiographical genre (or genres) is less suitable to the abstract discussion of ideas than to an exploration of moral dilemmas that arise in espousing and advocating them. In his study of French autobiography, Michael Sheringham highlighted the genre's usefulness as a vehicle for ideological testimony, debate, or conflict. In the nineteenth century especially, this often took the form of an "account of a conversion from a dominant value-system to a more personal and subjective one, an alternative ideological configuration regarded as more congenial to the subject."[96] Renan's case is paradigmatic in this regard, and it is no accident that Houtin makes reference to Renan's writings at important points in his own narrative. Like Renan, his own deconversion is represented as a triumph of objectivity over irrational belief. Also like Renan, Houtin has great faith in his ability to reach the truth of things and the truth of self. And again, as with Renan, "a critical sense of the interpenetration of subjectivity and ideology is wholly lacking."[97] The positivist spirit that Houtin brought to his historical and biographical writings is operative in his autobiographical efforts. It appears to be a significant factor in his confidence that he has avoided the self-deception he so often detected in others. Sheringham's characterization of Renan therefore applies equally well to Houtin. He "never draws attention to the process of writing his text, to the difficulty of reaching the truth, to the slipperiness of the categories he uses. the spirit of 'critique' does not seem to apply in the arena of the self."[98]

Notes

[1] In his *Nature et liberté*. Quoted by Albert Houtin, *Une vie de prêtre. Mon expérience 1867–1912* (Paris: F. Rieder, 1926), 428. Eng. trans. *The Life of a Priest: My Own Experience 1867–1912,* trans. Winifred S. Whale (London: Watts & Co., 1927), 255. References to this first volume of Houtin's autobiography will be to the English edition, with a reference to the French original following in parentheses.

[2] Letter of Leo XIII on historical studies, *Saepenumero Considerantes*, 18 August 1883. Quoted in Albert Houtin, *La Question biblique chez les catholiques de France au XIXe siècle* (Paris: Alphonse Picard, 1902). Houtin also reproduced it in *Life*, 145 (246), and had earlier utilized it as epigraph to *La controverse de l'apostolicité des Églises de France au XIXe siècle*.

[3] Albert Houtin, *Histoire du modernisme catholique* (Paris: chez l'auteur, 1913), vi. See George Tyrrell, *Christianity at the Cross-Roads* (London: Longmans, Green and Co., 1909), 5.

[4] *Mapping Ideology*, ed. Slavoj Zizek (New York: Verso, 1995), editor's "Introduction," 11.

[5] Ronald Burke, "Loisy's Faith: Landshift in Catholic Thought," *Journal of Religion* 60 (1980), 153. Pierre Guérin's assessment is being summarized here.

[6] Prior to his ordination to the subdiaconate, Houtin was instructed by his seminary director to write an account of his life. This, together with his journals and correspondence, over a long period was crafted into *Une vie de prêtre*. A second volume, *Mon expérience II: Ma vie laïque 1912–1926* (Paris: Rieder, 1928), was still very much in draft form at the time of his death. It is relatively short, occupying pages 15–84 of the volume, most of which consists of additional documentation. Beyond the two-volume autobiography, one may also mention *Mes difficultés avec mon évêque* [1903], much of which was incorporated into *Une vie de prêtre*, and a series of articles on the "clergy crisis" (1904–1905) later published as *La crise du clergé* (1907, 2nd ed. 1908) that he cites as a catalyst for autobiographical reflection. "Of this [crisis] I was no mere spectator, but a victim. In describing it, I had but to tell what I had myself experienced and what I had seen around me. I lived my whole life over again—my childhood, my youth, my life in the seminary, at the noviciate, as professor in the Low Seminary." *Life*, 199 (337).

[7] *Life*, 60 (104), 62 (108).

[8] On Goffman, see Tom Burns, *Erving Goffman* (New York: Routledge, 1992); Philip Manning, *Erving Goffman and Modern Sociology* (Stanford: Stanford University Press, 1992); *Le parler frais d'Erving Goffman* (Paris: Les éditions de minuit, 1969); *The View*

from Goffman, ed. Jason Ditton (London: Macmillan, 1980); *Erving Goffman: Exploring the Interaction Order,* ed. Paul Drew and Anthony Wooton (Boston: Northeastern University Press, 1988); *Beyond Goffman: Studies on Communication, Institution, and Social Interaction,* ed. Stephen H. Riggins (New York: Mouton de Gruyter, 1990).

[9] See, for example, Anthony P. Cohen, *Self Consciousness: An Alternative Anthropology of Identity* (New York: Routledge, 1994), 10, 27, 68–71, 98–100.

[10] John D. Barbour, *Versions of Deconversion: Autobiography and the Loss of Faith* (Charlottesville: University Press of Virginia, 1994).

[11] From the conclusion of *L'Avenir de la science.* Quoted in Albert Houtin, *La crise du clergé* (Paris: Emile Nourry, 1908), 226–27.

[12] *Life,* 4 (12).

[13] *Ibid.,* 5 (14), 6 (15–16).

[14] *Ibid.,* 15 (31).

[15] *Ibid.,* 44 (78–79).

[16] *Ibid.,* 19 (37). Houtin's sketch of the system of seminary formation which he experienced can be fleshed out by consulting Christian Dumoulin, *Un séminaire français au 19ème siècle: Le recrutement, la formation, la vie des clercs à Bourges* (Paris: Téqui, 1978). A provincial seminary also under Sulpician direction, Bourges would be very similar to Angers.

[17] *Ibid.,* 54–55 (94–96). Cf. 61 and 61n. (106–07 and 107n.). Cf. Joseph Turmel's similar evaluation of his seminary formation in chapter 3.

[18] See Robert H. Brown, *A Poetic for Sociology* (Chicago: University of Chicago Press, 1989), esp. ch. 4.

[19] Erving Goffman, *The Presentation of Self in Everyday Life* (New York: Doubleday Anchor, 1959), 112.

[20] *Ibid.,* 141–42.

[21] *Ibid.,* 79, 104.

[22] See Desmoulins, 206ff. *Life,* 55 (97).

[23] *Presentation of Self,* 214.

[24] *Life,* 52 (91), 55–56 (97–98). Cf. 22–23 (43–24).

[25] *Ibid.,* 56 (98).

[26] *Ibid.,* 50 (87–88), 55 (96–97).

[27] Thomas S. Kuhn, *The Structure of Scientific Revolutions* (Chicago: University of Chicago Press, 1970), 80.

[28] *Life,* 62 (108).

[29] Erving Goffman, "Role Distance" in *Encounters* (Indianapolis: Bobbs-Merrill, 1966), 87.

[30] Dumoulin, 176. He cites an instance in which a seminarian died in the course of his formation—a not entirely unknown occurrence, as Houtin's narrative also testifies. When his parents presented themselves in the visitors' parlor, his father was allowed into the infirmary to view the deceased, but the seminary rule prohibited both mother and sister from like access.

[31] "Role Distance," 106. Another facet of Goffman's earlier work that is of obvious relevance to the Tridentine seminary system is his analysis of "total institutions," characterized by the subsumption of all aspects of life under a single authority (the seminary rule), the conducting of activities in the company of others, all of whom are treated alike (homogenization of dress, address, deportment, etc.), a rigid timetable of events (the late nineteenth century French seminary was especially regimented), and the subordination of all activities to institutional aims. While it is tempting to pursue this

line of analysis, it must remain beyond the scope of present concerns. See Erving Goffman, *Asylums* (New York: Doubleday Anchor, 1961). This aspect of Goffman's work is discussed in Manning, ch. 5 and in Burns, ch. 6 and 7.

[32] Erving Goffman, "The Nature of Deference and Demeanor" in *Interaction Ritual* (Chicago: Aldine, 1967), 77.

[33] *Life*, 56 (99), 59 (103). He observes, "This fine outward pose concealed diverse sentiments, but the continuity of effort and the influence of behavior on morals transformed these eager disciples completely and very early," 59 (103). Houtin's expressed dissatisfaction with this sort of demeanor was, once again, less with what it revealed than what it concealed. This facade of clerical gravity hid a lack of educational grounding and further studies. Beneath a correct exterior lay concealed great intellectual poverty. Cf. *Life* 57 (99).

[34] J. Brugerette, *Le prêtre français et la société contemporaine 3: (1908–1936)* (Paris: P. Lethielleux, 1938), 252.

[35] *Ibid.*, 44 (79).

[36] Quoted in *Life*, 191 (322). Houtin had earlier quoted this in *La crise du clergé*, 72.

[37] *Life*, 82 (142), translation modified.

[38] See Dumoulin, 206ff.

[39] *Life*, 110–11 (187–88).

[40] *Ibid.*, 127 (216–17).

[41] Anthony Giddens, *Modernity and Self-Identity* (Stanford: Stanford University Press, 1991), 112, 143.

[42] *Life*, 98 (167).

[43] Gabriel Daly, *Transcendence and Immanence: A Study in Catholic Modernism and Integralism* (Oxford: Clarendon Press, 1980), 19–20.

[44] Christoph Théobald, "L'entrée de l'histoire dans l'univers religieux et théologique au moment de la 'crise moderniste'" in Jean Greisch et al., *La crise contemporaine: Du modernisme à la crise des herméneutiques* (Paris: Beauchesne, 1973), 10–11.

[45] The "crude positivism" characteristic of Houtin's historicism could, in its opposition to scholasticism, "occasionally win small points but in the long term only compounded woes and was at no point capable of the hard theological analysis demanded. An historical critical method, be it ever so 'critical,' can lead in only one direction if employed in a theological and religious vacuum." Thomas M. Loome, *Liberal Catholicism, Reform Catholicism, Modernism* (Mainz: Matthias-Grünewald-Verlag, 1979), 174.

[46] Théobald, 12.

[47] *Life*, 102 (174–75).

[48] *Ibid.*, 101 (172–73).

[49] *Life*, 117 (200).

[50] In a general vein, Giddens's use of Goffman's work has led to a renewed interest in the latter theorist. More specific to present concerns, Giddens introduces several refinements into the Goffmanian self that are useful. See Manning, 179–83, 14. Giddens has provided an outline of his theoretical framework in *The Constitution of Society* (Berkeley: University of California Press, 1984). See also Anthony Giddens and Christopher Pierson, *Conversations with Anthony Giddens* (Stanford: Stanford University Press, 1988). For exposition and critical evaluation of Giddens's approach see Ira J. Cohen, *Structuration Theory: Anthony Giddens and the Constitution of Social Life* (New York: St. Martin's Press, 1989); Ian Craib, *Anthony Giddens.* (New York: Routledge, 1992); *Social Theory of Modern Societies: Anthony Giddens and His Critics*, ed. David Held and John B. Thompson (Cambridge: Cambridge University Press, 1989);

Giddens' Theory of Structuration: A Critical Appreciation, ed. Christopher G. A. Bryant and David Jary (New York: Routledge, 1991).

[51] *The Constitution of Society*, 5–14.

[52] *Ibid.*, 4.

[53] Joseph Rouse, *Knowledge and Power: Towards a Political Philosophy of Science* (Ithaca: Cornell University Press, 1987), 30.

[54] *Life*, 105–06 (179–81).

[55] *Ibid.*, 184–85 (311–13).

[56] Ulrich Beck, Anthony Giddens, and Scott Lash, *Reflexive Modernization* (Stanford: Stanford University Press, 1994), 63–66, 84–85, 104.

[57] *Life*, 115 (196–197).

[58] *Modernity and Self-Identity*, 195; *Reflexive Modernization*, 84. For extended discussion of this contrast, see 85–95.

[59] *Life*, 127 (216).

[60] From *Discours et Conférences*. Houtin used this quotation as the conclusion of the first volume of his autobiography. *Life*, 260 (437).

[61] Letourneau is reported to have said, "If you were to write the history of the Biblical controversy as you have written that of the apostolical succession, we should be lost."At that point (1901), Houtin was more optimistic regarding the possibility of a *modus vivendi* between the Church and biblical criticism. *Ibid.*, 137 (232); *nous serions perdus* is italicized in the original. On Letourneau, see the necrology in *Bulletin trimestriel des anciens élèves de saint-Sulpice* 27 (1926): 570–77, and Phillipe Richer, "Un curé de Saint-Sulpice: Monsieur Letourneau (1900–1926)," *Bulletin de Saint-Sulpice* 22 (1996): 228–36.

[62] *Life*, 125 (212–13).

[63] *Life*, 145 (246), translation slightly modified. See note 2 *supra*.

[64] Cf. the reviews in *Revue de métaphysique et de morale* 11 (1903): supp., 5; *L'Année philosophique* 13 (1902): 189; *Catholic World* (190): 689–90; *The Quarterly Review* 199 (1904): 271; Reinach's review in *Revue critique d'histoire et de littérature* 53 (1902): 459–60; and the reviewer in *The Church Quarterly Review* LX (1905): 173.

[65] E.g., *Revue d'histoire ecclésiastique* 3 (1903): 137.

[66] E[ugène] Mangenot in *Polybiblion* 95 (1902): 332. Cf. Joseph Brucker in *Études* 92 (1902): 398–404.

[67] *Presentation of Self*, 165. In light of this comment, Houtin's representation of Cardinal Meignan's career is instructive. See *La Question biblique chez les catholiques de France au XIXe siècle*, ch. 13. One could push Goffman's analytical framework further by examining orthodox responses to the book as exercises in "impression management."

[68] *Life*, 180 (305).

[69] This second inventory is set forth in *Life*, ch. XV.

[70] *Ibid.*, 190 (320, 321).

[71] See note 36 *supra*.

[72] *Life*, 257–58 (432).

[73] *Ibid.*, 258–59 (433–34).

[74] *Ma vie laïque*, 82. This fourth inventory is dated 1926.

[75] Barbour, 106–07.

[76] *Life*, 122 (208).

[77] *Ibid.*, 143 (243).

[78] Barbour, 107. Chapter 6 is devoted to "Hypocrisy and the Ethics of Disbelief."

[79] *Ibid.*, 2.

[80] *Life*, 188 (317).

[81] Helen Rose Fuchs Ebaugh, *Becoming an Ex: The Process of Role Exit* (Chicago: University of Chicago Press, 1988), 23–25. In his study of Seventh-Day Adventist ex-pastors, Peter Ballis cautions that the exit process can be more complex and less orderly than depicted by stage models such as Ebaugh's. Such models can be useful as organizing frameworks; they should not be rigidly applied to exiters' accounts. Peter H. Ballis, *Leaving the Adventist Ministry: A Study of the Process of Exiting* (Westport, CT: Praeger, 1999).

[82] *Ibid.*, 123.

[83] *Life*, 186 (314), 166 (281–82).

[84] See *Ibid*, ch. XIX and XX. Barbour observes that "The loss of faith was often associated with a movement toward more radical politics" (36). Houtin had traveled a fair distance from the monarchist sentiments he had imbibed from his first tutor.

[85] *Ibid.*, 166 (281).

[86] *Ibid.*, 257 (432).

[87] Barbour, 176–77.

[88] Manning, 44–54, summarizes these criticisms.

[89] *Ibid.*, 55.

[90] Barbour, 106.

[91] See Annette C. Baier, "The Vital But Dangerous Art of Ignoring" and Amélie Oksenberg Rorty, "User-Friendly Self-Deception" in *Self and Deception*, ed. Roger T. Ames and Wimal Dissanayake (Albany: State University of New York Press, 1996), 53–72 and 73–89 respectively. Rorty's observation that "normal science is served by training scientists to follow a conservative epistemic policy, one that makes them susceptible to self-deceptive denials of evidence contrary to dominant theories" (84) is applicable to a theological tradition communicated by textbooks.

[92] Cf. Ebaugh, 52–53.

[93] *Life*, 61 (106–07).

[94] Cf. *Mes difficultés avec mon évêque.*

[95] Barbour, 208–09.

[96] Michael Sheringham, *French Autobiography: Devices and Desires* (Oxford: Clarendon Press, 1993), 170. Chapter 6 is devoted to "Autobiography and Ideology."

[97] *Ibid.*, 183.

[98] *Idem.*

3

Multiple Identities:
Joseph Turmel, *Moderniste Démasqué*

C.J.T. Talar

*Without a privileged peek backstage or a rupture in the performance
we have no way of calling into question the status of what might be
a convincing but feigned performance.*

James Scott[1]

erhaps a good place to begin consideration of Joseph Turmel
(1859–1943) is by retrieving one of the observations made at the
conclusion of the study on Albert Houtin. There it was suggested that the genre of autobiography is more suitable for exploration
of moral dilemmas that arise in the course of espousing and advocating
ideas than for abstract discussion of the ideas themselves. Certainly
Turmel's autobiographical *Comment j'ai donné congé aux dogmes*
(1935) and *Comment l'église romaine m'a donné congé* (1939) confirm
this.[2] Although he published extensively both under his own name and
under an astonishing variety of pseudonyms, little of that content finds
its way into these accounts. Instead, he privileges his moral evaluation
of the Church, on the one hand, and his moral justification of his own
conduct on the other. In the case of the latter, there was a great deal to
justify. Although Turmel had lost his faith in 1886, he continued to
teach in seminary until 1892, functioned as chaplain for the Little Sisters
of the Poor until 1903, and thereafter continued to say mass up to (and
indeed beyond) his excommunication in 1930. From 1898 onward, he
published, both under his own name and pseudonymously, works that
were subversive of the Catholic faith. Let it be emphasized: not simply
subversive of the dominant theology, with a view toward ecclesiastical
reform; but rather, intentionally destructive of Catholicism itself.

67

At one point in his narrative he describes an encounter with the Abbé Gendron, instrumental in Turmel's vocation, and acknowledged as his benefactor. It occurred in 1899, as his series of articles on angelology were appearing in the *Revue d'histoire et de littérature religieuses*.[3] They evoked from Gendron the query, "What are you doing? Where are you heading with the writings you are publishing?" and the pronouncement, "If you no longer have faith, stop saying Mass, leave the Church."[4] Turmel's autobiographical accounts could well be characterized as a sustained reply to those anguished questions and a justification for failing to heed that pronouncement.

Before proceeding to Turmel's defense of his conduct, we would do well to spend a moment on his moral evaluation of the Church. For Turmel, "The Church which systematically hid the truth from me, and which fed me lies, acted like a brigand set upon his victim. The methods differ; the dishonesty is the same."[5] And since he viewed that dishonesty as part of the Church's very nature, repeatedly manifested over the course of centuries, it was impossible for him to cherish any hopes of ecclesiastical reform. Thus, unlike Alfred Loisy and Albert Houtin, who preserved a spirit of cautious optimism toward Catholicism through the 1890s and into the new century, already in the 1880s Turmel adopted an antagonistic attitude toward the institution which had duped him. "The idea of revenge . . . became the supreme directive of my life."[6] On this basis, it is possible to distinguish Turmel from "modernists" properly so called. Alec Vidler did so, and in this was consistent with Houtin and with Turmel's biographer, Félix Sartiaux.[7]

By contrast, Jean Rivière consecrated a chapter of his *Le modernisme dans l'église* (1929) to Turmel, under the rubric, "*Offensive contre le modernisme masqué.*" The practice of pseudonymous publication subversive of dogma, coupled with the maintenance of an outwardly correct ecclesiastical persona, held to be a characteristic tactic of the modernists, was sufficient to install Turmel among their ranks.[8] In doing so, Rivière was able to draw upon predecessors who also had played a role in detecting Turmel behind his pseudonymous productions. For example, this conception permeates Eugène Portalié's 1908 study, in which he is, moreover, careful to highlight points of solidarity between Turmel's thought and Loisy's.[9] It is possible, of course, to seek to adjudicate this difference in perspective by granting that, by virtue of his actual motivation and aims, he is distinct from modernist partisans of reform, but was labeled a modernist by orthodox "moral entrepeneurs."[10] Still, more can be said. Turmel's self-definition distinguished him from the modernists, but not on the basis of fundamental aims so much as by virtue of the tactics employed in realizing them. In his mind, "[t]he goal common to all was destroying dogma." Whereas modernists did this utilizing "subterfuge," equivocal formulae which gave the appearance of "consolidating" dogma to the unwary reader, he proceeded more straightforwardly, refusing such "oratorical precautions" to cover "heretical intentions."[11] And here, in a kind of ironic confluence, Turmel joins *Pascendi*'s reading of modernism as inherently destructive of Catholicism.

Precisely because Turmel's work—especially that put forth under the pseudonyms "Guillaume Herzog" and "Antoine Dupin"—was (correctly) perceived by the orthodox as consciously corrosive of the faith, it confirmed perceptions of the true intentions of other writers and legitimated the papal measures taken to secure their extinction. While with historical perspective Turmel's position may be distinguished from those of modernists, at the time of the crisis, if anything, their positions were assimilated to his. It is arguable that, far from being merely a marginal, idiosyncratic figure, Turmel can shed some light on the dynamics of the modernist movement.

Having suggested why a treatment of Turmel contributes to an understanding of modernism, it is necessary to speak briefly to how he will be analyzed here. The divergence between his private beliefs and public self-representation render him an extreme case of a disparity between "front-stage" and "backstage" personae over a lengthy period. Likewise, the perceived discrepancy between the "official Church" and the historical facts that were routinely concealed or avoided was heightened in Turmel's case. Goffman's framework, helpful with Houtin, can be employed again with profit. Moreover, since Turmel, like Houtin, was largely a self-made critic, Gidden's emphasis on practice would apply to him as well. And Barbour's work on deconversion finds points of contact with Turmel's life. But the comparatively early occurrence of Turmel's loss of faith, coupled with the decision to remain in the Church as a priest—maintaining, in effect, a largely "secret deviance" for a protracted length of time—argues for a focus somewhat different than that used with Houtin. Turmel had to justify his persistence in a deviant status, first to himself. On a number of occasions he was obliged to justify his conduct in private conversations with Abbé Gendron. After the full extent of his pseudonymous activity had been "unmasked," he had to do so in a public forum. As intimated earlier, ideas occupy a subordinate place in Turmel's account, which is largely an exercise in moral self-justification. Frequently, "each side in a stigma contest tries to get other people to share and apply *its* value judgments, to make and impose *its* favored moral assessments."[12] To help sort through the various modes Turmel employs to accomplish his side of that task, conceptualization will be drawn from the sociology of deviance. Those same concepts will aid in understanding the categories which guardians of orthodoxy sought to fasten upon him. Just as one may speak of a "cognitive incommensurability" between proponents of rival paradigms (or, more prosaically, an intellectual "dialogue of the deaf"), so here one may discern a "normative incommensurability." On a moral level, Turmel and his critics tended to talk past one another.[13]

Deviating Orthodoxy

The system may have most to fear from those subordinates among whom the institutions of hegemony have been most successful. . . . The anger born of a sense of betrayal implies an earlier faith.

James Scott[14]

Turmel begins his narrative abruptly, with a passing reference to his subdiaconate (1880) and his assignment to studies at the Angers faculty of theology.[15] He brought with him a passion for independent study developed while at the Rennes seminary. But apparently he had found little there to trouble the theology being served up from the seminary manuals. Nor was the dogmatics taught at Angers by Louis Billot, S.J. (later a leading antimodernist and ardent supporter of Action Française), of a caliber to disturb a tranquil faith. Such disturbance as there was came from another source. Turmel began teaching himself German (along with Hebrew) and requested a German commentary on Isaiah, the subject of the Scripture course, from its professor. He received the three volumes of Gesenius and, although he did not penetrate very far into the first volume, it opened up a world of exegesis notably different from the one he had assimilated from Catholic commentators. This alternative world was only glimpsed; but he did see enough to discern an exegetical method significantly at variance with the one familiar to him. Put succinctly, the manual theologians decontextualized the text; Gesenius clarified it by respecting its historicity. While this did not affect Turmel's confidence in dogmatic reasonings, it did undermine his trust in theological exegesis. More ominously (in retrospect) it showed him that unbelievers were not simply motivated by pride or by hatred of the supernatural—as Catholic apologists had led him to believe—but proceeded from serious study of the texts. The result: "The whole of dogma still retained my adherence, a fervent adherence. But henceforth I had but diminished respect for the official interpreters of dogma."[16]

Following upon his ordination to the priesthood in 1882, Turmel was assigned to the seminary at Rennes as professor of theology. This accorded him the continuing incentive, opportunity, and resources to pursue his independent study. To further develop his Hebrew, he turned to the psalms, taking as guide the thoroughly orthodox commentary of the Abbé Lesêtre. More extensive acquaintance with the Catholic literature provided exposure to rationalist arguments, via attempts to refute them. As with Loisy, Turmel originally sought knowledge of critical exegesis to defeat the Church's adversaries with their own weapons. "Animated by a fervent love of the Church, my mother, I wished to defend her from the innumerable attacks to which she was exposed."[17] And, as was the case with Loisy, the would-be adversary of criticism became transformed into its advocate. The biblical work of Edouard Reuss is accorded a pivotal role in mediating this transition. (At the time, Reuss was a prominent conduit of German critical exegesis into France.)[18] He provided Turmel with compelling evidence that the chronology of the psalms, blindly accepted on Lesêtre's authority, was in fact significantly defective. Moreover, as Turmel continued his research, it became clear from the authors who Lesêtre cited that he was aware of this counter evidence. Turmel's conclusion: out of fear of being accused of causing scandal (if not of outright heresy) by the body of Catholic exegetes, out of fear of reprisals by the Holy Office, Lesêtre "had not dared to express his intimate thought; he had dissembled."[19] Delving further into Reuss's work uncovered more chronological discrepancies: Daniel, Deuteronomy, Leviticus. Conclusion: "forgeries." Next, the contradictory narratives in Genesis and Exodus. Conclusion: "little or perhaps even no historical value at all." Turning to the New Testament, he fared little better with the infancy narratives or the apocalyptic discourses in the gospels.[20]

As long as it was solely a matter of chronology, Turmel judged that he could insulate dogma from the effects of critical exegesis. But clearly more than chronology was at stake. The binary sort of mentality seen with Houtin reappears here. Either the Bible is inspired by God thoroughly and throughout, and therefore could not include forgeries or "narratives devoid of all reality, and contradictory besides." Or, the Bible actually does contain such things—and the foundational dogma of biblical inspiration is thereby "irremediably compromised."[21] By 1885, Turmel experienced his faith steadily giving ground before the seemingly unassailable results of scientific exegesis. Coupled with a growing loss of faith was the increasing conviction that Catholic apologists he had formerly revered were guilty of advocating theses whose falsity could not have escaped them. And in the case of those who could be considered sincere, their sincerity was gained at the price of a profound ignorance of the real issues at stake.[22] The tension which he experienced between his "front-stage" performance as seminary professor and his "backstage" convictions as scholar is neatly encapsulated in the comment, "for several months I thought as a rationalist and acted as a Christian."[23] The breakpoint occurred during the spring of 1886—he even assigned it a date: 18 March. On the feast of St. Joseph, which evoked for Turmel the "irreducible contradictions" of the infancy narratives, he opened the breviary to say first vespers. Scarcely having opened it, he closed it again abruptly, saying half aloud, "These stories are fables, the Bible is full of deceptions, Christian dogmatics is groundless; I will no longer say the breviary."[24] Making good on this decision left him with additional time each day for study, but did little to address the discrepancy between his public persona and private identity. To retrieve Barbour's phrase, he was confronted with "the ethics of disbelief."[25]

Summing up to this point, it is apparent that Turmel's deconversion proceeded rather rapidly when compared with Houtin's. Although Houtin's belief in the credibility of the received accounts of Church history was progressively undermined, for a time biblical inspiration interposed a barrier that preserved the veracity of Scripture for him. It was only in undertaking serious study of nineteenth century exegesis that this barrier fell—although hope for some form of transformed Catholicism remained, at least for a time. Turmel, with his self-taught Hebrew, growing acquaintance with critical exegesis, and increasing disaffection with Catholic interpreters, resembles Loisy more strongly. With Loisy, however, the accent falls on the positive potential in criticism for providing a more adequate apologetic for Catholicism. The Church that would emerge from such a winnowing process would be decidedly different; but above all it would retain its ability to function as a moral force in society. With Turmel, on the other hand, it is the destructive potential of criticism that makes the greater impact. It reveals the thoroughgoing inadequacy, not simply of the traditional apologetic, but of the tradition itself. It destroys any claim the Church might have to moral credentials. Given this fundamental difference, it is hardly surprising that Loisy's response to "the assured results of criticism" seeks to be creative. If the traditional notion of inspiration is no longer adequate to "the facts," then the task is to revise it so as to align it with them. Turmel simply accepts the traditional notions, inspiration included. In effect he agrees with Bossuet's major premise: if Catholicism is true, then it cannot have varied. In contrast to Bossuet, he will show its variation in essentials and uncover its duplicity. Thus, despite attempts such as Portalié's to assimilate Turmel's idea of development to Loisy's, they are going in very different directions in its application. When it comes to giving an account of the development of their lives, differences emerge as well. As long as Loisy retained the conviction that a renovated Catholicism could yet play a part in the future of humanity, he could legitimate his remaining in the Church in the role of reformer, despite his unorthodox beliefs. This option was closed to Turmel. Since he came to assume the discrepant role of "informer," he required a different rationale for its sustained performance.[26]

Undeviating Apostasy

Relations of domination are, at the same time, relations of resistance.
James Scott[27]

In one way, for Turmel the year 1886 marked a settling of accounts with the past. Henceforth, he would view Christian dogmas as purely the products of human imagination, their value on a par with "Buddhist dogmatics."[28] That same year opened up a route to the future. For it also marked a shift in his principal object of study, from the Bible to the history of Christian dogma, anticipating the direction of his published work. For his campaign of enlightening his fellow clergy, however, he initially stuck to the familiar terrain of the Bible. To a few friends he communicated a modest portion of what he had gleaned from Reuss: the multiple strands of tradition present in the Genesis flood narrative (carefully refraining from pointing out the contradictions between them), divergences in the chronology of the psalms as traditionally represented (prudently adding that this did not at all impinge upon dogma). This had the intended result of undermining confidence in Fulcran Vigouroux's manual, but the effect was limited to a mere handful of priests. Moreover, he decided that even these modest revelations had pushed the limits and that he could go no further.[29] Still, even in the absence of any clear idea of how he would disseminate the fruits of his research, he persisted in his program of patristic study. This state of affairs continued until August of 1892, when Turmel lost his faculty position as a result of a momentary lapse in his prudent reserve. A clearly heterodox remark made to a seminarian, which found its way to his superiors, sealed his fate.

Abbé Ceillier, the faculty colleague to whom, years earlier, he had confided some of his growing doubts, became his confessor. More at home on philosophical terrain (where, in Turmel's estimation, it was much easier to substitute convoluted argument for hard evidence), Ceillier failed to comprehend the impact of critical exegesis on his penitent's state of mind. He ascribed it instead to a mental breakdown caused by overwork, a diagnosis which Gendron and—more crucially —the diocese's vicar general, Abbé Guillois, shared. This saved Turmel from expulsion from the diocese and the priesthood. After an interval, he was assigned to the diocesan school for late vocations. These experiences seemed to deepen his self-perception as a "martyr" to the truth and to catalyze a spirit of "revenge."

> Degraded, humiliated before the entire clergy of the diocese, reduced to performing the task of a seminarian [at the school], separated from my books, bereft of opportunity to pursue my studies which, for more than fifteen years, were my life, I was treated like a criminal. I had, in fact, committed a crime, a crime horrible in the Church's view, since I had proven the groundlessness of its claims. And this proof had been the ineluctable result of study, undertaken at the beginning to defend dogma, and pursued with honesty, with fervor, and with tenacity.[30]

In December of 1893, Turmel assumed the chaplaincy of the Little Sisters of the Poor on the outskirts of Rennes. This afforded him greater insulation from surveillance and ample leisure for study. Gradually, he was able to resume his program of research, aided by the combined resources of university, municipal, and seminary libraries. The consistent focus of all this work remained the evolution of dogma. By autumn of 1896, he had read the greater part of the Latin patrology. Parallel with this he had gained acquaintance with the principal Greek Fathers of the first four centuries. For the previous two years, he had supplemented direct contact with the primary texts with extensive reading in German scholarship on the history of dogma, beginning with Adolf von Harnack. Like Houtin and Loisy, Turmel's mastery of his chosen subject area arose largely out of practical engagement with the texts. Guidance from secondary sources was supplementary, and his isolation from like-minded colleagues virtually complete. In September of 1896, he put pen to paper and began a history of the dogma of original sin. The following spring, he read a portion of the manuscript to a fellow diocesan priest, Abbé Pautonnier, who brought it to Loisy's attention. Its acceptance for publication in the *Revue d'histoire et de littérature religieuses* motivated the communication of a second study, on angelology, which actually saw publication first.

Pautonnier shared Loisy's evaluation of the angelology material with Turmel: "On the whole I believe that M. Turmel's history of dogmas will be able to rival the most scholarly produced by Germany, that it will have the advantage besides of being broadly conceived, without any *a priori* system and of being clearer in its exposition."[31] Loisy did recommend to Turmel directly that some of the language be toned down and that a number of the more provocative texts be excised. But, although it would put the theologians in an extremely bad light, the study on angelology did not engage any dogma. Despite Pautonnier's counsel that it be published pseudonymously, Loisy thought it safe to publish under Turmel's own name, and this fell in line with its author's own designs. "My revenge would have been incomplete if the Rennes clergy . . . had been able to think that I was squashed forever."[32]

Although given a favorable reception by some of the younger clergy, Turmel's articles were a source of serious disquiet—especially (and predictably) for theologians. The Jesuit Julien Fontaine alluded to one of the claims concerning belief in eternal punishment made in the first of them, drawing Turmel into a controversy. This broadened into a challenge to Turmel's pose to be functioning solely as an historian, not responsible therefore for the theological implications of his work, and a stigmatization of the work itself as "false, antiscientific and anticatholic."[33]

This exchange had results unanticipated by either party. To ensure that his accusations against Turmel's orthodoxy did not go unnoticed by those in a position to do something about them, Fontaine sent copies of his articles to some members of the hierarchy, including the archbishops of Rennes and Paris. In mid-1901, there was communicated to Turmel a directive of the Congregation of the Index that he publish nothing further without first submitting it to the approval of ecclesiastical authority. His own ordinary, Cardinal Labouré, saw the hand of Cardinal Richard in this and was not pleased at the interference of Paris in Rennes. Turmel's submission to the Index placed the matter in the hands of his archbishop, who decided to leave him in peace. Turmel continued to publish in the RHLR without prior ecclesiastical inspection, and Richard's hands were tied. This left Turmel unsure about the limits of what would be tolerated under this arrangement. Direct attacks against dogma were clearly out of bounds, but what about claims liable to scandalize the narrow minded? For a brief period, until matters appeared more settled, Turmel had recourse to pseudonyms: Denys Lenain and Goulven Lézurec.[34]

However, the same articles which had caught the attention of Fontaine had also been noticed by others, with more favorable response. The invitation to Turmel to collaborate with the *Revue du clergé français* put the archbishop of Paris once more in a position to insist on official approval. Rennes complied with the letter if not the spirit of the Congregation's directive by granting a *Nihil obstat* to whatever Turmel submitted. This not only placed his regular contributions to the RCF beyond Richard's control; it also conferred upon them the brevet of orthodoxy.[35]

A further mark of legitimacy was bestowed on Turmel by the publication of his *Histoire de la théologie positive depuis l'origine jusqu'au concile de Trente* in November of 1903. It appeared as the first offering in the *Bibliothèque de théologie historique*, published under the auspices of the Institut catholique of Paris. This book constitutes a good example of Turmel's method of procedure, provides an index via reviewers of how it was received, and is important in relation to subsequent controversy over his pseudonymous productions. In its introduction, Turmel presented himself in his customary guise of impartial historian who functions as a "faithful reporter," scrupulously avoiding the substitution of his own thought for that of the documents he quotes or summarizes. This is, of course, the same strategy adopted by Loisy and Houtin in many of their writings. As such it was not unfamiliar to contemporary followers of these controversies. Less familiar would have been Turmel's conception of "positive theology" adopted in the volume. He defined it as

> the exposition of the proofs which have served to support religious teaching. It must, to the degree to which the documents allow, go back to the origin of these proofs, indicate the moment of their appearance, then follow them over the course of centuries, laying out the developments they have undergone or the transformations they have assumed.[36]

While this approach was not entirely original with Turmel,[37] he was its unique contemporary French representative.

Reviewers did not always accept this delimitation of the field. Writing in *Études*, Jules Lebreton pointed out that marshaling texts was not the same thing as doing positive theology,[38] pointing to a crucial and characteristic defect in Turmel's approach. Within the chosen framework, however, it was generally agreed that Turmel had succeeded in his design with an admirable degree of erudition, producing "a work of the highest value."[39] Lebreton alluded to the author's earlier articles in the

RHLR, which had alarmed some "by the boldness and novelty of his historical theses," but admitted that in the volume under review he had been more circumspect.[40] Not sufficiently circumspect for the reviewer in *L'Ami du clergé*, who judged it unsuitable for seminarians or even the average priest, since "it would not be a lesson of love and respect for theology."[41] But apparently more than sufficiently circumspect for the person writing in the *Dublin Review*, who quoted approvingly the concluding words of Turmel's preface:

> Prominent bishops . . . have called upon the clergy to apply themselves to the Fathers of the Church, to familiarize themselves with their writings. Let the present volume serve that aim! Let it inspire in some young studious priests the desire to return to the sources of revelation and to apply themselves to the serious study of Scripture and Tradition![42]

Having been afforded "a privileged peek backstage" via Turmel's autobiographical self-revelations, it is impossible to refrain from seeing more than a little irony in these sentiments. That there were deeper purposes at work was not entirely opaque to contemporaries. Outside the Roman Catholic fold, E. Michaud saw this—or at least expressed it—most clearly. In the course of his review he remarked that "everything [Turmel] does not say is more interesting still than what he does say." A careful reading "between the lines" yielded the conclusion:

> The entire history of theological debates is filled with this butchering of liberty, of truth, and of science. And this butchering is all the more distressing in that the victors, in order to have their systems accepted, had recourse to *apocryphal* texts and that common opinion, in the Church, has thus been formed thanks to errors and falsifications. There is the positive, unimpeachable fact, that is easy to establish in reading M. Turmel's book attentively.[43]

Fortunately for Turmel, not all of his readers, especially Roman Catholic ones, were that attentive. But when later pseudonymous publications explicitly drew conclusions which were carefully left in abeyance in the *Histoire de la théologie positive*, or when, under his own name, the *Histoire du dogme de la papauté* (1908) advanced conclusions rejected in his earlier work, disquiet deepened over Turmel's true commitments.

Multiplying Deviants

Patterns of domination can, in fact, accommodate a reasonably high
level of practical resistance so long as that resistance is not publicly
and unambiguously acknowledged. Once it is, however, it requires a
public reply if the symbolic status quo is to be restored.

James Scott[44]

Disputes over disciplinary boundaries can be productive of deviant behavior. Claims for the autonomy of philosophy, history, and critical biblical study vis-à-vis theology posed a direct challenge to the very core of neo-Thomism. Conversely, the monopolization of professional authority resists inroads by seeking to maintain the status quo and deviantize innovators.[45] When the tactics used by innovators become matters of contention, disputes over disciplinary boundaries also become disputes over moral boundaries. In his initial attempts to enlighten a few clerical contemporaries with the results of his biblical research, Turmel seems to have quickly acquired a sense of the limits of the acceptable. A decade later, Turmel was able to benefit from Loisy's advice regarding what was prudent. In 1900–1901, he resorted briefly to pseudonymous publication while the articles on original sin previously accepted by the RHLR continued to run there with Turmel as their acknowledged author. The recourse to *identité masqué* appears more the effect of personal circumstances, a result of the directive of the Index, than any drastic change in the content of his work. However, when in 1906–1907 Turmel once more published pseudonymously, it was because dogma was at issue.[46] In the first of those years, "Antoine Dupin" examined the dogma of the Trinity in early Christianity, while in 1907 "Guillaume Herzog" produced a second series on Marian dogma. Both appeared in the RHLR.[47] Both were violently attacked as heterodox and led to the condemnation of the *Revue,* which published them by Cardinal Richard in May of 1907. And both touched off a controversy which made it clear that, while the defense of dogma remained primary, the pseudonymous nature of the attack was itself a volatile issue. Writing two decades after this controversy, when Turmel's identity had been established not only with Lenain, Dupin, and Herzog, but with a whole team of pseudonyms adopted subsequently, Jean Rivière cited "the case of this priest who, while remaining in the Church and adding his own name to the leading personages of ecclesiastical science, at the same time served the cause of rationalism and impiety under cover of various masks" as "an example of a very peculiar morality."[48]

The process of this unmasking constitutes an interesting story in itself. The material on the Trinity and on Mariology which Turmel sent to the RHLR in 1906 had been actually worked up by 1899, but had languished in manuscript form. He had incorporated portions of the work on Marian dogma into his *Théologie positive*, published in 1903, but had forgotten doing so at the time he sent off his manuscripts to the *Revue*. The close dependence of entire passages of Herzog's articles upon Turmel's book argued for some sort of relationship.[49] In a similar vein, Turmel had utilized his research on the development of the dogma of the Trinity in several articles which appeared under his name in the *New York Review* over 1905–1906. Once again, similarities were simply too striking to be attributed to coincidence.

Louis Saltet, professor of church history at the Toulouse Institut catholique, used internal criticism to establish (1) that Dupin had plagiarized Turmel, (2) that Herzog had also plagiarized Turmel, (3) that in reality Herzog and Dupin were one and the same person, and (4) that Lenain was but a third pseudonym of Herzog-Dupin.[50] Saltet began by noting the particularity of Turmel's conception of positive theology —and showing that the pseudonymous writers shared it. He went on to establish by close textual comparisons plagiarism of references, of entire passages and translations, of style, and of particular doctrines. Admittedly, in his *Histoire de la théologie positive* Turmel had limited himself to the role of reporter, while Herzog did not hesitate to render judgments on the texts and draw conclusions which remained unstated in Turmel's published work.[51] Nonetheless, these "antichristian *conclusions* of Herzog on Mariology" aside, "the entire substance of Herzog-Dupin (general ideas and references) are found in M. Turmel."[52]

To these points of internal criticism were added several external factors. First, it had not been possible to find a Guillaume Herzog in Lausanne (where he claimed to be domiciled) or an Antoine Dupin in Paris. Moreover, beyond the dependencies established by internal criticism of the texts was the chronology of those texts. Both Dupin and Herzog had published in the RHLR at a time when Turmel's name was conspicuously absent from its contributors. Turmel had, however, published several articles in the *New York Review*, in 1905 and 1906. Saltet demonstrated that Dupin had merely translated passages of these articles into French, and incorporated them into his own work. Dupin's article of July–August 1906 in the RHLR exhibited dependencies on Turmel's NYR piece which appeared in October–November 1905 —which Saltet termed plagiarism "*à la vapeur.*" More curiously still, Dupin's publication of July-August also showed crucial borrowings from Turmel's NYR article in the previous April–May fascicle. Saltet ironically styled this plagiarism "*télégraphique.*"[53] The network of dependencies was further complicated by the inclusion of Lenain. Relying once more on the kinds of factors he had used to establish connections between Herzog and Turmel, Saltet demonstrated borrowings by Herzog (1907) from Lenain (1901). But it was also possible to show dependencies in *Turmel's* 1903 book on the pseudonymous Lenain—so Lenain must have plagiarized Turmel's manuscript![54] Furthermore, Turmel's response to these revelations was less than satisfactory. He categorically denied identity with either Dupin or Herzog, but exhibited a notable lack of outrage at being plagiarized or regarding the use to which his own work had been put. He admitted that others had access to his manuscripts, but refused to point any fingers. Turmel did admit his identity with Lézurec and with Lenain. These were rather safe concessions, however, as Saltet himself judged Lenain's ideas "much more Catholic than Turmel's."[55]

Despite Turmel's denials that he was in fact Herzog-Dupin, other critics drew the conclusion Saltet had carefully refrained from making, but toward which his work led. Saltet's colleague, Eugène Portalié, pressed the question again in a series of articles that appeared in *Études* over the latter half of 1908, and did not hesitate to cite both a German and an American author who were convinced of Turmel's complicity by Saltet's arguments.[56] At that point, Turmel's disclaimer, made to his ordinary and in print, stonewalled critics.[57] However, Saltet's statement, made in May of 1908, that "The Herzog-Dupin Affair is not ended. It is beginning,"[58] would turn out to be prophetic.

In the wake of the controversy, the names Antoine Dupin and Guillaume Herzog disappeared from the ranks of published authors— along with Turmel's own. By way of compensation, over the next several years he generated a veritable team of pseudonymous identities, parceled out among various areas of historical theology. To "Louis Coulage" was allocated the formation of christology, while "Alexis Vanbeck" alternated with "André Lagarde" and "Alphonse Michel" in dealing with penance. "Armand Dulac," and later "Robert Lawson" exposed difficulties with the history of eucharistic dogma, and "Henri Delafosse" assumed responsibility for Christian origins. Turmel's former teacher, Louis Billot, was not neglected; "Edmond Perrin" functioned as his critic. The team was rounded out by "Hippolyte Gallerand," and by "Paul Letourneur" (whose articles on the origin of Christian institutions and beliefs subsequently appeared in book form under the name "Louis Coulage"). Meanwhile, Turmel outwardly conformed, maintaining his ecclesiastical status, albeit in a marginal role. He emerged from his eremitical existence to say mass and hear confessions.

Turmel weathered the "rupture in the performance" of his work of subversion caused by the detection of the relationships, both substantive and chronological, between his work and those of Herzog-Dupin-Lenain. He was eventually unmasked by a "privileged peek backstage" that had occurred early in the 1920s, but only became public in 1928. Its public disclosure was catalyzed by Jean Rivière's response to Hippolyte Gallarand's articles on the dogma of the redemption. In a footnote Rivière noted certain characteristic positions and phrases present in Gallerand and peculiar to Turmel. The critic remained content with indicating the plagiarism and did not openly accuse Turmel of authorship.[59] Two years later, Louis Saltet published proof of the identity of Gallerand and Turmel. Having come into a possession of a letter written by "Gallerand" to Rivière, and another by Turmel, Saltet compared the handwriting and concluded that they were the product of the same person. In the continuation of that article, he revealed that he had for some time been aware of Turmel's identity with Herzog-Dupin, but had declined to renew the controversy. Rivière's rejoinder now called it forth. It appears that when Abbé Paul Lejay, one of the editors of the RHLR, had died in 1920, he had not secured his correspondence and papers, which passed into the archives of the archdiocese of Paris. Among them was a card, signed by Turmel, requesting that Lejay publish the articles on Marian dogma under the name Herzog, instead of under Dupin as originally intended. He thought "Dupin" not sufficiently secure. This unmasked Turmel as the inventor of pseudonyms intended to throw orthodox pursuers off the scent.[60] These revelations were more than sufficient to reopen the question of Turmel's pseudonymous activity with his archbishop, now Cardinal Charost, and with Rome. In the face of such evidence he was compelled to admit his authorship of the offending Dupin and Herzog texts. In the hope (naive he judged in retrospect) of lifting the sanctions he thereby incurred, he went on to identify himself as the source of the pseudonymous team that emerged after the Herzog-Dupin controversy. In November of 1930, Turmel was excommunicated *vitandus* by the Holy Office. Thus concluded what the *Revue apologétique* had termed *"Un épisode actuel du modernisme."*[61]

Justifying Deviance

The ressentiment *attitude even plays a role in the formation of perceptions, expectations, and memories. It automatically selects*

those aspects of experience which can justify the factual application
of this pattern of feeling.

Max Scheler[62]

In light of all this, Turmel's morality looked very peculiar indeed. In 1908, he had not only denied to his ordinary any identity with Herzog-Dupin, he had gone on to affirm:

> As a Catholic priest, I profess all that the Roman Church professes and reject all that it rejects. As an affectionate and devoted son of the Virgin Mary, I believe in her Immaculate Conception, in her perfect and perpetual virginity, in her divine maternity; in a word, I adhere, in matters concerning the mother of God, to the complete doctrine of the Holy Church.[63]

Such declarations were hardly compatible with either his pseudonymous publications or his private positions. Moreover, when his own works were placed on the Index in 1909, 1910, and 1911, Turmel submitted. He took the Oath Against Modernism when that was promulgated in 1910.

The disparity between all this "impression management" and his subversive activity carried on under fictitious personae left Turmel with a formidable task of justification in his autobiography. First, he obviously felt constrained to justify his remaining a priest within the Church while publishing work, much of it pseudonymous, subversive of Catholicism's basic tenets. In short, he had to counter the accusation of "treason." Second, he had to answer the charge of "cowardice," leveled by Saltet and others, for having repeatedly concealed the truth from his superiors, both with regard to the true state of his beliefs and his responsibility for airing those in print.[64]

In this context, motivations take on a sociological dimension, insofar as they enable actors to relate themselves to social groups and are articulated in vocabularies that reflect moral standards. When elaborated, such vocabularies of motives are termed "motivational accounting systems."

> Motivational accounting systems allow the individual to justify his acts and to influence others. . . . The types of motivational accounting systems the individual chooses to use are not arbitrary inventions. They reflect the type of justification acceptable in a specific cultural matrix. . . . Whether internal or external, these mechanisms provide actors with the necessary vocabulary to justify past, present, and future deviancy.[65]

When used by deviants, such accounts may incorporate "neutralization techniques"—vocabularies used to construct a moral conception of self while engaging in proscribed behavior.[66] This reflects an underlying process of identity negotiation, as the behavior must be justified to oneself and—except in cases of secret deviance—to others. For our purposes it seems best to consider Turmel's neutralization techniques analytically rather than chronologically. This has the advantage of grouping his varied motives under a number of types, with a view toward clarifying them in the process.

Aspects of higher loyalties. A paramount concern for Turmel was the effect that an open break with the Church would have on his parents and his benefactor. To have openly declared his loss of faith would have only inflicted great suffering on them. Given the stigma attached to the lapsed priest, he would have had to find a place in which he was unknown to gain his livelihood, thereby separating himself from family.[67]

By continuing to function within the Church, Turmel was faced with more than simply justifying his persistence in a role. He also needed to construct an alternative identity that would be consistent with both private belief and public performance. In *Comment j'ai donné congé aux dogmes*, he writes of "the voice of duty" which "made itself heard," calling him to release others from the error from which he himself had been freed, and to consecrate a portion of his life "to the expansion of truth."[68] In *Comment l'église romaine m'a donné congé* he expressed this in terms of categories that became central to his self-understanding: "Martyr of the truth, I will be its apostle."[69] Fidelity to this higher vocation, this "apostolate of enlightenment,"[70] served to counter the charge of "treason."

The flip side of legitimation of motives via appeal to a higher loyalty involves delegitimation of any claims made by a "lower" one. The next two neutralization techniques directly address this.

Condemnation of the condemners. As with Houtin, Turmel clearly was more upset by what the Church withheld than by what it taught. He cites Renan's case as exceptional, in that Renan had access to the studies that opened his eyes while still a seminarian. For the vast majority of aspirants to the priesthood, everything that would weaken their commitment was systematically concealed in the "fortresses of lies" that were seminaries.[71] Even after ordination, the burden of pastoral duties left most with neither the time nor the means to instruct themselves. Naturally, what was withheld from the clergy remained hidden from the faithful. Both "do not have at hand anything other than books which sustain them in illusion."[72]

Turmel draws a moral distinction between the case of one who was able to pierce the tissue of pious fabrications prior to ordination—and who would go on to accept it anyway, performing the role while lacking belief—and one who discovers it only after receiving priesthood. In the latter case, representative not only of Turmel, but of hundreds of others by his reckoning, the Church itself is held responsible for the disorder of unbelieving priests saying mass. In short, given its conduct, Turmel did not think that the Church was *owed* the truth. Through its own lack of truth, it had forfeited the right. To the charge that he had failed in his moral obligation as the accused, he replied, "say rather that my judges began by failing first and foremost in their professional obligations and that their immoral conduct deprived them of all right to the truth."[73] And with it, all claim to moral authority over him.

In addition to his more general condemnation of the Church for its failure to admit the truth and its suppression of those who would reveal it, Turmel singled out individuals in order to impugn their motives. Saltet is accused of acting out of rancor over rejection by the *Revue* of an article submitted by him. Likewise, Turmel considered the change in attitude toward him exhibited by Duchesne in 1908 and Batiffol in 1922 to be personal in nature. In both cases, Turmel's published work had contravened positions put forth by the two scholars, which evoked from them decidedly negative evaluations of him. As a final example, certain details which surfaced after the sudden death of Cardinal Charost, and which cast doubt on his moral credentials, are glossed in the text and enlarged upon in an appendix.[74]

Denial of victim. This device admits that the deviant behavior in question causes harm, but denies that the offended party is truly deserving of victim status. The behavior finds its moral justification as a restitution for previous injustice the "victim" has inflicted on others. In a way, this provides a nexus between the previous two categories of neutralization techniques. To counter the systematic deception perpetuated by the Roman Church over the course of centuries, Turmel would undertake his apostolate of truth. It is significant that he described this as a work of "revenge," as noted earlier. Also of significance is the way in which this work is represented. The "harm" suffered by the "official Church" is severely mitigated by its responsibility in falsifying its own history in the first place.[75]

Claim of normalcy. Although his confessor and his faculty colleague initially found his situation anomalous to their experience,

Turmel eventually concluded that it was far from unique. In fact, he came to believe that the priest who lost his faith after ordination, then left the Church, constituted the exception rather than the rule. Nor could he be thought abnormal when weighed by the canons of critical scholarship.[76] As the modernist crisis escalated, he discerned clerical counterparts who seemed similar to him on both counts: "undeceived priests" distinguished for their critical scholarship.[77]

Claim of relative acceptability. This entails a kind of justification by invidious comparison. It has surfaced earlier in the context of situating Turmel in relation to modernism. While he perceived his aims to be congruent with those of modernists, clearly he thought his means of accomplishing those aims morally superior to theirs. In their pose as enlightened apologists, they employed orthodox formulae to convey ideas which were far from orthodox. But the price they paid was to live with duplicity. By contrast, Turmel portrays his objective as bringing to light the variations of dogmas by gathering up the texts in which these variations were evident. "The historian of dogma does not have the resources of equivocations with which Duchesne and Loisy shielded themselves. His specialization offers him no evasion."[78]

To recapitulate: motivational accounting systems do more than supply "good reasons" for a line of conduct. They are modes of influence—of influencing the self as well as others. They may render behavior possible by neutralizing specific proscriptions prohibiting it or by neutralizing the authority that legitimates those proscriptions. They may sustain a present course of action or retrospectively justify it in the past. As such they provide means of creating or sustaining a moral identity in the face of countervailing definitions.

Conclusion

The "multiple identities" of the chapter's title refer to the team of pseudonymous authors concocted by Turmel. In terms of his own self-interpretation after his loss of faith, the identity is unitary. His self-presentation as apostle and martyr of the truth is one side of the coin whose reverse is the collective identity of Catholicism as consciously duplicitous. Likewise, the *moderniste démasqué* of the title, an echo of Rivière's discussion of Turmel's pseudonymous activity, yields to a deeper sense of that term. If one grants to modernism, *pace Pascendi*, the aim of a constructive reconciliation between Catholicism and modernity, then Turmel's autobiographical revelations unmask him as something other than a modernist. Nonetheless, in circumstances in which extreme positions made the deepest impressions, one can see how more moderate stances were enveloped in a common stigma of destructive potential, perceived to be characteristic of all. Turmel's own apparent trajectory from the less radical positions of *Histoire de la théologie positive depuis l'origine jusqu'au concile de Trente* to those of *Histoire du dogme de la papauté*, plus the exploitation of his work by "Herzog" and "Dupin," were not lost on orthodox critics. It underscored the possibility of *is hodie, quis cras*?

Needless to say, the definition of the institution arrived at early by Turmel, and later by Houtin, was resoundingly rejected by their critics. The extrinsicism of the dominant theology, the tenor of the prevailing ecclesiology, and the generally defensive position of French Catholicism in face of the surrounding intellectual culture made any concessions to moral imperfection difficult. By contrast, the rather binary mentality reflected in both Houtin and Turmel, coupled with their socialization into a manual theology which provided few resources for creative reinterpretation, resulted in a stark truth-or-lies evaluation of the tradition. Any complete analysis of Turmel and his work would have to give more attention to the defects in theological method on both sides of the ideological divide, which contributed to the cognitive incommensurability characteristic of the modernist crisis. In line with an emphasis on a moral incommensurability, a more sociological perspective has been adopted here.

Notes

[1] James C. Scott, *Domination and the Arts of Resistance* (New Haven: Yale University Press, 1990), 4.

[2] Although Turmel wrote the story of his life as a single unit, completing it in 1931, circumstances dictated its publication in two parts at later dates.

[3] RHLR 3 (1898): 289–308; 407–34; 533–52; RHLR 4 (1899): 217–38; 289–309; 414–34; 537–62. A complete bibliography of Turmel's work may be found in Kurt-Peter Gertz, *Joseph Turmel (1859–1943). Ein theologiegeschichtlicher Beitrag zum Problem der Geschichtlichkeit der Dogmen* (Frankfurt: Peter Lang, 1975).

[4] Joseph Turmel, *Comment j'ai donné congé aux dogmes* (Herblay: Editions de l'idée libre, 1935), 111–12 (hereafter CJDCD).

[5] *Ibid.*, 47.

[6] *Ibid.*, 79. Cf. *Comment l'église romaine m'a donné congé* (Herblay: Editions de l'idée libre, [1939]), 126 (hereafter CER).

[7] Alec Vidler, *A Variety of Catholic Modernists* (Cambridge: Cambridge University Press, 1970), 61; Albert Houtin, *Histoire du modernisme catholique* (Paris: Chez l'auteur, 1913), 397; Félix Sartiaux, *Joseph Turmel: Prêtre, historien des dogmes* (Paris: Rieder, 1931), 212.

[8] Jean Rivière, *Le modernisme dans l'églsie* (Paris: Letouzey, 1929), 484–505.

[9] Eugène Portalié, *La critique de M. Turmel et "la Question Herzog-Dupin"* (Paris: Lethielleux, 1908).

[10] The term is derived from the sociology of deviance and covers both "rule creators" and "rule enforcers." See Howard Becker, *The Outsiders* (New York: Free Press, 1966), ch. 8. "Like distress over the condition itself, a lack of available means for its resolution may also provoke moral entrepeneurship." Erdwin H. Pfuhl and Stuart Henry, *The Deviance Process* (New York: Aldine De Gruyter, 1993), 86.

[11] Joseph Turmel, "Mémoire sur mes travaux." This was published posthumously and is accessible in Gertz, 302–09.

[12] Edwin M. Schur, *The Politics of Deviance* (Englewood Cliffs, New Jersey: Prentice-Hall, 1980), 141.

[13] "Their different versions of what the problem is may then become a central point at issue in a collective deviance struggle. *Ibid.*, 142. In *L'Ascétique moderniste* J.A. Chollet draws upon *Lamentabili* and *Pascendi* to contrast "modernist ethics" with the Church's traditional morality, in terms that could fairly be described as incommensurable. There is something different at work in *Comment j'ai donné congé aux dogmes* and in *Comment l'église romaine m'a donné congé*, however. At stake is not a valuation of morality, but a moral evaluation of tradition and its guardians. J.A. Chollet, *L'Ascétique moderniste* (Paris: P. Lethielleux, n.d.), 7–51.

[14] Scott, 107.

[15] Although Turmel does not dwell on his earlier seminary formation, the instruction he received at Rennes was comparable to that received by Houtin at Angers. See Jean Delumeau, ed., *Le Diocèse de Rennes* (Paris: Beauchesne, 1979), 241–43.

[16] Turmel, CJDCD, 16.

[17] *Ibid.*, 21. In his biography of Turmel, Sartiaux fills in the background related to his subject's early upbringing. Turmel came from a very poor family (neither of his parents could write), but they nutured an intense piety. He owed his being raised above these circumstances to the generosity of one of the parish clergy, who saw to his education. Sartiaux, *Joseph Turmel*, 40–42. Vidler comments: "As in the case of a number of other French priests who were involved in the modernist movement, this pious upbringing, this dependence on the Church for pastoral care, and this indebtedness to the Church for educational opportunity, should be borne in mind when one seeks to understand their subsequent love-hate relationship to the Church that mothered them" (56–57).

[18] On Reuss's biblical scholarship, see Paul Lobstein, "Edouard Reuss (1804–1891). Notes et souvenirs," in *Revue d'histoire et de philosophie religieuses* 1 (1921): 428–45. Also see A. Causse, *La Bible de Reuss et la renaissance des études d'histoire religieuse en France* (Paris: Félix Alcan, 1929).

[19] Turmel, CJDCD, 24.

[20] *Ibid.*, 26–30.

[21] *Ibid.*, 33–34.

[22] In this connection he mentions the efforts of Paulin Martin to uphold the Mosaic authenticity of the Pentateuch. J.P. Martin, *Introduction à la critique générale de l'Ancien Testament: De l'origine du Pentateuque*, 3 vols. (Paris: Maisonnueve and Leclerc, n.d.). As the direct recipient of Martin's teaching at the Paris Institut catholique, Loisy was no more convinced by these attempts. See Alfred Loisy, *Choses passées* (Paris: Nourry, 1913), 54.

[23] Turmel, CJDCD, 38.

[24] *Ibid.*, 39.

[25] See John D. Barbour, *Versions of Deconversion: Autobiography and the Loss of Faith* (Charlottesville: University Press of Virginia, 1994), ch. 6.

[26] "The informer is someone who pretends to the performers to be a member of their team, is allowed to come backstage and to acquire destructive information, and then openly or secretly sells out the show to the audience." Erving Goffman, *The*

Presentation of Self in Everyday Life (Garden City, New York: Anchor Books, 1959), 145. Cf. the material on the "whistleblower" in *The Politics of Religious Apostasy,* ed. David G. Bromley (Westport, CT: Praeger, 1998), especially ch. 2.

[27] Scott, 45.

[28] Turmel, CJDCD, 43.

[29] *Ibid.,* 55–57.

[30] *Ibid.,* 78.

[31] Loisy to Pautonnier, 4 March 1898. CJDCD, 109.

[32] *Ibid.,* 111.

[33] See *Revue du monde catholique* 137 (1899): 193–225 (the original allusion appears on pp. 219–20n.); 138 (1899): 209–218 (the charges cited occur on 215–16); 139 (1899): 226–44; 140 (1899): 144–80; 608–15.

[34] Under Denys Lenain he published in RHLR 5 (1900): 552–62 and RHLR 6 (1901): 454–65 and 531–36. Goulven Lézurec appeared in *La Justice sociale* (13 July 1901): 1–2.

[35] Turmel, CJDCD, 119–32.

[36] Joseph Turmel, *Histoire de la théologie positive depuis l'origine jusq'au concile de Trente* (Paris: Gabriel Beauchesne, 1904), v (hereafter *Hist. de la théologie pos.* I; A second volume was published in 1906).

[37] Louis Saltet pointed out that it was characteristic of Jean de Launoy in the seventeenth century and J. Langen in the nineteenth. Louis Saltet, *La Question Herzog-Dupin* (Paris: P. Lethielleux, 1908), 20–21.

[38] J. Lebreton, Review of *Hist. de la théologie pos.* I, in *Études* 98 (1904): 861.

[39] Cf. reviews in *Canoniste contemporaine* 27 (1904): 629–30; *Dublin Review* 135 (1904): 198–99; *Polybiblion* 101 (1904): 141–42.

[40] *Études* 98 (1904): 860.

[41] *L'Ami du clergé* 27 (1905): 438.

[42] *Dublin Review* 135 (1904): 199. Cf. Turmel, *Hist. de la théologie pos.* I, ix.

[43] E. Michaud, Review of *Hist. de la théologie pos.* I, in *Revue internationale de théologie* 12 (1904): 494–95.

[44] Scott, 57.

[45] Ben-Yehuda, *Deviance and Moral Boundaries,* 121.

[46] Turmel, CER, 8.

[47] RHLR 11 (1906): 219–31; 353–65; 515–32 and RHLR 12 (1907): 118–33; 320–40; 483–607 respectively. Both series were also published separately as brochures.

[48] Rivière, 502.

[49] Turmel, CER, 7–17.

[50] Saltet, *op. cit.*

[51] *Ibid.,* 42–43n.

[52] *Ibid.,* 259.

[53] *Ibid.,* 59–65.

[54] *Ibid.,* 232.

[55] *Ibid.,* 259–60.

[56] Published separately as *La Critique de M. Turmel et "la Question Herzog-Dupin,"* *op. cit.,* 29–30n. and 74n.

[57] Turmel was able to show Msgr. Dubourg instances where his published work had been plagiarized by others. That textual evidence, together with correspondence establishing the communication of his manuscripts in response to requests, lent plausibility to similar appropriation by Herzog and Dupin. See CER, 25–32.

[58] Saltet, 119.

[59] Jean Rivière, "Le dogme de la rédemption chez saint Augustin," *Revue des sciences religieuses* 7 (1927): 429–32.

[60] Louis Saltet, "La suite des pseudonymes de M.J. Turmel," *Bulletin de littérature ecclésiastique* 30 (1929): 83–90, 104–25, 165–82.

[61] Bruno de Solages, "Un épisode actuel du modernisme," *Revue apologétique* 49 (1929): 385–403.

[62] Max Scheler, *Ressentiment*, trans. Lewis B. Coser and William W. Holdheim (Milwaukee: Marquette University Press, 1994), 54.

[63] This formulary was drawn up by his archbishop. Turmel copied it in his own hand and signed it in May of 1908. CER, 31.

[64] Turmel, CER, 123–47.

[65] Nachman Ben-Yehuda, *Deviance and Moral Boundaries* (Chicago: University of Chicago Press, 1987), 212. The concept is further elaborated in his *The Politics and Morality of Deviance* (Albany: State University of New York Press, 1990), 18–31 and may be traced to the ethnomethodological work of Harold Garfinkel. See John Heritage, *Garfinkel and Ethnomethodology* (Cambridge: Polity Press, 1996), 135–178. Although such systems may function on the macrolevel of institutional ideologies and values, their operation on the microlevel is of principal interest here.

[66] For discussion of various types of neutralization devices, see Pfuhl and Henry, 61–70.

[67] CJDCD, 45. "Mémoire sur mes travaux," 303. In Sartiaux's view, Turmel even achieves a certain nobility in this: "In remaining he made only himself suffer." Sartiaux, *Joseph Turmel*, 46.

[68] Turmel, CJDCD, 55.

[69] Turmel, CER, 126. Cf. "Mémoire sur mes travaux," 308.

[70] Turmel, CER, 138.

[71] "Mémoire sur mes travaux," 305.

[72] Turmel, CJDCD, 41.

[73] Turmel, CER, 140.

[74] *Ibid.*, 21n., 41–43, 119–20, 149–52.

[75] Cf. Turmel, CER, 127–28.

[76] Cf. Sartiaux, *Joseph Turmel*, 84–85.

[77] Turmel devotes an appendix of CJDCD (135–145) to Alfred Loisy, comparing the latter's situation as revealed in *Choses passées* and the three-volume *Mémoires* with his own. Among the ranks of the "undeceived" he also places Cardinal Meignan, Archbishop Mignot, and Duchesne. This is reminiscent of Houtin's evaluations of his fellow modernists, especially in *Ma vie laïque*.

[78] Turmel, CER, 131.

4

Slattery's O'Connell:
Americanism and Modernism
In the
Biographie de J. R. Slattery

William Portier

Introduction

The Question of Americanism and Modernism

For us Americans, the most striking feature in Modernism is that it served to bring the American Catholic Church into the story of the Universal Church. Just as the Spanish-American War made the United States a world Power, so about the same time the seething and the turmoil, the condemnations and the abandonments of Catholicism going on in Rome and elsewhere, made American Catholicism an integral part of the Roman Church. To this result, of course, the establishment of the Catholic University at Washington, the creation of the Delegation Apostolic, and specially the meteoric career of Archbishop Ireland in the politics of the two hemispheres contributed chiefly.

Anonymous[1]

In 1899, Pope Leo XIII sent the apostolic letter *Testem Benevolentiae* to Cardinal James Gibbons of Baltimore. In it he censured a set of ascetical and doctrinal aberrations known as Americanism. Five years later, in the midst of the French modernist crisis, Albert Houtin (1867–1926) published the first history of Americanism. He argued for a continuity between Americanism, as an attempted "adaptation of the church to modern ideals," and the historical, biblical, and political crises then raging in France.[2]

In 1907, Pope Pius X published his antimodernist encyclical *Pascendi Dominici Gregis*. By this time, Albert Houtin and John R. Slattery (1851–1926) had become good friends. Seven of Houtin's books, including *L'Américanisme*, had been placed on the Index of Forbidden Books. Slattery had already renounced Church and priesthood in 1906. At about this time, they began collaborating on Slattery's autobiography. Completed around 1912 but never published, the autobiography is preserved in the Papiers Houtin under the title *Biographie De J.R. Slattery*.[3] Slattery, like Houtin, took for granted the positive connection between Americanism and modernism, describing the latter as "an enlarging or an extension of intellectual liberalism under the influence of Loisy."[4]

American Catholic historians have generally resisted this interpretation. In 1949, the eighty-seven year old Abbé Félix Klein (1862–1953), a veteran of the controversies over Americanism and modernism in France, published the fourth volume of his memoirs. Translated into English in 1951 as *Americanism, A Phantom Heresy*, Klein's title provided a generation of scholars with a slogan to designate Americanism. The Catholic theological climate after *Pascendi* had little room for development and pluralism in theology. Suggestions that Americanism involved any home-grown theological ideas would have rendered distinguished American prelates doctrinally suspect. For the generation of John Tracy Ellis (1905–1992) and Thomas T. McAvoy (1903–1969), Americanism had to be a phantom heresy and could have nothing to do with modernism.

With the second Vatican Council, Catholic thought became more hospitable to developmental and pluralistic approaches to theological truth. A new generation of historians would revise the phantom heresy approach in an explicitly theological direction. In 1981, making a qualified appropriation of Houtin's interpretation, Margaret M. Reher argued for the continuity of Americanism and modernism in the United States.[5] R. Scott Appleby's 1992 study of American Catholic modernism proposed a "liberal to modernist trajectory" for which William L. Sullivan (1872–1935) and Slattery provided the most important examples.[6]

But, compared to the episcopal leadership, Slattery, and especially Sullivan, were lesser figures in the Americanist movement. To them I propose to add Denis J. O'Connell (1849–1927). Along with Archbishop John Ireland (1838–1918) and Bishop John J. Keane (1839–1918), O'Connell belonged to the Americanist inner circle. The relationship between Slattery and O'Connell, as portrayed in Slattery's autobiography, adds a new and significant dimension to the old question of the continuity between Americanism and modernism. For Slattery claims that he and O'Connell traveled Appleby's trajectory together. This essay examines that claim. It concludes that Slattery's auto-biography offers strong corroborating evidence for a positive connection between Americanism and modernism in the person of leading Americanist and apparent antimodernist Denis J. O'Connell.[7]

Biographie De J R Slattery

By contrast with modernists whose primary work was in the area of scholarship, Slattery's way into modernism was more indirect. From 1877 to 1902, he led Catholic efforts to evangelize African Americans in the southern United States. In the years after the modernist crisis, he would turn to autobiography for many of the same reasons other modernists did. The *Biographie* not only casts Slattery's passage from missionary to modernist into the form of a first-person narrative, but also, and most importantly, tries to justify that passage in moral terms by way of the category of honesty.

In approaching the *Biographie*, one comes immediately upon questions about how the manuscript found its way into the Papiers Houtin and why it was never published. Answers to such questions have to do with Slattery's relationship with Houtin. Between 1903 and 1911, Slattery worked closely with Houtin. It was, in fact, Denis O'Connell who first put them in contact.[8] Slattery no doubt supplied Houtin with information for *L'Américanisme*. Though Houtin never mentions his name, he twice cites Slattery's anonymous 1903 article "A Root Trouble in Catholicism."[9] In 1906 and again in 1909, Houtin dedicated books "*A John Richard Slattery Hommage reconnaissant.*" Slattery probably financed the publication of these works. Together Houtin and Slattery attended international meetings of religious liberals at Geneva in 1905 and at Boston in 1907. In 1910, Slattery translated and wrote a six-page introductory note for Houtin's *Un prêtre marié*.[10]

The second volume of Houtin's own autobiography describes a falling out with Slattery in 1912 over Houtin's repeated refusal to accept Slattery's offer to finance his education in law or medicine so that Houtin could leave the field of religious controversy.[11] After this, Slattery seems to have erased himself from the historical record. We are left to wonder how, after their falling out, a manuscript of Slattery's autobiography remained in the Papiers Houtin and why it was never published. My own best guess is that Slattery didn't know Houtin still had a copy of the autobiography and that Houtin was waiting, as in the case of Alfred Loisy, for Slattery, who was sixteen years older, to predecease him. They both died in 1926. At that time, Loisy expressed his surprise at the announcement of a biography of Slattery in the works Houtin had left unpublished at his death.[12]

Slattery's autobiography offers an American reconstruction of the modernist crisis. As might be expected, Appleby's cast of characters is featured in the *Biographie*. But these characters make only brief appearances and are not an integral part of the story. William L. Sullivan was twenty-one years younger than Slattery. They barely knew each other.[13] When the first issue of the *New York Review* appeared in the summer of 1905, Slattery was in Geneva with Houtin.[14] The *Review*'s editors were also younger men. Slattery was not trained in biblical studies like James Driscoll and Francis Gigot. Nor was he a scientist like John Zahm. With O'Connell, Ireland, and Keane, Slattery was more an intelligent ecclesiastic than a scholar. Surprisingly, in view of phantom heresy historiography's emphasis on the discontinuity between Americanism and modernism, it is his Americanist friends who Slattery paints as his closest companions in the modernist crisis.

His encounter with critical history and issues associated with modernism came in the course of his work as an ecclesiastic. Even as a missionary pastor and seminary administrator, Slattery carried on a vigorous intellectual life. He published extensively on the church and the "Negro question." As founding rector (1888) of St. Joseph's Seminary in Baltimore, he read widely for his regular course on the origins of the Church. Church history was the medium in which Slattery experienced the modernist crisis and became "a tragic casualty" of it.[15] Over the years, critical history raised questions about the Church, and especially about the priesthood, which Slattery could never honestly answer. Disillusionment with racism in the Church and cumulative discouragement with his twenty-five year struggle to support the Josephite mission fueled Slattery's historical doubts and precipitated his own crisis between 1899 and 1902.

Slattery's crisis became public on June 22, 1902, when he preached at the first mass of African American Josephite John Henry Dorsey. As founder of the American Josephites (1892), Slattery had championed the cause of African American priests and been frustrated by what he perceived as a lack of both lay and hierarchical support. In an incendiary sermon, preached in the presence of Cardinal Gibbons himself, Slattery brought together the twin issues of racism in the Church and the gradual evolution of Catholic doctrine and Church structures.[16] The "Dorsey Sermon" precipitated a newspaper and pamphlet controversy. In 1903,

Slattery resigned as Josephite superior general. His wealthy father died in 1905. He was then free to publish in *The Independent* his "public declaration of apostasy" and "official goodbye to the Church."[17]

The *Biographie*, however, is not concerned primarily with the intellectual questions that Slattery raised publicly in 1902 and 1903. His unfinished business with the Church was more personal than intellectual. Slattery believed that, by refusing to travel the entire length of the liberal to modernist trajectory, his former Americanist companions had betrayed themselves and him. The autobiography made a moral case against them.[18]

> I pin my faith on the human race, yes without God, without state, without church, without business and only with one possession: Honest manhood.[19]

Slattery concluded his autobiography with this appeal to "honest manhood." It was by this criterion that he would judge and condemn his former friends and companions. He hoped to bring readers to share his negative moral estimate of the Catholic Church and those Americanists who remained loyal to it. He wanted to convince his readers that many other ecclesiastics had realized, as he had, that history could not support the Church's claims. But these others played falsely. Chapter XIX of the autobiography is entitled "La Rupture." As he concludes it, Slattery incorporates the closing paragraphs of "How My Priesthood Dropped from Me" (1906).

> Now my readers need not regard me as an isolated case. Obliged to go about the country a great deal, here and there have I met learned and thoughtful priests; so also in my travels in England, France, Germany, Switzerland, and Italy. The same thoughts seemed uppermost. "I wonder," was my remark to a very scholarly professor, "how long have men discussed as we are now doing?" They have always done so on the quiet. Some put dogma above history, science, and aught that might tarnish it; others rest upon symbolism; others again take up other studies in order to divert their minds. Some have left the Church; others drift along. "How am I going to live?" was a not infrequent question. (XIX, 11)

Slattery's honor required that readers not regard him "as an isolated case." The *Biographie*, therefore, must implicate others in Slattery's own religious crisis. He portrays John Ireland, John Lancaster Spalding, and many others as carrying on ecclesiastical business as usual in spite of their own religiously disabling doubts and lack of faith.

Slattery had his finger on the Victorian crisis of belief. But his autobiography is filled with bitter and fatalistic self-righteousness. In the absence of corroborating evidence from other sources, this self-serving tone leads the reader to be suspicious of Slattery's assessments of individual cases. Still, despite the autobiography's unremitting and often libelous negativity, Denis O'Connell emerges from it with a genuinely human, albeit elusive, shape. Given O'Connell's "Machiavellian" reputation for ecclesiastical intrigue, this is a surprise. Slattery and O'Connell first met as college students at St. Charles Seminary, Ellicott City, Maryland. Later they would both reside at Bishop Keane's Richmond cathedral in the early 1880s. As protégé of James Gibbons, O'Connell went on to become rector of the North American College at Rome, Roman agent for the American bishops, and then for the Americanist movement. Slattery's autobiography portrays O'Connell as his closest companion on the road from missionary to modernist. His eighteen letters to O'Connell between 1899 and 1902 corroborate the autobiography's portrait of O'Connell as sharing in what Slattery calls "notre crise commune."[20]

But O'Connell reversed his field to become anti-modernist rector of Catholic University (1903–1909), and eventually bishop of Richmond. The most natural choice to play the villain of the autobiography, O'Connell is instead rendered by Slattery with depth and a certain wistful affection. Amid the foul air of self-pity and recrimination, O'Connell circulates through Slattery's narrative like a breath of real life. Slattery's failure to treat O'Connell as harshly as he did Gibbons and Ireland, for example, is intriguing. His apparent inconsistency as a moralist will be considered below. At this point, it is enough to note that his uncharacteristic, and therefore unexpected, care to treat O'Connell fairly counts heavily in favor of the plausibility of Slattery's O'Connell.

Americanism and Modernism in the *Biographie*

Slattery wrote before the ascendency of phantom heresy historiography, with its corollary of a radical discontinuity between Americanism and modernism. He presumes that Americanism and modernism are serial chapters in the story of Catholic responses to political and intellectual modernity. The Americanist movement (1886–1899), therefore, is the intellectual and emotional vector for Slattery's modernist experience between 1895 and 1902.

Slattery became a clerical satellite of the Americanists around 1893 when John Ireland chose him to edit the American speeches of Francesco Satolli, future apostolic delegate to the United States, and, as a curial cardinal, one of the putative authors of *Testem Benevolentiae*. O'Connell had escorted Satolli to the United States and temporarily into the arms of the liberal party. And O'Connell probably recommended Slattery to Ireland as Satolli's American editor. *Loyalty to Church and State, The Mind of His Eminence, Francis Cardinal Satolli, Pro-Delegate Apostolic* (Baltimore, 1894) became one of Slattery's fund, raisers for the Josephite missions. But Slattery edited the work more out of Americanist commitment than to raise money. He describes Satolli's speeches as "so liberal, so American" that he would have edited them without payment "for the sole love of my ideal." Satolli's speeches "gave authority to my dream of seeing the Church adapt itself to the scientific and social conditions of new generations."[21]

The autobiography presents Slattery's Americanist dream for rapprochement between Church and age as obviously continuous with what European modernists sought. In the United States, *modern* meant political liberty. "Even today," Slattery wrote in 1909, "the relation of the United States to the church is so modern that France alone in Europe has accepted it."[22] But, for Slattery and O'Connell, politics was inseparable from real theological questions about revelation, religious experience, and especially Church history in a critical key.

In August of 1897, O'Connell spoke on Americanism at the International Catholic Scientific Congress at Fribourg, Switzerland, along with John Zahm, C.S.C., on evolution, and Marie-Joseph Lagrange, O.P., on the biblical question. Entitled "A New Idea in the Life of Father Hecker," O'Connell's address advocated that the Church move away from Roman law and toward Anglo-Saxon law, specifically the American constitutional arrangement of separation of Church and State. O'Connell's speech was a key episode in the French side of the Americanist controversy ignited by Félix Klein's translation and adaptation of Walter Elliott's *The Life of Father Hecker* (1891).[23]

Already in 1895, the Americanists had experienced the first in a series of ecclesiastical setbacks that would culminate in *Testem Benevolentiae*. Pope Leo XIII's 1895 encyclical *Longinqua Oceani* warned Americans against making separation of Church and State into a universal paradigm. The Vatican then removed both Denis O'Connell and John Keane from their positions as rector of the North American College and Catholic University respectively. In 1898, Ireland failed in a key role in Vatican diplomatic attempts to avert the Spanish American War. Then came *Testem Benevolentiae*. It precipitated what Slattery termed, in the title of Chapter XVI of his autobiography, "La Crise (1899–1902)." Slattery read in *Testem* "the condemnation of all my ideas". . . . This was a painful blow, although my faith in the truth of Catholicism and my hopes for its future had been diminished greatly over the past four years."[24]

In the winter of 1899, shortly after the publication of *Testem Benevolentiae*, O'Connell, Ireland, and Keane gathered in Rome. Slattery decided to bring his proposal for an African American catechetical college to the Vatican and join them. He arrived on March 26, Tuesday of Holy Week, and found his friends in disarray. They spent Holy Saturday morning discussing Americanism. The autobiography reports a conversation that Slattery had with O'Connell and Ireland on the evening of April 23, 1899 in the garden of their Genoa hotel.

> After dinner, as the evening was magnificent, we had a long con-
> versation in the hotel garden. We discussed the fundamental points of
> religion including the existence of God. The archbishop, Big
> John—as we called him among ourselves, O'Connell and I—showed
> himself as completely skeptical and radical as his two companions.
> As it struck eleven, a clock alerted us that the conversation was taking
> too long. What is left to us?, said Ireland, getting up quickly. Extreme
> unction, I replied.[25]

This conversation would remain crucial to Slattery's belief that Ireland acted dishonestly during the modernist crisis. But the auto-biography's record of it is not alone sufficient to make the case. Though it is Ireland's remark and state of mind that Slattery finds noteworthy, most interesting in this passage is Slattery's assumption that O'Connell shared his religious skepticism. Four years later, this same O'Connell would reinvent himself as Catholic University's anti-modernist rector.

Given O'Connell's previous liberal views, as well as his friendship with Slattery, Gerald Fogarty considers the possibility that O'Connell may have "surrendered his intellectual integrity for the sake of ecclesiastical preferment." For Fogarty, however, O'Connell's "uncom-promising stance against modernism" is surprising only if one confuses Americanism, which is about law, with modernism, which is about biblical criticism.[26] Using Loisy as a model, Fogarty limits modernism's historical dimension to issues of biblical criticism. But for ecclesiastics such as Slattery and O'Connell, whose deepest self-understanding had to do with the priesthood, biblical criticism spilled over into early Church history. In what sense did Christ found the Church? Were the present claims of the Church, especially the structures in which the priesthood made sense, continuous with its beginnings in the apostolic age? From the perspective of early Church history, Loisy's mentor,

Church historian Louis Duchesne (1843–1922), rather than Loisy, is the key figure.[27] Describing his seminary course on the "first age of the Church," Slattery puts Duchesne in the middle of things.[28] Houtin would call Duchesne modernism's father.[29]

Liberty Hall: Where Americanism and Modernism Met

Fogarty himself documents O'Connell's ties to Duchesne. After his dismissal as rector of the North American College in June of 1895, O'Connell continued in Rome as the vicar of Cardinal Gibbon's titular church, Santa Maria in Trastevere. In Slattery's words, "His apartment, which he himself christened as 'Liberty Hall,' was the gathering place of all the liberals."[30] Fogarty describes Liberty Hall as "the meeting place for . . . those churchmen and laymen, either living in or visiting Rome, who were dedicated to the modernization of the Church."[31] Baron Friedrich von Hügel was a regular visitor to Liberty Hall when he was in Rome. In 1897, O'Connell would arrange for von Hügel to meet the American Protestant biblical scholar, Charles A. Briggs.[32]

Louis Duchesne moved to Rome in 1895 as rector of the École Française. O'Connell was "particularly interested" in Duchesne's critical studies in Church history.[33] Duchesne became a regular member of the "Lodge." In fact, O'Connell would refer to it as "Duchesne & Co." Between 1896 and some time in 1900 or 1901, the "Club" or "Lodge" met regularly at Liberty Hall on Tuesday evenings. The "vocation" of Liberty Hall was, in Slattery's words, "to bring together, Catholic minds and hearts who gravitate outside the charmed circle of the Curial and mold them into oneness of thought and action."[34] After the condemnation of Americanism, Ireland warned O'Connell that Liberty Hall had to stop. At the end of 1899, O'Connell wrote to Ireland, "I informed Duchesne & Co., there would be no more Tuesdays."[35] But they must have continued. A year later, Slattery sent O'Connell $100 to help continue the work at "Liberty Hall."

Given the quality of O'Connell's intellect and his contacts with so many figures involved with both Americanism and modernism, it is difficult to imagine that he separated the intellectual issues involved as easily as Fogarty was inclined to think in 1974. More recently, Fogarty has made a case for a connection between Americanism and the biblical question. But it existed primarily in the minds of those European conservatives who criticized both. O'Connell, Fogarty thought at this time, saw no "direct relationship" between them.[36]

Slattery, at least, saw a strong connection between Duchesne's critical Church history and the reform proposals in O'Connell's Fribourg address. Critical history had relativized the Church's present forms. They are not from Christ in the way that the prevailing neoscholasticism would have explained. This left Americanists and other progressives free to propose reforms that would modernize church life and structures. *Testem* frustrated their dreams for reform. But, to the extent that they were aware of critical history (and their correspondence makes clear that Slattery and O'Connell were), they were left, as were the modernists, to account for contemporary Church life in developmentalist or symbolist categories. After 1899, this became increasingly difficult as Slattery saw the Church at odds with the age's democratic temper. Critical history threatened to undercut his ecclesiastical identity as a priest. The defeat of Americanism blocked the way forward. This is what Slattery calls "La crise."[37]

Slattery and O'Connell:
"Notre Crise Commune"

Between 1899 and 1901, Slattery and O'Connell corresponded regularly and met in Europe during the summers. We do not have the complete O'Connell-Slattery correspondence. O'Connell's letters to Slattery are not in the Josephite Archives. But when the autobiography is supplemented with Slattery's seventeen letters to O'Connell from this period, preserved in the Archives of the Diocese of Richmond, a fuller portrait of O'Connell's mind emerges, and his Americanist politics become difficult to disentangle from the religious questions of the modernist crisis.[38]

The period of these letters corresponds to a growing deterioration in the relationship between O'Connell and John Ireland. Since 1898, O'Connell had been working to take the Americanist movement in the direction of an alliance with Germany. He became the intermediary in Franz Xavier Kraus' (1840–1901) negotiations on behalf of the German government with liberal papal hopeful, Cardinal Serafino Vannutelli. As pope, Vannutelli would agree to abandon the goal of restoring the papal states, and to make room for modern scholarship in the Church. O'Connell had promised Ireland's support. The latter reneged on a promise to visit Germany in 1899. Ireland's subsequent public statements in support of France and in favor of the pope's temporal authority left O'Connell isolated and exposed at Rome where he had no official position.

Slattery took O'Connell's side in this rift. The growing pessimism of his letters corresponds to Ireland's activities at the time. O'Connell and Slattery interpreted Ireland's actions as base ecclesiastical ambition in pursuit of the cardinal's red hat. In the winter of 1900, O'Connell could still urge Ireland, "henceforth [to] speak out bravely from your own soul as a man, an honest man." A year later, Slattery wrote to O'Connell, "In John Ireland's debacle another idol is shattered."[39]

These developments had their theological parallels. Slattery claims that, between 1899 and 1901, he and O'Connell had become doctrinal "symbolists." Disillusionment with fellow missionaries combined with his reading of the "modern historians of its [the Church's] origins" to make Slattery "hesitant about the doctrines relative to the very notion of the Church." This left him with a "symbolic" view of doctrine, a view which he also ascribed to O'Connell.[40]

> I came to conceive the Catholic Church as an institution whose doctrine, taken at least symbolically, can have a happy influence and whose organization, despite its faults is still the most useful for doing good.[41]

The ten substantive letters Slattery wrote to O'Connell between April, 1899 and July of 1900 focus on two interrelated theological issues. First, they appropriated critical history for understanding the Church's origins. O'Connell sent Slattery books by Duchesne and Giovanni Semeria. They read Gregorovius and Creighton on the papacy and Harnack on the history of dogma. With critical history having shown the inadequacy of neoscholastic accounts of the Church, they moved toward doctrinal "symbolism." They discussed moral experience, conscience, and sin, as symbolic of the supernatural order, as possibly revelatory of God.

A letter of June 8, 1899, gives a glimpse into the second issue. Slattery sent Charles Monroe Sheldon's popular *In His Steps* (1897) to O'Connell. Slattery liked its appeal to the following of Christ. This was in part a response to something O'Connell had said about "natural powers in the moral world." Slattery made an argument that, allowing for sin, "the great movements of modern life may be called supernatural." Speaking of "sin and conscience," he says "our ideas are not in the Old Testament and need the theologians to be found in the New Testament." O'Connell recommended Wilfrid Ward's anonymous article on "The Ethics of Religious Conformity" in the *Quarterly Review* for January of 1899. Slattery recommended Auguste Sabatier's "Christian Dogma and the Christian Life" in the *Contemporary Review* for November of 1899. Both articles explore "symbolic" interpretations of traditional Christianity.

Clearly this is a shared discussion. They respond to each other's points and questions, suggest and send readings, and comment on them. Slattery refers to "our ideas." At O'Connell's suggestion, he begins to keep a daily record of his thoughts. This will grow into Slattery's "notes on the development of the church."[42] They are the likely source for the historical claims in Slattery's "Dorsey Sermon," the "Aftermath" brochure that followed it, and the anonymous "A Root Trouble in Catholicism" (1903).

As he enters 1901, the year that Slattery describes as the "most unhappy of my life," his letters to O'Connell become heavier in spirit. The contrast between the ways of science and the ways of the Church intrudes itself persistently. He sends O'Connell his article on "Scholastic Methods, Their Advantages and Disadvantages."[43] Most of the discussion is focused on the need for Church reform and the diminishing possibility for it. O'Connell sends Gioberti's *Church Reform*.

> But a more serious turn of mind, which seems hinted at in your note, engages Bro Joe [Slattery]—It ·is that Christianity itself is a Curialism, especially in its system of doctrines and morals. . . . Hence Mr. Browning's words, "Head doubts, heart doubts, doubts within and without," now of four or five years standing, take on a fierce earnestness in my brains. What if the structure falls? If the streams of Biology and Electricity and kindred sciences burrow under the Relics? And yet think we must. We are flung into it all and put in an age when science goes in leaps and bounds to the pinnacle. And again we cannot drop out. Life is the awful mystery.[44]

In his last letter before traveling to Europe for the summer of 1901, Slattery tells O'Connell, "I have so much to talk over with you." The letter concludes: "It is with the greatest pleasure I look forward to a few weeks with you in quiet rest, discussing the many thoughts seething in our minds and hearts."[45] Slattery and O'Connell met in Heidelberg on July 30, 1901, and traveled together until August 27. "During this trip." Slattery writes, "my companion was a delight to me. . . .I did not hide at all from him the kind of travail that was going on in my mind. Nor did he conceal at all from me that he had walked just as far."[46]

In a garden at Fribourg, they saw two caged birds. "'Voici Gilpin et Joe,' he [O'Connell] said to me dejectedly," Slattery writes. He goes on to explain that these were the code names they used in their correspondence. Slattery often signed his letters to O'Connell "Bro Joe." "Gilpin, the fox," he explains, "obviously stood for O'Connell." It is here that Slattery makes reference to "our common crisis." He goes on to specify how he understood their respective experiences of this crisis.

In our common crisis, there was nevertheless one difference. While for me the dogmas remained agonizing enigmas; for him they were only symbols of moral ideas more or less just, more or less profound. He defined religion as *the ethical faculty*, or again, as the entire oneness of man individually, socially, in the state as in the home.

The next sentence says: "Il ne croyait ni en Dieu, ni en l'immortalité de l'âme." The first part of the sentence, referring to belief in God, is crossed out. The two words that replace it are difficult to read. A negative is written in before "en l'immortalité de l'âme." In this passage, Slattery attributes to O'Connell a position of radical "symbolism." He wasn't sure whether he thought O'Connell believed in God. He didn't think O'Connell believed in the immortality of the soul.

The revisions in the manuscript show Slattery's concern to represent O'Connell's mind faithfully. The paragraph cited above, beginning with "In our common crisis," is also a revision. Slattery had originally written:

In our common crisis, there was nevertheless one difference. Living in Rome, in the atmosphere of the papal court, my friend had fallen into a sweet and benevolent skepticism; for him the dogmas were poetic symbols. For me, a man of the north, they remained agonizing enigmas.[47]

The revised version is more precise and appropriately distant, but the phrase "un skepticisme doux et bienveillant" captures better Slattery's sense of the mind and soul of this romantic Gilpin, who had so charmed the Countess Sabina di Parravacino Revel and her conciliationist Italian allies, gained the confidence of Franz Kraus, and attracted and inspired "the Club" at Liberty Hall.

O'Connell and Slattery parted company at Strasbourg on August 27, 1901. Returning to Baltimore, Slattery found it increasingly difficult to separate "Catholicism itself" from the "mythology" it had produced and which he rejected. He reports that the greater part of his spare time in 1900 and 1901 was devoted to reading and rereading the works of Cardinal Newman, "who many liberal Catholics portrayed as the greatest apologist and theologian of modern times." Newman represented a developmentalist alternative to symbolism. Slattery remarked "This study failed to confirm my faith. I became the pawn of doubt. It consumed me. I can say that the year 1901 was the most unhappy of my life."[48]

The O'Connell Papers contain no letters from Slattery between August of 1901, when they parted in Strasbourg, and August of 1902, when they came together again at Geneva. It is hard to imagine that they didn't correspond during that year. But O'Connell's life was taking a new direction. Already between the summer of 1900 and November of 1902, when Catholic University's new rector would be elected, O'Connell had begun to plan for the end of his Roman exile. During the same summer of 1901, when he traveled through Germany with Slattery, he also met in Switzerland with Charles Grannan (1846–1924), professor of scripture at Catholic University and a member of the liberal party. O'Connell had regained Satolli's favor and was gathering support for his appointment as rector of Catholic University.[49]

Shortly after the Dorsey Sermon on June 22, 1902, Slattery left for Europe and his annual rendezvous with O'Connell. But things had changed in a year. Slattery was on his way out of the Church. Cardinal Gibbons had refused to accept him into his archdiocese. The Dorsey sermon was Slattery's last attempt to force Gibbons to accept his resignation and allow him to function as a priest *sub titulo patrimonii.* O'Connell was moving in a different direction. Public association with Slattery could only damage his impending ecclesiastical rehabilitation. They met at Geneva on August 6, 1902. On August 10, O'Connell left to visit Grannan at Rigi-Scheidigg, Switzerland. On August 22, O'Connell rejoined Slattery at Zurich. After traveling around Germany for two weeks, they separated. Slattery went to Berlin, where he would study during the next academic year, and O'Connell returned to Switzerland, perhaps to consult again with Grannan.[50]

> During the month we spent together, he treated me as the same good friend he had always been. Concerning my future, he was reserved, but without saying a word that could be taken as blame in case I should leave the Church. He asked only, so as not to compromise him, that henceforth I no longer meet him in America, nor in Ireland where he was equally known. He led me to believe that his conduct would have been different, if he had been rich and independent, and, in this regard, he revealed his financial situation to me.[51]

Slattery claims O'Connell confided that, in 1895, he had invested $17,000 with the religious community of John Ireland's sister in St. Paul. He had never received the promised six percent interest. Slattery advised him to try to embarrass Ireland, "many times a millionaire" from land speculation, to make good on O'Connell's investment. O'Connell did not want to alienate Ireland.[52]

Slattery spent the fall in Germany studying German and writing "A Root Trouble in Catholicism." Rumors of his impending departure had preceded him to America. Ireland wrote to O'Connell in December.

> One dense cloud now hangs over the horizon,—Slattery. The reports in Baltimore and Washington are that he has thrown everything to the wind. If he does not turn up soon, the press will talk and the sensation will be dreadful,—all his friends suffering. My God,—I cannot believe what I heard. If you know his address, write to him at once and beg him quickly to silence reports. The Cardinal is affrighted.[53]

The inclusion of this letter in the *Biographie* suggests that O'Connell sent it to Slattery.

By the time Slattery returned to the United States in early January, newspapers were already announcing O'Connell's appointment as rector of Catholic University. Slattery cabled his congratulations to Rome. O'Connell thanked him by cable. During August 1902 in Germany, they had discussed O'Connell's prospects. In Slattery's estimate, O'Connell thought the rectorship would provide an indirect but sure route to the episcopacy, "the great dream of his life."[54] An interview with Slattery about O'Connell's new office appeared in the Baltimore *Sun* for January 18, 1903. O'Connell later told Slattery that he had received more than 100 copies of this interview and numerous letters warning him to avoid Slattery. One came from a bishop (Slattery thought it was Ireland) who advised O'Connell to treat Slattery like a "corpse." On February 6, he received a cable from O'Connell with two German verbs on it: Schweigen, Erwarten. Be silent and wait. "The dear prelate doubtless wanted me to keep absolutely silent and wait and take no steps to leave the Josephites so as not to cause him any embarrassment at the time of his return to the United States."[55]

After O'Connell's installation on April 22, 1903, Slattery and O'Connell met only twice and that under strained circumstances.[56] Slattery would describe O'Connell as a "priest who had sacrificed everything to his ambition."[57] As if to underline this, he noted Loisy's report, at the end of July, that O'Connell had not visited him before leaving Europe and that he had heard nothing from him since then.[58]

In Chapter XXI, Slattery returns to O'Connell for the last time. After May 23, 1903, Slattery did not hear from O'Connell for more than three years. In July 1906, O'Connell wrote to ask if they could meet in Switzerland or Italy. Slattery says that he had already bought his ticket home. Shortly thereafter, O'Connell was finally named a bishop by Pius X in December of 1907, just months after the publication of *Pascendi*.[59]

Slattery sent a congratulatory telegram from Paris. Ironically recalling O'Connell's dejected remark in the Fribourg garden, it said simply: Gilpin Hurrah Joe.[60]

By 1911, O'Connell was auxiliary bishop of San Francisco. Slattery was in the city with his uncle at Christmas. He and O'Connell visited at the bishop's residence and at Slattery's hotel. They talked as old friends, "returning to their favorite topics of conversation": God and the Church and their old Americanist comrades. "He spoke to me of God, who he conceived as a great force, working in the universe." The words "conscious of itself perhaps, perhaps not conscious" are crossed out at the end of the previous sentence. O'Connell on God was as elusive in 1912 as he had been in 1901. Slattery says that O'Connell spoke of Ireland and Gibbons as understanding that "they no longer had a role to play in the Church, that their liberal hopes had been empty, and that all that remained to them was to die."[61]

As old friends are wont to do, they also lied to each other. O'Connell claimed to be perfectly happy. Slattery claimed to feel content and free, his former priesthood now only a dream. Of O'Connell he said: "He showed neither astonishment, nor blame, nor regret, and we parted as good old friends, united always in heart, but who have taken different paths in life." Slattery recalled that in 1895 Cardinal Vaughan had warned: "O'Connell is a man of intrigue [a skimmer]; look out." "It was severe, but fitting," he comments.[62]

As he brought his story of their friendship to a close, Slattery struggled for the right word for O'Connell. He first translated Vaughan's "skimmer" with *ecumeur* (pirate). He settled on *intrigant*. His final word on O'Connell began by calling him an "ecclesiastical adventurer" or "man of intrigue" (intrigant de l'église). That phrase had replaced "corsaire théologique," a "theological buccaneer." All are apt for O'Connell and together they provide a thicker sense of him. We do not know whether Slattery and O'Connell ever saw each other between Christmas of 1912 and Slattery's death in 1926. For now this is Slattery's final word on O'Connell.

> An ecclesiastical adventurer, he got it in his head early on to gain a miter. Under Leo XIII, he tried by adopting the liberal tactics that the pope seemed to encourage on account of circumstances. Under Pius X, he tried by feigning (en affectant) a perfect orthodoxy. He has succeeded. He has had the brilliant career he dreamed of. He has applied his vast intelligence to it. But I do not know if he is happy. He appeared to me a bit of a misanthrope and I fear that, after having been at the center of things, he may be disenchanted.[63]

Conclusion

Slattery surely believed that O'Connell's "perfect orthodoxy" was "feigned." He thought O'Connell a "sweet and benevolent skeptic," a doctrinal symbolist for whom religion was morality. He could not be sure that O'Connell even believed in a personal God. He portrays O'Connell as having come to these positions by a critical study of Church history during the years of the modernist crisis, as well as by his experience of "ourialism." Denis O'Connell, one of the three most prominent Americanists, was also a theological modernist. Is this a picture we should believe?

This essay has traced the autobiography's story of Slattery's friendship with O'Connell. O'Connell's place in the *Biographie* bears out Fogarty's description of Slattery as "one of O'Connell's closest friends."[64] But the portrait that emerges, especially when the *Biographie* is supplemented with the correspondence from 1899 through 1901, is one not only of friendship but also of intellectual and spiritual companionship. Slattery's testimony that he and O'Connell shared a common crisis is at least as plausible as Fogarty's portrait of O'Connell. Fogarty did not have the *Biographie* available to him. His O'Connell doesn't see a connection between advocating modern political institutions for the Church's life and the historical critical study of the Church's origins carried on by so many of his friends and allies. Both portraits must rely on the man of intrigue's own seemingly careful theological silence.

Accepting Slattery's O'Connell makes a difference in two important respects. First, and most importantly, like Slattery himself, his O'Connell presumes a substantive connection between Americanism and modernism. Slattery's O'Connell traverses the entire length of Appleby's liberal to modernist trajectory. Against "phantom heresy" historiography, Slattery's O'Connell adds significant weight to the arguments of historians such as Reher and Appleby for a real continuity between Americanism and modernism. If we accept Slattery's O'Connell, Americanism and modernism are not two disconnected marginal episodes in American Catholic history. Instead they are a central part of the continuing conversation about being Catholic in what Slattery thought to be the most modern of nations.

Second, if we accept Slattery's portrait, we have an O'Connell who is intellectually consistent. We don't have to say that O'Connell failed to see the connections between his proposals for Church reform and fundamental issues of theology raised by the modernist crisis. We can think instead that O'Connell was quite aware of connections among the lives and works of the various people he gathered at Liberty Hall and with whom he corresponded.

But if O'Connell was intellectually consistent, what then of his moral consistency? His anti-modernist posture at Catholic University appears as an even baser form of ecclesiastical careerism than that of which he accused Ireland. How did O'Connell escape judgment by Slattery's criterion of honest manhood? Isn't Slattery himself inconsistent in his failure to judge O'Connell more harshly?

Slattery's apparent inconsistency as a moralist is due, in some measure at least, to the fact that he had shared, to a lesser degree, O'Connell's dependence on the patronage of Gibbons and Ireland. Slattery claimed that both he and O'Connell had reason to blame the "egoist" Cardinal Gibbons and the "shattered idol" Ireland for having abandoned them to ecclesiastical limbo in order to maintain or advance their own positions. Slattery saw O'Connell as a fellow victim of "curialism," and specifically of the ecclesiastical ambitions of Gibbons and Ireland.[65] Slattery had money and O'Connell had none. But O'Connell was closer to "honest manhood" than Gibbons and Ireland. In the end, for Slattery, Gilpin and Joe were still prisoners in the same cage.

Notes

[1] "Catholic Modernism," unsigned review of Albert Houtin, *Histoire du Modernisme Catholique, The Independent*, December 26, 1912, 1499–1500.

[2] Albert Houtin, *L'Américanisme* (Paris: Emile Nourry, 1904), 457.

[3] The manuscript is located in the Papiers Houtin (NAF 15741–42) at the Bibliothèque Nationale in Paris. Written mostly in French, the *Biographie* runs to approximately two hundred handwritten pages. Despite its title, internal evidence clearly indicates that it is an autobiography. The text has twenty-one Roman-numbered chapters. It is not clearly consecutively paginated. My references to the text will be, therefore, by chapter number and page number within the chapter. Translations from the French are my own. See William L. Portier, "A Note on the Unpublished *Biographie De J.R. Slattery,* in ed. Ronald Burke, Gary Lease, and George Gilmore, *Historiography and Modernism* (Mobile: Spring Hill College, 1985), 74–5.

[4] *Biographie*, XX, 3.

[5] Margaret M. Reher, "Americanism and Modernism—Continuity or Discontinuity?" *U.S. Catholic Historian*, 1 (Summer, 1981), 87–103. Philip Gleason reviews the historiography of Americanism and thoroughly documents the shift with respect to its relation to modernism in "The New Americanism in Catholic Historiography," *U.S. Catholic Historian*, 11 (Summer, 1993), 1–18.

[6] R. Scott Appleby, *"Church and Age Unite!" The Modernist Impulse in American Catholicism* (Notre Dame: University of Notre Dame Press, 1992), Introduction and Chapter 5.

[7] Gleason notes that a reversal of positions has occurred on the question of the relationship between Americanism and modernism. For Gleason this shift is clearly theologically driven, "for very little relevant historical evidence has been adduced that was not already known to scholars of the Ellis-McAvoy generation." "The New Americanism in Catholic Historiography," 14. The present essay offers new historical evidence in the form of the *Biographie*.

[8] *Biographie*, XIX, 6.

[9] "A Root Trouble in Catholicism" by a Presbyter, *The Independent*, 55 (March 19, 1903), 662–65. *Biographie*, XVII, 5 affirms Slattery's authorship. Houtin cites Slattery's claim that "The Americanization of the world spells the Americanization of the Church." See *L'Américanisme*, 282–83, 170. Slattery probably had a hand in *The Independent's* (July 21, 1904, 166) favorable editorial notice of *L'Américanisme*. He described himself as a close friend of the editor, William Hayes Ward, and as one of its "correspondents" for religious affairs. *Biographie* XXI, 5.

[10] Albert Houtin, *A Married Priest*, translated from the French by John Richard Slattery (Boston: Sherman, French & Co., 1910). See also Thomas Kselman, "The Perraud Affair: Clergy, Church, and Sexual Politics in Fin-de-Siècle France," *The Journal of Modern History*, 70 (September 1998), 588–618.

[11] Albert Houtin, *Mon Expérience, II, Ma Vie Laïque, 1912–1926, Documents et Souvenirs* (Paris: Les Editions Rieder, 1928), 18–19.

[12] Alfred Loisy, *Mémoires Pour Servir A L'Histoire Religieuse De Notre Temps* (Paris: Emile Nourry, 1931), Tome III, 61.

[13] Slattery mentions Sullivan in *Biographie*, XX, 36–7 and refers to him in "The Workings of Modernism," *American Journal of Theology*, 13 (October, 1909), 572. Sullivan's correspondence shows that Sullivan and Slattery met at least once. Sullivan to William Wendte, New York, January 6, 1912, Sullivan Papers, Register BMS 467/10, Folder 18, Andover Harvard Library. Cambridge, MA.

[14] *Biographie*, XIX, 7.

[15] James Hennesey, S.J., *American Catholics* (New York: Oxford University Press, 1981), 216. On Slattery's life and his work as a Josephite, see Stephen J. Ochs, *Desegregating the Altar, the Josephites and the Struggle for Black Priests, 1871–1960* (Baton Rouge: Louisiana State University Press, 1992), Chapters 2 & 3; William L. Portier, "John R. Slattery's Vision for the Evangelization of American Blacks," *U.S. Catholic Historian*, 5/1 (1986), 19–44.

[16] The "Dorsey Sermon" is preserved in pamphlet form in the Josephite Archives, Baltimore, along with various newspaper articles and another pamphlet, Slattery's response to his critics, entitled "Aftermath of the Dorsey Sermon," written at Berlin in December of 1902. Slattery's account of the gradual evolution of Catholic doctrine and Church structures includes reference to the work of Giovanni Semeria (1867–1931) on Christian origins and to Loisy's *L'Évangile et L'Église*, which had appeared in November 1902 between the June sermon and the December pamphlet.

[17] John R. Slattery, "How My Priesthood Dropped from Me," *The Independent*, 61 (Sept. 6, 1906), 565–71. See *Biographie*, XXI, 1; XIX, 11.

[18] Slattery's autobiography bears out C.J.T. Talar's claim, apropos of Houtin "The autobiographical genre (or genres) is less suitable to the abstract discussion of ideas than to an exploration of moral dilemmas that arise in espousing and advancing them." Talar, "Identity Formation, Identity Reconstruction, and Identity Transformation: Albert Houtin," above, 58.

[19] *Biographie*, XXI, 17.

[20] *Biographie*, XVI, 10.

[21] *Ibid.*, XII, 11; 14–15.

[22] John R. Slattery, "The Workings of Modernism," 570.

[23] On O'Connell's Fribourg speech, see Gerald P. Fogarty, S.J., *The Vatican and the Americanist Crisis: Denis J. O'Connell, American Agent in Rome, 1885–1903* (Roma: Università Gregoriana Editrice, 1974), 263–68. The text of O'Connell's speech is included as an Appendix, 319–26. It is O'Connell's only known publication.

[24] *Biographie*, XIV, 13.

[25] *Ibid.*, XVI, 5.

[26] Fogarty, *The Vatican and the Americanist Crisis*, 296, 305–06. "Yet O'Connell was in no sense a biblical scholar himself nor could he agree with Loisy and those modernists who denied supernatural revelation and maintained that Christianity arose from that which was most noble in human nature. He was primarily a religious man whose faith was enhanced rather than threatened by modern scientific discoveries" (305). And yet Slattery's autobiography, corroborated by his letters to O'Connell, shows that in 1902, the year before he was named rector of Catholic University, it was precisely O'Connell's ability to affirm "supernatural revelation" that Slattery questioned. See William L. Portier, "Modernism in the United States: The Case of John R. Slattery (1851–1926)" in ed. Ronald Burke, Gary Lease, and George Gilmore, *Varieties of Modernism* (Mobile: Spring Hill College, 1986), 81–85.

[27] "While the biblical question generated a great deal of attention then and since, questions of Church history were seen as contributing to a larger—and hence increasingly threatening—critical front that threatened orthodoxy. Houtin's work points to the historical dimension of the crisis, while bringing Duchesne's role into greater prominence." C.J.T. Talar, "Pious Legend and 'Pious Fraud': Albert Houtin (1867–1926) and the Controversy over the Apostolic origins of the Churches of France," unpublished paper in possession of the author, cited from the concluding paragraph. On Loisy and Duchesne, see Marvin R. O'Connell, *Critics on Trial, An Introduction to the Catholic Modernist Crisis* (Washington, DC: Catholic University of America Press, 1994), Chapter 4.

[28] "It was in Rome, in 1895, that I ran across Duchesne's 'Origines.' The stumbling chapter I read five or six times, and discussed it with several others many more times." "How My Priesthood Dropped from Me," 566. See Louis Duchesne, *Christian Worship, Its Origin and Evolution* [1889], trans. M.L. McClure (fifth edition; London: SPCK, 1923), Chapter I.

[29] Albert Houtin, *Histoire du Modernisme Catholique* (Paris: Chez l'auteur, 1913), Chapître XXI.

[30] *Biographie*, XVI, 2.

[31] Fogarty, *Vatican and the Americanist Crisis*, 257.

[32] Friedrich von Hügel, *Diaries*, November 19, 1897 in the von Hügel manuscript collection at the University of St. Andrews in Scotland.

[33] Fogarty, *Vatican and the Americanist Crisis*, 88. "Although Duchesne was regarded as too liberal by some people in Rome, O'Connell had him dine at the [North American] college and address the students." Fogarty remarks on O'Connell's interest in history. Duchesne's talks were intended to fill in possible gaps in the Roman education of North American College students.

[34] Slattery to O'Connell, Baltimore, December 7, 1900, O'Connell Papers, Archives of the Diocese of Richmond, from a microfilm copy at the University of Notre Dame Archives.

[35] Fogarty, *Vatican and the Americanist Crisis*, 293.

[36] Gerald P. Fogarty, S.J., *American Catholic Biblical Scholarship* (San Francisco: Harper & Row, 1989), Chapter 4 on "Americanism and the Biblical Question," 68. For an account of how the issues of political Americanism (separation of Church and State),

evolution, the biblical question and the figures involved with them came together with Italian conciliationists, see Ornella Confessore, *L'Americanismo Cattolico in Italia* (Roma: Edizioni Studium, 1984). O'Connell and his political alliance with Countess Sabina di Parravicino Revel (1865–1944) are at the center of this story. The last chapter, "Americanismo e Modernismo," distinguishes the political from the doctrinal in a manner congenial to Fogarty's interpretation. See his long review in *Catholic Historical Review*, 75/2 (April, 1989), 305–308.

[37] Slattery articulates this dilemma in the "Dorsey Sermon," the "Aftermath" brochure, and his anonymous "A Root Trouble in Catholicism." As in this 1909 formulation, the connection between critical history and reform proposals such as O'Connell's is clear: "Now the letter on modernism is a political document. The results of higher criticism had cut the ground from underneath papal pretensions. If scholarship be admitted, Rome's supremacy is gone—a supremacy in papal eyes of the Church over the State, the mistress over the handmaid. There was nothing else to do to save this supremacy but to repudiate modernism and modernists, root and branch." "The Workings of Modernism," 560.

[38] In 1957, Thomas T. McAvoy wrote: "If there was a theologian of the progressive group it was Denis O'Connell. Unfortunately O'Connell's activities were in an advisory capacity, and there are not enough of his writings to enable one to say what his full theological opinions were." *The Great Crisis in American Catholic History, 1895–1900* (Chicago: Henry Regnery Co., 1957), 86. Thomas Wangler reaches a similar conclusion regarding O'Connell's "theological framework." See "The Birth of Americanism: 'Westward the Apocalyptic Candlestick,'" *Harvard Theological Review*, 65 (1972), 419. Though the *Biographie* does not give us access to O'Connell's "full theological opinions" or his complete "theological framework," it provides a fuller context in which to interpret O'Connell's correspondence and strongly suggests a framework of theological "symbolism."

[39] Slattery to O'Connell, no place, March 29, 1901. For an account of O'Connell's turn to the "German orientation" and Ireland's loyalty to France, see Robert C. Ayers, "The Americanists and Franz Xaver Kraus: An Historical Analysis of an International Liberal Catholic Combination, 1897–1898" (Ph.D. dissertation, Syracuse University, 1981). See 259 for O'Connell to Ireland, Rome, February 28, 1900. For John Ireland's side of the story, see Marvin R. O'Connell, *John Ireland and the American Catholic Church* (St. Paul: Minnesota Historical Society Press, 1988), Chapters XVIII and XIX.

[40] *Biographie*, XVI, 10–11.

[41] *Ibid.*, XV, 11–12. For an account of Slattery's understanding of symbolism, see his "How My Priesthood Dropped from Me," 569–70. The issues are clearly the reality of the supernatural order and the nature of revelation. Houtin uses the word *symbolisme* to describe positions of Auguste Sabatier and Marcel Hébert on the eve of *Testem Benevolentiae* and of Loisy around 1902. See *Histoire du Modernisme Catholique*, 35–39; 125–6.

[42] See the letters of January 2, March 14, and March 16, 1900.

[43] *American Ecclesiastical Review*, 21 (November, 1900), 483–92.

[44] Slattery to O'Connell, New York, March 13, 1901.

[45] Slattery to O'Connell, New York, May 19, 1901.

[46] *Biographie*, XVI, 10–11.

[47] Here is my transcription of the relevant parts of the French text under discussion: "Durant ce voyage mon compagnon fût charmant pour moi. Je ne lui cachai point quel travail s'opérait dans mon intelligence. Il ne me dissimula point qu'il avait lui aussi beaucoup marché. . . . Dans notre crise commune, il y avait cependant une différence. Tandis que pour moi les dogmes restaient d'angoissantes énigmes; pour lui ils n'étaient

que des symboles d'idées morales plus ou moins justes plus ou moins profondes. Il definnissait la religion: *the ethical faculty*, ou encore, the entire oneness of man individually, socially, in the state as in the home [English in original]. . . . Dans notre crise commune, il y avait cependant une différence. Vivant à Rome, dans l'atmosphere de la cour pontificale, mon ami était tombé dans un skepticisme doux et bienveillant; pour lui les dogmes étaient de[s] poétiques symboles. Pour moi, homme du nord, ils restaient d'angoissantes énigmes." *Biographie*, XVI, 11.

[48] *Biographie*, XVI, 12.

[49] Colman Barry finds O'Connell's rapid rehabilitation "a bit surprising and difficult to understand." See *The Catholic University of America 1903–1909, The Rectorship of Denis J. O'Connell* (Washington, DC: Catholic University Press, 1950), 24 and the discussion to 33. See also Fogarty, *Vatican and the Americanist Crisis*, 296–302. Slattery claims that a remark about Cardinal Satolli led to O'Connell's dismissal as rector of the North American College in 1895. In a conversation with a friend of Archbishop Michael Corrigan of New York, the leader of the conservative party, O'Connell is reported to have asked, in an attempt to portray Corrigan in a negative light, "Did not Corrigan say that Satolli was the son of Leo XIII?" This remark was reported to the cardinal, in notarized form, as a declarative sentence: "Satolli is the son of Leo XIII." *Biographie*, XIII, 19–20.

[50] *Biographie*, XVII, 1–3. Barry has Grannan spending the summer of 1902 in Europe with O'Connell "laying the groundwork" for November's trustee meeting. See Barry, *Rectorship of O'Connell*, 27.

[51] *Biographie*, XVII, 4.

[52] *Ibid.*, XVII, 5.

[53] *Ibid.*, XVII, 6.

[54] *Ibid.*, XVII, 16.

[55] *Ibid.*, XVIII, 1–2.

[56] *Ibid.*, XVIII, 3–5.

[57] *Ibid.*, XVIII, 12.

[58] *Ibid.*, XIX, 3. As indicated by Loisy's *Mémoires*, O'Connell was part of the group of ecclesiastics in regular contact with Loisy. See, for example, II, 484, 507; III, 35, 61 (a mention of Slattery identifying him as "ami de Mgr. O'Connell"), 75, 86.

[59] In 1892, O'Connell had recommended Loisy to Ireland as a scripture professor for his new seminary in St. Paul. By 1904, biblical scholars Charles Grannan, O'Connell's former ally, and Henri Poels (1868–1948) would experience the rector's newfound antimodernism. See Fogarty, *American Catholic Biblical Scholarship*, 155 and Chapters 5 & 6.

[60] *Biographie*, XXI, 2.

[61] *Ibid.*, XXI, 3,

[62] *Ibid.*, XXI, 3–4.

[63] *Ibid.*, XXI, 4.

[64] Fogarty, "The Vatican and the Americanist Crisis," 332; see 305.

[65] Slattery judges Gibbons as "au fond . . . un égoïste." "American in heart and spirit, he took on the mentality of an Italian curialist," *Biographie*, XII, 5–6. According to Slattery, O'Connell never forgave Gibbons for allowing him to be dismissed without a fight as rector of the North American College in 1895. See *Biographie*, XXI, 2. Slattery also claims that, at this time, Gibbons asked O'Connell to return all his letters and O'Connell refused. See *Biographie*, XIII, 16.

5

Telling the Story:
Maude Petre
as Autobiographer

Ellen Leonard

I n Maude Petre's autobiographical work, *My Way of Faith*, Petre intertwined her own story with the story of Roman Catholic modernism.[1] This intertwining was, to a certain extent, inevitable. Petre had been an important figure in the loose group of Roman Catholics interested in modernizing the Church at the beginning of the twentieth century, and she had refused to take the anti-modernist oath in 1910 when it was imposed by the Catholic hierarchy in an effort to eradicate modernism from the Church. As a result, she had been forbidden to receive the sacraments in her own diocese. Through the initiative of her brother-in-law, unsuccessful efforts were made in 1934 to regularize her ecclesiastical position. In a letter to Bishop Amigo she expressed her desire "for the few years that remain to me, to work for religion—it is all I care for," while making it clear that she would not repudiate those whom she loved and respected.[2] Unfortunately the bishop remained as resolute in his insistence that she renounce her "modernist opinions" as Petre was in her refusal to do so. These unsuccessful attempts surely informed her "present consciousness" as she shaped the materials for her memoirs. The book would provide her answer as to why she had remained a Roman Catholic in spite of pulls from without and pressure from within. In the process, it would demonstrate her fidelity to the Church.

At the same time, Petre subordinated her own story of fidelity and endurance to the story of the male modernists. She was a public figure who had been the provincial superior of a religious congregation of women known as the Filles de Marie, the president of the Women's Institute in Storrington, a recognized speaker and writer. And yet she explained in the foreword that *My Way of Faith* was not an autobiography, "even if a thread of autobiography run(s) through it." "I trust," she added, "that my mirror reflects things far more interesting than my own person," and she generally presented her part in the modernist movement in terms of her friendship with Baron von Hügel, Henri Bremond, and, above all, George Tyrrell. "I bestirred myself at times, and struck my oar into the waters; but I was more concerned with the thoughts and actions of others than with my own."[3] Petre's work (sixteen published books and numerous articles) was subsumed under that of Tyrrell and seen by her as a continuation of his mission.[4] In this respect, Petre followed a pattern typical for female autobiographers. The characteristic of women to write their stories through the stories of others has been noted by feminist theorists who suggest that women's sense of self is intimately entwined with their relationships to others. Their autobiographical texts, reflecting more fluid ego boundaries than are found in men, are therefore more relational in character. Petre's story thus seems to fall into the genre of female lives of prime devotion to male destiny.[5]

Is it possible to reconcile Petre's presentation of her own faithfulness in an autobiographical work with her subordination of her story to the story of others? Is it possible to read the book as a coherent whole that is about both Petre herself as an independent figure and also about her conscious subordination to Tyrrell? This essay will argue that Petre's emphasis on her own suffering in *My Way of Faith* links these seemingly disparate elements in her self-presentation. Her relationships, particularly her friendship with George Tyrrell, were part of her own religious quest. Both the quest and her devotion to Tyrrell caused her personal suffering. Therefore she may perhaps best be understood as a martyr, one who courageously endured suffering and who was a faithful witness.

Petre's Devotion to Male Destiny

Maude Petre, like most women throughout history, saw herself primarily in a supportive role. In her last book, Petre reflected on modernism.

> No one can live within the Church at present without realizing that "Modernism" has been absorbed as well as condemned; that it has, in

its own measure, brought about a larger spirit; and that much is said
which could not have been said had men like Loisy, Tyrrell, von
Hügel, not lived and spoken.[6]

One notes that Petre does not name herself among those who had
spoken. And yet her voice continued loud and clear longer than any of
the three men.

This tendency to downplay her own role shaped much of her
autobiography. In 1890, at age twenty-seven, she joined the Filles de
Marie. She remained a member for eighteen years and served as
provincial superior in England and Ireland. Yet she devoted only two
pages of *My Way of Faith* to her experiences with the Filles de Marie
(which she did not name).[7] Instead she concentrated on her involvement
with Tyrrell and the modernist movement. Her friendship with Tyrrell
had begun during a retreat which he preached to the Filles de Marie
from July 22 to 31, 1900,[8] and she quickly came to see this friendship
and her commitment to support Tyrrell as a new vocation. "I had already
chosen my life purpose, in accordance with what I understood to be my
vocation; but now a new call supervened to which the other was
eventually sacrificed; to which, indeed, my whole life was consecrated
so long as Tyrrell lived."[9]

Tyrrell's life as a Catholic priest mattered more than anything else
to Petre. As she stated in *My Way of Faith*, she "would certainly have
died to secure his spiritual safety."[10] In her diary she insisted that she did
not want to add to his difficulties by being a "temptation" to him. "I
know I would give him up at once if it were for his good. But he does so
need someone to love him just now—to love him through thick and
thin."[11] She therefore left her religious community and devoted her life
to trying to "make his life as tolerable as possible."[12] This included
providing for his material needs through an annuity and a quiet home in
Storrington.

Tyrrell's death at her home in Storrington in 1909 was thus one of
the most important events in Petre's life. The ten days before his death
were, she said, "a large part of my life, into which was pressed and
concentrated much of my past and most of my future." "For then heart
met heart in a union for which no danger any longer existed; he knew,
better than ever, what he was to me, and I knew, at last, what I was to
him. No! not as much as he was to me, but a great deal all the same."
His death became for her the great liberator and revealer. "We see what
we never saw before; we understand much that perplexed us." She took
comfort in the fact that he believed in her abiding friendship, and she
saw "his final testament and dispositions" as proof of his trust.[13] She

thought that von Hügel was surprised that Tyrrell had left everything to her "and not to him, who was the greater mind and person."[14]

Petre also described Tyrrell's death in the *Autobiography and Life of George Tyrrell*, which she edited and wrote. There her voice, which had been explicitly muted in earlier sections of the work,[15] suddenly emerged.

> As I was with him, except at short intervals, the whole time, and as I was consequently able to understand his low, semi-articulate speech, as another, not following his illness from the first, could not do, I will not apologize for speaking in the first person, and giving the narrative exactly according to my own knowledge and impressions.[16]

Yet she still subordinated her voice to his. "The life of George Tyrrell," she said, "is the story of one who did not outlive the day's labor, but fell, tired and wounded, on the very battlefield." He had no opportunity "to reject what was wrong, confirm what was right." She expressed her deepest desire for the work: "May the history of his life explain much which, in his indifference to self, he never explained, and fill out something of the work which every man leaves unfinished!"[17] Petre saw this as her mission and life work.

Even after Tyrrell's death, their friendship decisively shaped Petre's life. "My acquaintance with George Tyrrell," she claimed in her autobiography, "changed the course of my life, and affects it even now. Had it not been for my burden of fidelity to him it might have been easier to regain my former position in the Church."[18] In spite of the costliness of her friendship, she remained convinced that "from the hour in which George Tyrrell entered my life something happened for good."[19] Shortly after Tyrrell's death in 1909, Petre added the following statement to her will:

> Being now in full possession of my ordinary faculties, I desire to say that I regard it as a privilege to have been able to work for Fr. T's memory; that I would gladly do more than I am doing, had I the requisite ability; that I think God raised him up in spite of all his faults, to do a great work for the future of the Church; that I believe he was a martyr in the cause for which he labored. All my views may not have been the same as his, but the more independent my mind, the deeper can be the reverence in which I held and continue to hold him.[20]

This was an extraordinary statement to include in a will. In her autobiography, she expressed the same sentiment this way: "And now, looking back on the period of that great friendship, so much a part of my life then and since . . . I could as well wish myself another being as wish it had not been."[21] For Petre, Tyrrell was a Christ figure, a martyr who suffered in body, mind, and heart. "On his deathbed none could have failed to be struck by the expression of Christ-like sorrow on the bowed head."[22] It is in keeping with her self-construction to imagine that Petre saw herself as one of the holy women at the foot of the cross.

Maude Petre, Religious Seeker

Maude Petre began to write the story of her "pauvre vie" in 1932 in part in order to tell once again her version of the "modernist story" and in part because she needed to sort out her position as a Catholic and a "modernist."[23] Here, too, she wrote in self-deprecating terms. In her diary she expressed her hope that she might be recognized as a Catholic writer, but accepted the fact that this was unlikely. "I must work on—not try to be recognized as a Catholic writer. Perhaps better so! The issues are greater than that!"[24] A few months later, she repeated in her diary that she hoped her new book would be "a reflection of things greater than myself."[25] Carolyn Heilbrun notes that this attitude toward one's own story is typical of women's autobiography. "One must be called by God or Christ to service in spiritual causes higher than one's own poor self might envision, and authorized by that spiritual call to an achievement in no other way excusable in a female self."[26]

And yet, as in many religious autobiographies, particularly those by women, Petre presented her experience as a religious seeker as a source of wisdom for the Church. The fact that Petre's is a woman's story thus adds a dimension that is otherwise missing in modernist studies and one which Petre consciously noted in her writing, often reminding her readers, "I am a woman."[27] She wrote, she claimed, "not as a teacher, but as a specimen—the specimen of a soul that has spent a long life in the battle between faith and doubt."[28] She saw herself as "attempting nothing didactic . . . offering only her personal experience." But she questioned religious apologists "who speak as though the truths of Copernicanism had never really entered into philosophy, and as though they could still view life and the universe from the Ptolemaic standpoint."[29] Petre knew that such a world no longer existed and that it was important for the Church to address the modern world. She saw her position of "solitude and abandonment" as perhaps offering an opportunity to draw lessons for the Church and for Christianity from the crisis.

Petre presented modernism as the clash of knowledge and faith, dividing the issues with which modernism wrestled into inner and outer problems. Those that arose from the character, doctrine, and discipline of the Church itself and which the Church could address were inner problems. They centered on the question of the rights and limits of religious authority. Though this question was troubling, even more disturbing were the outer problems, those problems over which the Church had no power but which arose from "new and devastating discoveries in science and history."[30] She distinguished three waves of doubt and disbelief that had swept the world during her lifetime: doubts arising from science, from historical criticism, and from what she described as the "sociological," the rejection of God that she saw reflected in the world about her.[31] About these problems she asked, "What was to be done if the acquisitions of human science, in whatever order, were unamenable (sic) to the Church's presentation of Catholic doctrine?"[32]

For Petre, these questions and doubts were not abstract. Rather, they pained her personally. "I have suffered from wounded self-love; I have suffered from wounded affections; I have suffered from the passion of love: but none of those pains have been worse—most of them not so bad—as the suffering from a tried and tortured faith."[33] Scholastic philosophy was to have provided a remedy to her persistent doubts. On the advice of her confessor, she had gone to Rome at the age of twenty-two to undertake this study. However, she described this period of her life with regret: "Looking back on my life I see how much less I profited by certain opportunities than I might have done." She added, "there have been too many pauses in my life's work."[34] Nonetheless, she offered her reactions to Thomism as those of "a religious mind, and at the same time, an innate skeptical mind, to this great philosophical system, which was offered to me, by my spiritual guides."[35] In the end, she found Thomism unable to answer the questions that the modern age raised so persistently.

By contrast, Petre saw the modernism of men like Tyrrell as "prepared to meet the full blast of unbelieving questions that were blown out of the studies of the exegetist and any other scientist."[36] She admitted that modernism had not solved the problems, "for it is only by a long process of spiritualization that human knowledge and faith are finally accorded."[37] But the official Church evaded the problems altogether. "Looking back on it all, I can see how impossible it was for the Church not to make some pronouncement." But she added, "Because she [the Church] was supreme teacher she forgot that she must also be supreme learner."[38] Nevertheless, Petre maintained that it was important that the questions had been asked.

Furthermore, Petre argued, modernism had affected the Church for good regardless of the campaign of the Catholic hierarchy against it. She was convinced that, because of modernism, the modern challenges were being addressed indirectly in spiritual books and hinted at in sermons.

> The controversy of Modernism is dead, but not the great questions with which it dealt. And as I have said, many are breathing more freely through windows that were opened by those they will never thank. In time to come some of those, who were apparently worsted, may be recognized as pioneers of a greater and fuller spiritual Christianity.[39]

Despite the limitations of the modernists, modernism at least addressed the right questions in a more satisfying way than did Thomism.

Intellectually, Petre was never fully satisfied, but the heart that desired God continued to hold fast. She saw her life as a struggle to bring mind and heart together. At times she fell back on a theory of gender complementarity, suggesting that one of the inner conflicts of her life had been that she thought like a man and felt like a woman.[40] Along with many women, she experienced the tension of not fitting into the established roles for women of her class. At the same time, she expressed ambivalence about her ability "to think like a man." "My mind," she explained, "had gone ahead of my training, but it had not acquired the true scholarly character." As with all the circumstances of her life, she accepted the fact and interpreted it in a positive way. "But there it is—a scholar I am not, nor can ever be, and I can only try to reap some consolation from the hope that I have thereby preserved an even greater independence than I should have had under more favorable intellectual conditions."[41]

Petre retained both her independence and her modernist convictions until the end of her life, as appeared in her final work, *Alfred Loisy: His Religious Significance*. Completed shortly before her death in her eightieth year in December, 1942, this book gave her a final opportunity to tell the story of modernism and to reflect on her part in the drama. In it Petre allowed her own voice to be heard. She described her work as that of "a Catholic, a member of the Church from which Alfred Loisy was excluded, but one who believes that, in spite of the vicissitudes of his religious life, he had a message of religious significance to deliver to mankind from which Christianity, and even Catholicism, can draw profit."[42] One senses that she identified with the scholar in what she perceived as his lonely exile from the Church which meant so much to her.

The last chapter of *My Way of Faith* returned to the question of why, given both her modernist convictions and the rejection of modernism by the Catholic hierarchy, she remained a Catholic. "And as for myself, I ask, at the end of this review of my life and thought, what the Church has been to me, what she still is." Her response was simple and profound.

> The Church has lighted my way. Instead of struggling through a wilderness I have had a road—a road to virtue and truth. Only a road—the road to an end, not the end itself—the road to truth, not the fullness of truth itself. . . . In one word, she has taught me how to seek God.[43]

As a religious seeker and despite her occasional self-deprecation, Petre resolutely continued on that road in spite of the religious hierarchy. She was and remained a modernist whose experience, she was convinced, contained valuable lessons for the universal Church.

Maude Petre, Martyr

In *My Way of Faith*, Petre followed what Estelle Jelinek describes as a fairly consistent pattern in women's autobiographies. "Unlike most men's progressive, unidirectional forms, most women's life studies tend to be disjunctive or discontinuous narratives—often interrupting the chronological order with flashbacks, anecdotes, and character sketches."[44] This is an apt description of *My Way of Faith*, one acknowledged by Petre. "Such a study is inevitably discursive, and without chronological consistency; one cannot cut the thought of one's life into definite periods."[45] Nonetheless her work consistently came back to, even revolved around, the suffering entailed by her religious quest as well as by her relationship with Tyrrell. It is this emphasis on suffering that gives *My Way of Faith* coherence and unity despite its discursive form and the apparent tension between her self-construction as a religious seeker with wisdom to share and her self-construction as Tyrrell's supporter.

Although *My Way of Faith* presented Petre's personal experiences, she made a conscious effort to set these experiences within a larger social and ecclesial context and to maintain a certain detachment. A different picture of Maude Petre emerges from her diary.[46] Petre began to keep a journal in 1900, shortly after she met Tyrrell and at his suggestion. She continued this practice with some lapses until the day before she died in December, 1942. These personal accounts of her activities and of her deepest feelings allow the reader to appreciate the daily life of an active woman and the immediacy of her reactions to events. They also reveal her moments of joy and even more her long periods of suffering as she struggled with uncertainties, periods of depression, religious doubts, misunderstandings, and ecclesiastical censure. One meets in the diary a passionate, generous woman who offered support to others even while she herself was suffering profound loneliness. The passionate voice which can be heard through the pages of her diary is deliberately muted in her published works. However, it comes through at times in *My Way of Faith*, where she constructs a version of herself as a Catholic religious woman who has had to struggle to remain faithful and who has suffered for her convictions in the spirit of the saints and martyrs. The cost was high, but Petre gladly paid the price in order to be faithful to herself, to her friends, and to the mission which she had embraced.

Petre's version of self was thus martyr as well as friend of Tyrrell and religious seeker. Her models were the saints about whom she began to read as a child of six or seven. Her childhood ambition had been to become a philosopher, a saint, and a martyr, and she had chosen as a patron a female saint, Catherine of Alexandria, who represented this triple ideal.[47] In *My Way of Faith*, she explicitly recalled a book entitled *Early Martyrs* by Mrs. Hyde, as well as short lives of saints, which she had "devoured" and "set about to imitate rather literally."[48] These stories presented the message that to be a Christian one must suffer.[49] Furthermore, as a recusant Catholic, she came from a family who had suffered for their faith.[50]

This emphasis on suffering encompassed both her devotion to Tyrrell and her treatment at the hands of the Church hierarchy. As Petre reflected on her "emotional growth and development" in *My Way of Faith*, she pondered why she had not married and concluded, "on the whole, I am glad to have lived my own life, and shared the life of others in a measure which I could not have done as a married woman. And my true love affair was to come later, in a form which could never be crowned with fulfillment." She then described very simply her experience of falling in love: "I had that consciousness of eternity; that sense that nothing else mattered on earth or in heaven; that it was the one priceless pearl for which all else could be sold or cast away as dross."[51] Here there is no hint of the pain and uncertainty that she revealed in her diary written thirty-six years earlier: "A terrible feeling waves over me as though there were a fate stronger than myself, drawing me towards what can never be."[52] Still, she admitted in *My Way of Faith* that Tyrrell was not the ideal man of her imagination. She learned, she said, "the common lesson that one can love a man for his needs as for his perfection."[53] In fact, Tyrrell seems to have been an egotistic and difficult friend, vacillating between affection and appreciation for Petre and impatience and resentment toward her.[54] She realized that her very belief in him was a source of irritation. "I saw him in priestly garments, and he liked mufti." "My efforts were not always happy," she continued, "and I myself was often to blame; had I cared for him less, and desired less to be cared for in return, I should, perhaps, have succeeded better."[55]

Although she acknowledged the suffering entailed in her relationship to Tyrrell, Petre placed more emphasis in her autobiography on the suffering involved in her commitment to modernism. She began by noting that she found "nothing more painful and distasteful than to go back to those days." The people she cared for most were dead, and she herself felt like "a solitary, marooned being on a deserted island." Her response to the question why not forget those days of controversy was "simply because I am not allowed to forget. Because I could not leave my lonely island without being untrue to myself and others."[56] She confessed, "I am sure I made some mistakes," but, she added, "I adhered throughout to what I believed to be my call and my duty." By contrast, "I think things were done to me, by incensed opponents, which were certainly not essential to religion, even in its most rigid and orthodox character."[57] To ignore this past, even worse to take the anti-modernist oath, would be to cast her lot with these oppressors. She therefore resolutely maintained her refusal to take the oath, convinced that "if one's life did not bear sufficient testimony to one's faith an oath would not do so."[58]

Nonetheless, she acknowledged her pain in being isolated, particularly in her chapter on "The Twilight of Modernism," where she explicitly addressed her own canonical situation. "Religious solitude is not good for the soul," she said, "and for one whose true home is the Catholic Church, and who can find no home elsewhere, ostracization implies very real suffering."[59] About those who refused to take the anti-modernist oath, she wrote, "though I will not admit of the use of the word *martyr* to describe those who felt it their duty to refuse it, or who took it with pain and inner revolt, yet it certainly was, in many cases, a weapon of spiritual torture."[60] Concerning the "orthodox" who accused such persons of pride and self-will, she added, "If only they knew what it costs to leave the shelter, and what a horror some have of taking a part which must be *exceptional*, they would regret their facile criticisms."[61]

She herself lived with the "spiritual torture" and the "facile criticism" for over thirty years. Despite her refusal to use the term "martyr" to describe herself, she clearly identified with the martyrs and did not hesitate to use the term for Tyrrell, whose martyrdom she shared. In her unique way, then, Maude Petre fulfilled her ambition to become a philosopher, a saint, and especially a martyr. In the end, the fulfillment of this ambition was the central story of *My Way of Faith*, despite the importance that Petre accorded Tyrrell and to modernism more generally.

Conclusion

The purpose of the religious autobiographies studied by John Morris in *Versions of the Self: Studies in English Autobiography from John Bunyan to John Stuart Mill* was to testify to God's mercy and to stir others.[62] This was also Petre's purpose. In the introduction to *My Way of Faith*, she referred to a friend who "has more than once urged me to write my own life, and explain how and why I have 'kept my faith,' because she thinks, I suppose, that I might help others by revealing my own secret." Petre hastened to point out that she had "no secret—no wondrous formula—no philosopher's stone of faith." But she had passed through a period of religious crisis which she was willing to share, inviting her readers "to take what interests them and leave the rest." Her story of fidelity to the Church of her baptism was both a contrast and a companion to the popular stories of conversion to the Roman Catholic Church. As she stated in the introduction to *My Way of Faith*: "My tale is to be one not of change, but of adherence; not of conversion, but of stability. I mean stability in the sense of constancy."[63] It was the stability and constancy of the martyr who bears witness even in the midst of suffering.

Carolyn Heilbrun in *Writing a Woman's Life* noted that before 1970 only the female life of prime devotion to male destiny had been told, although she recognized spiritual autobiographies in which God or Christ may be put in the place of a man with the same results: "one's own desires and quests are always secondary."[64] Petre's autobiography apparently fits into Heilbrun's category of prime devotion to male destiny. And yet Petre puts this devotion to male destiny in the context of her own religious quest and specifically her self-construction as martyr. As a result, her autobiography does, despite its emphasis on Tyrrell, present an independent self. Modernism, including her friendship with Tyrrell, provided the context for her own story of fidelity to the Church and her self-construction as a martyr, a faithful witness who suffered for her faith.

Notes

[1] Petre, *My Way of Faith* (London: J.M. Dent & Sons, 1937); hereafter *MWF.*

[2] Petre's correspondence with Bishop Amigo is in the Vigilance Committee file, Archive of the Diocese of Southwark, London. Quote from letter September 6, 1934. For an account of this correspondence, see Ellen Leonard, *Unresting Transformation: The Theology and Spirituality of Maude Petre* (Lanham: University Press of America, 1991). Petre also wrote to the pope about her situation; Petre Papers, British Library, Add. MS 52377, October 28, 1932. In March 1939, she wrote to the newly elected Pius XII and received in response a paternal blessing from Cardinal Maglione; Petre Papers, BL, Add. MS 52381.

[3] *MWF*, 253.

[4] Some of her work was quite literally the continuation of Tyrrell's mission. *The Soul's Orbit or Man's Journey to God* (London: Longmans, Green & Co., 1904) was based on notes taken by Petre of Tyrrell's retreat conferences and consisted of Tyrrell's interpretation of the *Spiritual Exercises* of Ignatius. In addition to her own work, Petre edited a number of works by Tyrrell after his death.

[5] See, for example, Carolyn G. Heilbrun, *Writing a Woman's Life* (New York: Ballantine Books, 1988); Linda Wagner-Martin, *Women's Lives: The New Biography* (New Brunswick, NJ: Rutgers University Press, 1994); Estelle C. Jelinek, *The Tradition of Women's Autobiography: From Antiquity to the Present* (Boston: Twayne Publishers, 1986); Mary G. Mason, "The Other Voice: Autobiography of Women Writers," in *Autobiography: Essays Theoretical and Critical*, ed. by James Olney (Princeton: Princeton University Press, 1980), 207–35; *Revealing Lives: Autobiography, Biography, and Gender*, eds. Susan Groag Bell and Marilyn Yalom (Albany, NY: State University of New York Press, 1990).

[6] *Alfred Loisy: His Religious Significance* (Cambridge University Press, 1944), 53–54.

[7] *MWF*, 152–54.

[8] This retreat, the last given by Tyrrell, replaced one that he had been scheduled to give in Dublin to Jesuits preparing for ordination. The change was one of the restrictions imposed on him as a result of problems over his article, "A Perverted Devotion." *Autobiography and Life of George Tyrrell*, 2 vols. (London: Arnold, 1912), 2, 130.

[9] *MWF*, 276.

[10] *Ibid.*, 279.

[11] Petre Papers, BL, Add. MS52372, December 19, 1900.

[12] *MWF*, 284.

[13] *Ibid.*, 284–288.

[14] *Ibid.*, 267.

[15] The first volume consisted of Tyrrell's autobiography which he had sent to Petre. In the introduction, she referred to the recipient of this material as "a friend." *Life of Tyrrell*, 1, v.

[16] *Ibid.*, 2, 423.

[17] *Ibid.*, 1, x–xi.

[18] *MWF*, 270.

[19] *Ibid.*, 272.

[20] Petre's niece, Mrs. Katherine Pirenne, kindly allowed me to make a copy of this will.

[21] *MWF*, 270.

[22] *Ibid.*, 296.

[23] Lewis May's book on *George Tyrrell and the Modernist Movement* (London: Spottiswoode, 1932) had raised once again questions about events surrounding Tyrrell's death.

[24] Petre Papers, BL, Add. MS 52377, May 4, 1932.

[25] Petre Papers, Add. MS 52377, August 12, 1932. Tyrrell had described the autobiographical fragments which he wrote for Petre as "ma pauvre vie." These fragments became the first volume of Petre's *Autobiography and Life of George Tyrrell*.

[26] Heilbrun, *Writing a Woman's Life*, 23.

[27] See, for example, *MWF*, 269.

[28] *Ibid.*, 188.

[29] *Ibid.*, 170.

[30] *Ibid.*, 211.

[31] *Ibid.*, 167–168.

[32] *Ibid.*, 229.

[33] *Ibid.*, 162.

[34] *Ibid.*, 171.

[35] *Ibid.*, 174.

[36] *Ibid.*, 233.

[37] *Ibid.*, 235.

[38] *Ibid.*, 241.

[39] *Ibid.*, 250.

[40] *Ibid.*, 270.

[41] *Ibid.*, 171–172.

[42] *Loisy*, 1.

[43] *MWF*, 340–341.

[44] Jelinek, *The Tradition of Women's Autobiography*, 53

[45] *MWF*, ix.

[46] The difference between an autobiography and a diary has been noted by Roy Pascal: An autobiography is conventionally "a review of a life from a particular moment in time, while the diary, however reflective it may be, moves through a series of moments in time." Quoted from *Design and Truth in Autobiography* (Cambridge, MA, 1960) 3, by John Morris in *Versions of the Self: Studies in English Autobiography from John Bunyan to John Stuart Mill* (New York: Basic Books, 1966), 172. For details on Petre's life drawn from her diaries, see Leonard, *Unresting Transformation: The Theology and Spirituality of Maude Petre*.

[47] *MWF*, 65–66.

[48] *Ibid.*, 50.

[49] Judith Perkins in *The Suffering Self: Pain and Narrative Representation in the Early Christian Era* (London and New York: Routledge, 1995), 200–214, shows how the *Acts of the Martyrs* and the lives of the saints, especially female saints, represented Christianity as the community of sufferers and illustrated that to be a Christian *was* to suffer.

[50] Petre, *The Ninth Lord Petre: Pioneers of Roman Catholic Emancipation* (London: SPCK, 1928), describes not only Petre's great-great-grandfather and the old English Catholics but Maude Petre herself.

[51] *MWF*, 152.

[52] Petre Papers, BL, Add. MS 52372, September 21, 1900.

[53] *MWF*, 152.

[54] Tyrrell's letters to fellow Jesuit, Henri Bremond, contain a number of negative remarks concerning Petre. See *Lettres de George Tyrrell à Henri Bremond*, ed. A. Louis-David (Paris: Aubier Montaigne, 1971).

[55] *MWF*, 281, 284.

[56] *Ibid.*, 207

[57] *Ibid.*, 243.

[58] *Ibid.*, 246.

[59] *Ibid.*, 245. Petre omitted the details of her struggles with ecclesiastical authorities, but her journal pages reveal the extent of her suffering, including moments of self-doubt.

[60] *Ibid.*, 245; emphasis is Petre's.

[61] *Ibid.*, 339.

[62] Morris, *Versions of the Self*, 143–144.

[63] *MWF*, ix, xi.

[64] Heilbrun, *Writing a Woman's Life*, 60, 21.

6

Luis Martín (1846–1906)
The Black Pope of the Modernist Period

David Schultenover, S.J.

"In the final analysis... the prerogative of autobiography consists in this: that it shows us not the objective stages of a career—to discern these is the task of the historian—but that it reveals instead the effort of a creator to give the meaning of his own mythic tale"

Georges Gusdorf[1]

G eorges Gusdorf cautions anyone who attempts to write a biography to do so with consummate trepidation. Who, after all, is so self-aware that he or she can write his or her *own* life, let alone someone else's? One can attempt a precise recounting of "facts," as, for example, the artist who paints a historical battle scene in exquisite detail of uniforms, weapons, topography, and deployment; but the result will fall hopelessly short of the real soldiers' real experience. Or one could abandon the effort to reproduce detail and try instead to capture the experience by poetic interpretation, as Picasso did with *Guernica*, and come arguably far closer to the original experience. This paper attempts something of the latter on the subject of Luis Martín Garcia (1846–1906), superior general of the Society of Jesus at the time of the Modernist Crisis, as it works from copious autobiographical sources left by Martín.

Theorists of autobiography have argued that every memoir, autobiography, or confession is a narrative interpretation. No matter how many data are recalled and with what precision, the fact remains that the autobiographer uses memory to draw the past into the present, not as objectified—as it were, on film (which can capture only objective superficialities of events, not their complex prehistories, contexts, and meanings interior to the actors)—but as remembered with a motive; and the latter is the engine of the narrative. No, the autobiographer, no matter how attentive to detail, no matter how many documents he or she quotes, first of all selects events for recounting and marshals documentation to support that recounting. Far more objective material is always left out than is recorded. Then, having made the selections, the autobiographer weaves them into a narrative that interprets the writer's life according to some overriding motive. Often that motive is *to set the record straight*, that is, to correct false impressions gained by observers of the writer's observable deeds; in other words, the autobiographer writes to "save" his life, to liberate himself from interpretations he sees as false or out of harmony with his own view of himself, "to give the meaning," as Gusdorf says, "to his own mythic tale."

My aim here is to try to capture the meaning that Luis Martín gave "to his own mythic tale" in his *Memorias*,[2] and see what light that meaning sheds on his role in the modernist crisis and particularly on the events leading up to the crisis—he died in spring, 1906, on the eve of the fateful condemnations. I will begin with some cultural-political background, as it was a major component of Martín's self-construct. Then I will focus on his formative years, both because his account of these years provides the most extensive description of his self-perception, but also because the issues that arose then perdured through the rest of his life and provided for him self-reflective continuity. The self of his autobiography was a construct based on selective memories of his earlier years. We do not know the self of Martín's early years, only the self he remembered "with a motive" from the vantage point of his final years, so that in some very real sense the two are continuous, but not the same.

Martín's Political Background

Luis Martín's Spain was fraught with tension and violent encounters between political liberals and monarchists, which no Spaniard, however removed from the neuralgic centers, could escape. The typical Spaniard was a person of deep and complete feeling, whose self-identity sprung from the family and radiated out to village, province, and nation, in that order. Since the early nineteenth century, Spain had been a loose federation of small, mutually hostile republics that periodically exploded into revolution or war. So, although the Spaniard's sense of self was centered in the family with its immediate environs—usually the village—that center was always in tension with the nation. Thus the Spaniard's life was highly politicized and explosive.[3]

For modern Spain, 1808 was a watershed year.[4] Napoleon defeated the Spanish and enthroned his brother Joseph in place of Ferdinand VII. In the ensuing chaos, when the Spanish government ceased to function, two agencies rushed into the power vacuum: the army and the church; and these, with attendant constituencies, became the principal protagonists of the century's struggle. Of the two, the church was stronger, the army having been routed by the French. However, the army allied with Wellington's British regulars, and, using guerrilla tactics, gradually drove the French from the peninsula, thereby regaining stature. This coalition of the Spanish and English armies was the beginning of that contagion of liberalism against which the Spanish church contended throughout the century.

In 1812, a cortes met in the southern coastal city of Cádiz to draft a constitution, but, because the French still controlled Spain's interior roadways, representatives came mostly from the liberal-dominated southern and eastern seaboards. The resulting constitution, therefore, reflected the liberal agenda: a laissez faire economy, strict separation of church and state, secularization of schools and much of the church's property, and the abolition of the Inquisition (whose recent target had been freemasonry). Spain, however, lacked the large, well-educated middle class required for liberalism to work—free trade, free thought, and constitutional government meant nothing to the masses of landless peasants— so the program languished before the well-organized and still powerful church.

Ironically, however, the liberal party's weakness against the church led to a more radical and doctrinaire liberalism. A mutual scapegoating for the ills of the post-Napoleonic chaos resulted. Liberals and the church vilified each other as the enemy, liberals becoming wholly anticlerical and church leaders wholly anti-liberal—violently so in proportion to Spain's entrenched clericalism.

Following Napoleon's defeat in 1814, Ferdinand VII returned to Spain and faced a choice between the army and the church. Given the liberal party's weakness, the choice was clear: the old alliance between throne and altar had served Ferdinand well, and the church was now clearly the stronger party, whereas the army was now aligned with republican liberals.

Supported by church authorities, Ferdinand abolished the constitution and inaugurated nineteen years of despotism, which only exacerbated the liberals' anticlericalism. For their part, the liberals, like the weakened army which had turned to guerrilla warfare to defeat the French, now turned to freemasonry to prosecute their aims. Founded in Spain by the English in 1728, freemasonry faced harsh repression by the church-dominated party, so that it never gained popular support. Nevertheless, it remained the church's *bête noire*, particularly as the army in 1820 forced Ferdinand to reinstate the constitution of 1812 in exchange for helping him pursue his reconquest of the empire, thereby banning the Inquisition and thus lifting the pressure on freemasonry.

This move angered the reactionaries and convinced them that Ferdinand was drifting toward liberalism. Many of the clergy, particularly in the north, concluded that the church would never be safe until Spain had a monarch who would be completely answerable to them. This group defined themselves against both Ferdinand and the liberals. They were the founders of Carlism. The majority of the clergy supported Carlism vs. the liberal, anti-clerical parties.

The first Carlist war broke out in 1833. The liberals, with military aid from England—which the Carlists never forgot or forgave—and concessions from the regent Queen Mother María Cristina, enjoyed open season on religious orders, which were in any case easy targets.[5] In summer 1834 a cholera epidemic in Madrid occasioned vicious scapegoating. Jesuits were the primary target, as the rumor spread that they had poisoned the wells. They, along with other religious orders, lost many lives and property and were dispersed until 1851.[6] Many of those involved in the mob action against the religious, however, were not liberals but members of the urban working class not in sympathy with the clergy's political role. One of these was Don Calixto, the friend of Luis Martín's father, with whom Luis lived while attending seminary in Burgos.

Between 1835 and 1844 the liberal party expropriated most unused church land and sold it in public auction, hoping thereby to create a liberal rural middle class. Martín's father seems to have benefitted from this auction, but he never warmed to the liberals. The majority of new landlords, however, found themselves conflicted. Traditionally they favored Carlism, but a Carlist victory would return their lands back to the church, so they supported the liberals. Meanwhile, liberals who acquired property found themselves joining Carlist landlords in a new landed oligarchy which negotiated an end to the war in 1839.

The effect on church life of the Carlist-liberal contest was catastrophic. It meant loss of revenue from property rentals and dependence on the state for economic support. This situation might have occasioned church reform, but it did not. To maintain the style of life to which it had become accustomed—to maintain the enormous churches, schools, and other institutions—the church curried favor with the nouveau riche oligarchy and turned away from the proletariat. As a result, the church lost the masses, yet blamed the liberals for irreligion in Spain.[7]

The Society of Jesus occupied a precarious position in Spain from the Enlightenment on. Pope Clement XIV, on 8 June 1773, bowing to political pressure spearheaded by Spain, signed a bill suppressing the order. Restored by Pius VII in 1815 following the defeat of Napoleon, it reestablished itself in Spain that same year. During the next 100 years, however, Spanish Jesuits suffered three distinct dispersions: 1820–23, 1834–51, and 1868–75.[8] In 1846, the year Pius IX became pope, during the middle period of Jesuit exile, Luis Martín was born in the pro-Carlist province of Burgos. Five years later, on 16 March 1851, a concordat between Pius IX and Isabella II restored the Jesuits to Spain, only to be exiled again in 1868—Luis Martín with them. Spanish Jesuit houses of formation were founded in southern France and remained there until France dispersed all Jesuits in 1880. Luis Martín, therefore, spent nearly twelve years in exile, not being allowed to return home to bury his only surviving brother and his parents.

Sources for Martín's Construction of His "Self"

After Martín's death in 1906, Peter Chandlery, a curial secretary and Martín's daily walking companion, serialized an important, if hagiographic, biography of Martín in *Letters and Notices of the English Province of the Society of Jesus*.[9] Chandlery wrote almost entirely from the outside observer's viewpoint, hardly ever betraying inside knowledge. The same is true of all the briefer biographical notices and eulogies published by other authors on the occasion of Martín's death, most of them derivative of Chandlery's. It seems that Martín confided intimacies only to his own massive but incomplete *Memorias*—a manuscript of 5424 quarto pages! These memoirs are extraordinary on several counts. First, their sheer size—which might lead one to expect verbosity. Indeed, he was wordy, but the historian will forgive that in the light of Martín's always careful and detailed accounts, replete with names, scenarios, and commentaries rarely found anywhere, let alone in Vatican and curial archives. Second, so far as is known, this is the only autobiography of any of the anti-modernist figures, so it takes a certain pride of place among all the archival sources for (anti)modernist studies. Third, it is the only autobiographical account of a Jesuit superior general since Ignatius of Loyola's very brief relation.

But, whereas Ignatius was clear about why he wrote his story, Martín was not. It is difficult to imagine that he had ever intended his *Memorias* for public scrutiny, especially the part about his early life. One might draw this conclusion from two remarkable anomalies: first, the fact that he wrote his memoirs in six languages, sometimes passing from language to language in mid-sentence—as an exercise, he said, to sharpen his skills; and second, his unusual candor about his upbringing, schooling, and private struggles. But the fact that he was so candid— sometimes brutally so—lends confidence to the judgment that he left a reliable account of his most private thoughts.

In a prefatory note, Martín gave the following ascetical rationale for his undertaking:

> In the name of Our Lord Jesus Christ, today (15 May 1895) I begin to write in French and in English these recollections of my life, in order to exercise myself in these languages and to acquire the habit of speaking them less incorrectly. I want to take up this story line or material rather than any other, because it will give me the opportunity to make a general examination of conscience for my entire life, to confess many sorrows, and to bless God who has shown himself to be so full of forgiveness and so infinitely merciful."[10]

But Martín's decision to enter on such a startling and colossal departure from tradition, Jesuit or otherwise,[11] requires more explanation than he offered here. The second sentence of his preface contains two pregnant words, "story line" and "sorrows," which do not capture the nuance of the original French. What Martín seems really to be saying is this: "I choose this method rather than some other for telling my story, because it lends itself better to a general examination of conscience and con- session of moral failures and sorrows." Thus my view is that Martín's underlying, personal motivation, at least with respect to all of the personal reflections and insertions that dominate his memoirs up to 1892 and recur infrequently thereafter, is confessional. I will argue, based on Martín's own words, that he was driven by an interior need not only to make sense of his life, but also to "set the record straight" and "save" himself in the process—in Gusdorf's terms, "to give the meaning of his own mythic tale."

Introspection is characteristically modern and Western. People of Mediterranean culture, like Martín, were characteristically anti-intro- specie. However, when one joined a religious order, one took on a culture within a culture, one that included systematic soul-searching, examination of conscience (or "consciousness," in its current patois) as an ascetical discipline. Keeping a journal of interior movements was not uncommon. So Martín's introspection, although uncharacteristic for a Spaniard, was not uncharacteristic for a Jesuit. Writing the results of his introspection for eyes other than his own, however, was highly uncommon, particularly on such a scale. Moreover, it will become clear as we go along that, both by personality and circumstances of life, Martín fell rather toward the extreme end of the introspective spectrum.

The historical detail of the *Memorias,* especially of the later years, demands some other explanation of motive than the one Martín provided. The congregation of 1892 that elected him general mandated the writing of histories of each Jesuit province, as well as a general history of the whole Society. Martín energetically devoted himself to this task, not only because he was a dutiful servant, but also because he was personally intensely interested in history—and again not only because he was interested in others but also because he was intensely interested in "saving" himself by empathetic comparison.[12] To write the Society's history, he assembled competent archivists and writers, personally instructed them at great length on modern historical methods, and moved the Jesuit archives to Exaeten in Holland where they would be more accessible to scholars and less subject to confiscation by hostile governments.[13]

As part of this ambitious project, Martín himself undertook the history of his own generalate, beginning with his own personal history. Amazingly, he worked in almost total secrecy—amazing because of the project's enormous scope, the time commitment involved, the documents required, and the constraints of space in the curia.[14] None of his general assistants knew about it. Only one man knew—Father Eduardo Gallo, the secretary of Martín's Spanish assistant. Martín and Gallo went back a long way,[15] and it was he whom Martín, on his deathbed, charged with the mission to smuggle the *Memorias* back to his home province of Castile for safe keeping. So, when Martín died and his successor was elected, Gallo consigned the *Memorias* at the last minute with the luggage of the Castillian provincial superior, Ignacio María Ibero, as he boarded the northbound train for Spain. Ibero did not know the contents of the box.[16]

Martín began writing his memoirs in 1895, four and a half months after he had moved the general curia from Fiesole to Rome; he continued writing them probably until sometime in 1902 when his fatal cancer first appeared. After that, he worked at them only sparingly if at all.[17] Given his open and confessionary stance, it is most regrettable from the historian's viewpoint that he did not live long enough to retrospect the post-1901 years of the modernist crisis and integrate all of the relevant correspondence into his narrative. But what we do get is a privileged perspective on the all-important *background* to the modernist crisis, as well as to several other not unconnected ecclesiastico-political crises, such as the Spanish-American War, seen through the eyes of one of the key figures of fin de siècle European and ecclesiastical history. His actions and views regarding modernism and specifically George Tyrrell can, however, be ascertained from copious documents available in the Roman archives.[18]

The year 1892, when Martín assumed the post of superior general, was a fateful year. It brought together a constellation of the three main protagonists of the events played out on the eve of the modernist crisis: Martín, Leo XIII, and Leo's chamberlain, Monsignor Rafael Merry del Val, who would become Pius X's secretary of state and principal executor of the Vatican decisions that precipitated the modernist crisis. When, in 1895, on the mandate of the general congregation, Martín moved the Jesuit curia from Fiesole back to Rome, it was he, with his great intellectual and moral resources and special relationship to the papacy, whom Leo and his successor, Pius X, would call on more than anyone else to devise and/or execute strategies to meet the impending crisis.[19]

Martín's Formative Years

I enter upon this part of my essay keenly mindful of Gusdorf's admonition. No recounting of "facts" or their interpretation can faithfully translate a life. Nor do I presume to do so. My hope is to do what the artist does: paint an *interpretation* of a life according to a frankly admitted agendum—to illuminate the modernist crisis by trying to grasp something of the self-construct of one of its protagonists. I am also keenly aware that I will be opening myself to the charge that *I* am constructing Martín's "self" rather than drawing from the sources *Martín's* construction. My hope is that, although I will be appealing to analytical techniques unfamiliar to Luis Martín, he—were he to read the results— would recognize the "self" here constructed as clearly his.

One can hardly grasp the mind of Luis Martín without understanding his roots: his primary socialization in a middle-class family in a region of Spain dominated by Carlism; his secondary socialization first in a Burgos seminary, then in the Society of Jesus during the violent struggles leading to and following the deposition of Isabella II (1868) when Jesuits were expelled from Spain; finally the effect on him of his years as a religious superior—first as rector of the venerable major

Seminary of Salamanca (today a pontifical university); then as provincial of the Jesuit province of Castile during the post-restoration era when ecclesiastical-political factionalism among "liberals" and several cabals of conservative partisans constantly threatened the peace, even within religious houses; finally as superior general of the Society of Jesus (1892–1906) when he had to try to be "all things to all people," while his beloved Spain was losing world power to the upstart United States, culminating in the Spanish-American War, and while factionalism at home continued unabated, leading to the assassination of Prime Minister Antonio Cánovas del Castillo (1828–1897), and while France was undergoing similar church-state convulsions leading to the laws of separation, secularization of church properties, periodic expulsion of Jesuits with loss of schools and parishes. The man had a few things on his plate—which makes the writing of his memoirs during this time all the more amazing.

On 19 August 1846, during the seventeen-year period of Jesuit exile (1834–1851), Luis Martín Garcia was born in the pro-Carlist province of Burgos in the village of Melgar de Fernamental. Five years later, on 16 March 1851, a concordat between Pius IX and Isabella II restored the Jesuits to Spain.

Today, the visitor to Melgar will find fixed to the side of a small house a short distance from the grand church of Our Lady of the Assumption a substantial marble tablet bearing the inscription:

IHS
In honor
of the Most Reverend Father Luis Martín y García
who was born in this house
on the 19th of August 1846
and was elected Superior General of the Society of Jesus
on the 2nd of October 1892
The Municipal Government of the Village of Melgar de Fernamental

Two weeks after Martín's election, the whole town turned out for a spectacular celebration. Villagers decorated the modest Martín house, processed from there to the church for a solemn Mass, afterwards shot off fireworks, danced to music, and feasted on delicacies. Melgar renamed its main street for Fr. Martín, the twenty-fourth general and the fifth Spaniard in that post. His election was clearly the biggest event in the history of that village of 2,116 inhabitants.[20]

Martín's parents were Don Clemente Martín Arroyo (1816–1877) and Doña Francisca Garcia (1817–1878),[21] both natives of Melgar and descendants of middle class families. Don Clemente was a dealer in packsaddles and harness. He also managed some small pieces of farm land and in his later years leased a flour mill.[22] Luis was baptized on 20 August 1846, as Luis Hipólito, because he was born on the feast of St. Louis of Toulouse, a bishop who had died in 1297 at the age of twenty-three, a fact that would take on some significance for Luis in the light of the premature deaths of his six siblings. The second name was that of his patron, St. Hippolytus of Rome (c. 170–c. 235).

Luis testifies that, although his father was not himself educated,[23] he saw to it that his sons were. After primary schooling, Luis studied Latin in Melgar under a certain Don Jerónimo Lorenzo and succeeded not brilliantly, but sufficiently well to advance to the next chair.[24] In 1858, he was admitted to the school of philosophy at the Seminary of San Carlos in Burgos—at the age of twelve! For his three years of philosophy and first year of theology, he was an extern, living with the family of Don Calixto, a business friend of his father. For his last two years of theology, he was an intern. Academically, Luis began slowly, then, at a certain point, to excel. "His academic records show that in the last four years he received the grade of *Meritissimus* in the principal subjects and nothing less than *Benemeritus* in the rest." The public defense of his thesis in philosophy on 14 March 1861, earned him a "very good" and in theology on 18 February 1864, an "excellent."[25]

As to his general comportment, his fellow students later testified that his moral conduct was "most exemplary."[26] There was probably no external reason to judge otherwise. Testimony to his virtuous life was consistent throughout, otherwise he would never have held one position of leadership after another all the way to superior general of the Society of Jesus.[27] However, throughout most of his life, Luis was living quite another life interiorly, and the discord between the two lives—judging by his own testimony—seemed to express itself in a series of somatizations, the last one finally ending his life.

Martín returns to this point regularly in his *Memorias*, like a theme that ties his whole life together. It is the primary, most interior, and personal element of his life that was most distressing and unintegrated and therefore about which he sought, by writing his *Memorias*, to "save" himself. It is important to be clear about this crucial factor from the beginning, because it runs throughout his life like a pedal point, freshly sounded by the twice daily examinations of conscience. It colored his entire perspective.

First, a word about the phenomenon of "somatization." It was a term given me by John Pilch, a student of cross-cultural illnesses, when

I described to him Martín's illnesses and their largely failed treatment. Physician Arthur Kleinman, in a classic study, *Social Origins of Distress and Disease,* defines *somatization* as "the normative expression of personal and social distress in an idiom of bodily complaints and medical help-seeking."[28] While I am no expert in this area, I am well enough read in it to affirm that the descriptions supplied by Kleinman and a host of other scholars in the field of culture-associated disorders make sense of Martín's recurrent references to and discussions of his *mal* and *enfermedad crónico.*[29]

My view is that the self Luis Martín constructs and works out of is rooted in a chronic depression due to the incalculable loss sustained by his family in the deaths of six of their seven children. When Hermenegildo died on 11 June 1869, Luis was the lone survivor of his parents' offspring. On the burial of his mother, 3 February 1878, the simple entry in the death register of the village of Melgar ended dolefully, "She left a son called Don Luis."[30] The birth/death data of the children are themselves cruelly revealing:

> Eugenio, 19 November 1843 to 30 October 1846.
> Francisco, 26 January 1845 to 3 March 1845.
> Luis, 19 August 1846 to 18 April 1906.
> Augustín, 28 August 1848 to 20 November 1854.
> Constantina, 11 March 1850 to 8 September 1851.
> Hermenegildo, 13 April 1852 to 11 June 1869.
> Emeterio, 3 March 1854 to 21 August 1855.

Two deaths occurred before Luis would have been aware of them. Eugenio died at age 3, the year Luis was born, while Francisco died the year before, after less than two months of life. Constantina died at 1.25 years when Luis was 5. Augustín died at age 6 when Luis was 8. Emeterio died at 1.5 years when Luis was 9. Hermenegildo died at age 17 when Luis was 23 and in the Society, leaving his parents with no one to carry on the family name.

These data on deaths in the Martín household are similar to those in the Kierkegaard household and prompt a comparison of effects. Søren Kierkegaard was, like Luis, the only survivor of seven siblings and reflected that, as a result, his father incurred an overwhelming guilt that beshadowed not only his own life but his family's as well.[31] Luis Martín's experience was parallel, if not as dramatic in its etiology. The recurrent experience of sibling deaths would have affected him profoundly, particularly through his parents' reaction.

The impact of those losses can be viewed from a couple of perspectives. Psychodynamics suggest that Luis would not have been cognitively aware of the first two deaths; or, while he would have been consciously unaware of those deaths, he would have unconsciously experienced the losses through his parents' grief, particularly his mother's. As his cognitive powers developed, however, the experiences of sibling deaths in his fifth, eighth, ninth, and twenty-third years would have been more and more his own but still much affected by his parents' reactions. [32]

During much of this time, Luis would likely have been deprived especially of his mother's attention. If she was emotionally unavailable to him in his early years, he would not have received adequate "mirroring" of his experiences, curiosity, and strivings and would therefore have suffered some retardation of development. In the face of this inadequacy, when Augustín died, not only would Luis have been aware of his personal loss, but—to invoke Kohlberg's theory of moral development—he would probably also have wondered if he had "done something wrong" to cause his brother's death, thereby incurring a sense of guilt. [33] Subsequent deaths would have reopened the same unconscious/conscious questions of culpability.

As Luis probably grew up with a sense of guilt and culpability surrounding his siblings' deaths, it is not unlikely that he also struggled with guilt feelings about joining the Jesuits and thereby not carrying on the family name as the only remaining son of his parents. In this respect, his last sibling's death, occurring when Luis was already a Jesuit, very likely would have not only retriggered his earlier emotional reactions but even heightened them. While this analysis would fit the children of any culture, Luis probably would have felt the added pressure that befalls a Mediterranean son whose family ties and responsibilities are exceptionally binding.

We can also view the Martín deaths demographically. Data on infant mortality in Spain in 1860 show that the mortality rate of 17.4% was not out of line with that in other countries of Europe. Thus, while Luis's parents would have experienced infant death as not unexpected, its scale in their family was quite anomalous. It would very likely have enhanced their felt-need to continue to have heirs and to contextualize their losses in religiosity. All of this trauma and attendant parental guilt and spiritualization of it would have had a profound effect on Luis. Certainly one can legitimately surmise that his later pattern of spiritualization of "miseries" reflected that of his parents.

Just what effect did all of this trauma have on Luis Martín? Quite possibly it slowed his development and perhaps even led to certain personal disorders. The editors of his *Memorias* concur that Luis was a thoroughly unremarkable child until his fourth year in the seminary. This fact coheres well with what child psychologists say can happen to a child who suffers grievous loss. Erna Furman observes that bereavement can result in "developmental arrests, impairments, and deviations, leading to maladjustments and/or symptom formation" in children who mirror their parents' reactions but without adequate coping mechanisms. If the parents suffer depression, the child would internalize that response. If the parents see the death of a child as God's judgment on them or as willed by God, a surviving child's conscience "may become excessively harsh and threatening. . . . Such a development is often marked by strong guilt feelings, fears and nightmares, low self-esteem, unrealistically high standards for oneself, reluctance to make mistakes and to compete or the reverse, namely an unrelenting drive to excel. Some effects . . . do not become evident until [the child] needs to cope with a new developmental phase," for example, puberty. The child might "manage the ongoing daily life" but might be "unequal to the new stresses and conflicts which progression brings."[34]

This observation suggests that Luis, with no healthy way of negotiating the negative feelings attendant on the deaths of his siblings, was probably driven subconsciously to "make it up" to his parents by "being the best" or "being perfect" and by burying his own feelings. These dynamics could well explain, without denying the authentic agency of grace, why he would have gravitated to something so typically detached from human emotions as religious life. At the same time, he may have found religious life attractive because it offered a structure that was enduring and would not subject him to repeated losses. It offered him an honorable way of "saving" both himself and his family, to "make it up to them" by carrying the whole family to God, thereby transcending their loss through a socially recognized apotheosis. I am not suggesting that Luis was driven to religious life or "escaped" in it— I believe with Thomas Aquinas that "grace builds on nature." Consciously and culturally, Luis would have been responding to the grace of God given in and through his circumstances, but entering religious life could be seen as his culturally/religiously blessed effort to give his life ultimate meaning by transmuting it from tragedy to comedy. While this reflection on the impact of the colossal losses suffered by the Martín's must necessarily be hypothetical—given the absence of direct confirmation in the sources—it makes sense of the rich data that Luis supplies in his *Memorias*. My view is that Luis Martín's childhood depression impaired his development. At a specific moment in his adolescence, a conversion experience broke the spell and enabled him to direct his energies in exceptionally productive directions. Before we get to that moment of conversion, however, we must highlight the events that led to it.

Childhood Depression Brought to Crisis by Sexual Abuse

At the age of twelve, Luis began studying at the College of San Carlos in Burgos with a view to an ecclesiastical career. For his first four years in Burgos he lived as an extern with a good friend of his father's —a certain Don Calixto[35]—who was a manufacturer of harness, but, unlike Luis's father, was a liberal anticlerical. He and his devout wife Petra seemed to have had no children of their own—at least none are mentioned in the *Memorias*, but two nieces lived with them for varying periods, along with a fourteen-year old servant boy.

For two and a half years Luis had to share a bed with this older boy. He confessed that this boy, whom he studiously avoided naming and spoke of only pejoratively,[36] while he was "endowed with many external qualities which made him very attractive and likeable, . . . attempted many evil conversations and reprehensible actions [with me]" and did "me much harm during those next three years."[37] Luis regularly referred to him as the *mal criado*, which in the idiom does not mean simply "ill-bred" but "perverse." While Luis vowed that he tried with all his strength to resist the temptations, the trauma and shame of that experience remained fixed in his memory: "I must say that all the year long [he was here speaking of his first year, but it continued throughout the next two as well] this familiarity was a steady occasion of many other faults that I have regretted very much all my life through."[38] Nowhere does Martín say precisely what occurred between him and this *mal criado*, but, whatever it was, he clearly felt himself seriously compromised morally.

There is, of course, the possibility that what happened between Luis and the servant boy was mostly the invention of Luis's overheated imagination. We will never know for sure. The important issue—judging from his recurrent references to and interpretations of this shaming—is that, whatever the objective reality, the sexual curiosity awakened in him by this experience at puberty led to a lifelong and morbid preoccupation.

"Morbid" is not my subjective characterization. Martín himself, in returning to this issue with surprising candor throughout his *Memorias*, himself regularly connected it with his chronic ill health that led ultimately to his death.[39] The sexual abuse would have been one more experience of loss—the loss of innocence and personal boundaries—and would probably have thrown him back to the same responses that worked for him as a child in suffering the loss of siblings.

Journey to Self-Confidence: Appropriating a Self

Martín's third year of philosophy in Burgos (1860–61) was, he said, "decisive." During this year, the fourteenth of his life, he reached puberty and was given his own room in the house of Don Calixto. This move was crucial because it not only removed him from the most baleful influence of the *mal criado* but also gave him private space to study. He confesses that he increasingly enjoyed his privacy, and that his thoughts increasingly turned toward his future and how he ought to take his first steps on the way to salvation.[40] With less hassle from the *mal criado*, more time to himself, and more time for serious study, his classroom performance improved dramatically. One of his professors who showed the relevance of their studies to current events, particularly to church-state issues, inspired in Luis a life-long passionate interest in history and current affairs.

Luis recalls one particular moment from which all his subsequent success and self-perception as a leader seems to have sprung. One day during a review session, his professor called on one of the brightest students who could have been expected to distinguish himself with a thorough recounting of the material. As the student was embarrassing himself with silence, however, Martín found himself amazed that he knew the answer and could cover himself in glory, were he called on. Signaled by unmistakable body language, the professor called on Luis, who not only gave the desired answer but added an idea that had not occurred to the professor himself. All were amazed, and from that moment on, Martín never lost the taste for honor achieved. It would determine the whole direction of his life.

> From that day on I began persistently to aspire to be counted among the first in class. This aspiration imposed great sacrifices on me in terms of more assiduous and consistent application, because many others in the class had shown more talent and earned higher grades than I in previous years. Nevertheless, the honor and vanity of such

an aspiration goaded my spirit so that, in order not to lose the position I had just won, I vigorously subjected myself to work very hard and study with great earnestness.[41]

The work paid off. At midyear, Martín was designated to deliver the public disputation. When the appointed day arrived, he said, "proud of my work, I presented it as best I could. Of course, my natural timidity made me appear modest and respectful: the same fear of seeing myself gored by my opponents augmented my natural timidity, and so I remained respectful throughout all that spectacular discussion." That year he earned the highest grade of "meritissimus" and never looked back. He neglected to note, however, that fourteen others of his class also received that grade, among whom were six of his best friends.[42] Thus Martín displays here, as well as elsewhere throughout his *Memorias*, a tendency to hubris, particularly when referring to academic achievements. It is as though he had found in academics one area where he could excel and gain public esteem; and in the face of his own poor self-image—he thought of himself as physically ugly and certainly morally ugly as well—this accomplishment strengthened his fragile ego.[43]

This pattern of academic achievement, coupled with apparent modesty and respect, continued throughout his life. It accounts, I believe, for his being consistently advanced to positions of leadership from his earliest days in the Society to his last.

Having suddenly acquired a taste for study, he also began to read more widely, well beyond what was required for his lectures, particularly in current affairs. Among his reading that year were several works by the liberal Catholic thinker Jaime Balmes, who attempted to defend Catholicism as not unfriendly toward progress.

In general, Martín began to feel personally more secure because of his academic success and public honor. He was growing into a man; and, while the hidden area of his sexuality—"the sufferings and temptations occasioned by my dealings with the 'mal criado'"— continued to trouble him,[44] the strength he felt in his intellectual awakening spilled over into his moral life and moved him toward a conversion. During Lent of that year (1861), he attended the weekday services at the Cathedral of San Lorenzo, where the sermons of Archbishop Fernando de la Puenta along with the deep and prayerful piety of the throngs that packed the cathedral "impressed me profoundly and were the means that prepared me for my real and deep conversion."[45]

Thus, along with his intellectual awakening came a spiritual awakening and a sense of his own power to take control of his life and his future. He seems at this point to have been verging on what Kierkegaard called the ethical stage in life's three-fold dialectic, moving from "the sphere of the possible" to that of a "real subject . . . the ethically existing subject," and so through ethical decision gaining a sense of inner coherence that leads to a task and a vocation.[46]

He sensed, however, that the spirit of repentance awakened in him during Lent remained vague. He wanted something more and was looking for a guide to direct his next step, when, he said, Francis de Sales' *Introduction to the Devout Life* "fell into my hands." He read it with delight and followed Francis's suggestions about going beyond vocal prayer to interior, mental prayer. He recalls how he used to pray kneeling humbly amidst the bales of wool that crowded his little room: "I was sure that then God observed my feelings and actions with love and showered on me light and grace abundant enough to enflame my cold heart."[47]

This new way of praying and studying soon led Luis to feel the need to make a general confession of his whole life. A popular book of devotions guided him through a thorough examination of conscience, which he recorded on "many sheets of paper." These pocketed, he went to the nearby Carmelite church and called for his regular confessor, Father Pedro de Goiri y Aldama, the most esteemed priest of the monastery. Father Goiri arrived and entered the confessional. Luis then announced his desire to make a general confession and prepared to read his pages. Father Goiri, realizing that the light was inadequate for reading, gently ushered Luis into a nearby private room. Kneeling before the priest, Luis began his recitation but was soon overcome by emotion and began to sob. The friar remained calm, allowing Luis to continue reading, as best he could, "between sobs and sighs from the heart." When he finished and had stuffed "that wretched paper" into his pocket, the friar consoled him, enjoined a moderate penance, added some friendly words and sent him away. Luis tried to stop crying long enough to thank the friar for his kindness, but he could only kiss his hand and exit into the dim light of the church. "From that moment," he recalls,

> the peace and tranquility of my soul were incredible. It had been purified by contrition and the priest's forgiveness, grace had inundated me, and thus I began to enjoy an inner happiness such as I had never felt before. It was a perfect renewal of my entire being, as much interiorly by the love, confidence, and encouragement for the future, as exteriorly by the seriousness and dignity of my comportment, which I adopted from that happy day, toward all my friends and acquaintances.

Then follows Martín's typical expostulation of wonder and praise at the profound mercy and benevolence of God, showing that Luis saw himself very concretely as a loved sinner.[48]

For several years thereafter Luis enjoyed a sense of new birth, along with a new taste for spiritual realities and aversion to former ways. The theater and bull fighting he formerly enjoyed he now saw as potentially harmful to one's spiritual wellbeing. His conversion experience also confirmed his desire to be a priest, albeit not yet a Jesuit.

The next year (1861), Luis began his theological studies. Several Jesuits—three priests, four scholastics, and two brothers—had been on the staff at San Carlos,[49] but Luis had purposely avoided them, he said, to maintain complete independence. Now at the Seminary of San Jerónimo, however, he began to imagine himself a Jesuit, stimulated by his study of several Jesuit authors—Matteo Liberatore's *Ethicae et juris naturae elementa* and Giovanni Perrone's *Praelectiones theologicae* – and by the recommendations of his esteemed professor, Don Manuel González Peña (1834–?), a peritus at Vatican I, who introduced him to the Jesuit journal, *La Civiltá Cattolica*, and frequently referred to Jesuit authors, particularly Robert Bellarmine.[50] Incidentally, Luis, intrigued by a reference in class, purchased and read, albeit without much understanding, de Maistre's *Du Pape*.[51] His new-found intellectual powers and accomplishments, as well as the newly won esteem from his classmates, excited him and set him resolutely on his new moral path.

One of Luis's personal qualities, from which moral difficulties arose, was his overly vivid imagination, with a concomitant tendency to catastrophize. Perhaps the sickness and deaths in his family, along with his parents' consequent overprotectiveness, made him unusually susceptible to overstimulation. At any rate, events such as the theater and bull fights—and, later, sexually suggestive materials—seemed to invade his soul. He recounts, for example, the effect of having seen a circus act of lions whose roars so stimulated him that the "lions seemed to pursue me on my way home." To corral his sensitivities, he now replaced all such entertainments with ascetical practices, such as the strict fast during Lent (not yet required of one his age), more devotions, and hearing more sermons. He also romantically fantasized about the life of the seminary interns with their own private room, restrictions on family visits, and the strict discipline of bells and daily order.[52]

The next year, 1862–63, his second of theology, Luis realized his fantasy. His award-winning performance the previous year led his professor, Don Peña, to nominate him for a half-tuition scholarship as an intern. It also earned him an interview with the cardinal archbishop for a live-in apprenticeship to ecclesiastical office, although at the time of the interview Luis did not know its purpose. The cardinal saw at once that Luis was too low bred for the position[53] — he was shy and awkward before people of high standing—but the cardinal did endorse him as an intern at San Jerónimo. His romantic images of life as an intern fled before the reality of living with generally unrefined young men. Still, Luis considered it an advantage over living as an extern, as it removed him from the moral dangers of his previous life and prepared him psychologically and spiritually for his future as a Jesuit.

Luis valued most the seminary regimen. It introduced him to ascetical discipline and the spiritual life, which, until then, he had learned entirely on his own, primarily from reading Francis de Sales. Of all the exercises, Luis found hearing Rodriguez read in chapel to be "extraordinarily useful for our formation." However, he observed, "not all got the same fruit from it, since many, out of laziness or boredom, slept during such an important practice."[54] Clearly Luis was not one of them—he carried a penchant for religious rigor throughout his life.

Luis continued to work hard at his studies, seldom going out or visiting the rooms of classmates, so as not to veer from his path and to maintain his academic ranking. He even began on his own to read Thomas' *Summa* along with Cajetan's commentary, never mind that his slight learning in philosophy balked his comprehension. Jesuit authors, featured on lists of required reading, elevated Luis's esteem for the Society and influenced his choice of vocation. That year he ranked third in his class and received as a prize a (now second) copy of de Maistre's *Du Pape*.[55] That the seminary would select this book as a prize suggests the kind of ecclesiology Martín imbibed.[56]

Novels found place among the leisure reading of Luis's classmates. He himself skimmed several offered by friends but set them aside, believing that they cost many of his classmates their vocation.[57] Instead, induced by friendship with a new student, a particularly refined young man whose fluency in Vergil impressed him, Luis devoted his free time to mastering Latin, entirely on his own. He purchased five or six grammars, studied them comparatively, committed much of them to memory, and began reading the *Aeneid* and memorizing that as well. At one point, he wrote the author of his favorite grammar, asking why he had not noted that *misereor* can take the dative as well as the genitive— Luis was, of course, thinking of ecclesiastical Latin, as in the litany response, *miserere nobis*. The author, a classicist, did not respond. I mention this incident and Luis's self-chosen immersion in Latin to indicate not only how serious a student he was, but also how passionate he could become, indeed fixated, on issues and on details that for some reason tripped his interest.

In his final year of theology at San Jerónimo, 1863–64, Luis became even more retiring and selective of his friends, whom he chose almost exclusively from among the more serious students. They spoke of edifying topics, like the virtues of the Jesuit Fathers they had known, and worked together in the Conference of St. Vincent de Paul, organized in the seminary to give members an opportunity to do works of mercy. He also found time to indulge a growing interest in church-state issues. On the suggestion of a friend who convinced him that Pius IX's *Quanta cura* with its *Syllabus* warranted it, Luis subscribed to the traditionalist periodical, *El Pensiamento Español,* which carried on a running battle with the liberal press. Reading unapproved periodicals, however, was strictly forbidden, so he and friend would get their copy through an extern and retire to Luis's room where they devoured it, particularly the essays translated from *La Civiltà Cattolica*:

> La 'Civiltà Cattolica' was for me at that time the most incontestable authority on politics, and consequently my friend and I received its opinions and propositions like articles of faith. I still remember the respect and veneration with which we read the first pages of the periodical, excerpts of the "Civiltà," on the "Principles of 1789."[58] We did not read the Sacred Scriptures with more respect and enthusiasm than this periodical.[59]

Thus was Luis introduced to church-state politics, a move about which he felt somewhat ambivalent. He did not think the illicit reading itself ill advised, since it "widened my poor ideas and opened my mind to a new field for the future." But he could not recommend his duplicity, which was "very dangerous and indeed worthy of punishment." Moreover, he said, just as the year before he had exposed himself to moral danger by scanning novels, so now he realized that he had exposed himself, by this uncensored reading, to ideas that could have "infected me."[60]

However, even more dangerous than reading novels and periodicals, Luis thought, was his passion for Latin. He became obsessed with it, devoting to it virtually every spare moment, even moments stolen from his live theology lectures. Having mastered and compared five or six grammars, he determined to tidy up their discrepancies by perfecting his own grammatical chart. This project enthralled him and, Luis observed, might have broken his health had the end of term not intervened—at which he expostulated, "God protected me!"[61] A man clearly given to providentialism.

That year Luis gained first place in his class. His prize was Vives' edition of Thomas' *Summa*.

Although the term ended and Luis returned to Melgar for summer vacation, Latin remained an obsession. Literally day and night he worked at it, committing to memory hundreds of pages of grammar and syntax and working on his definitive chart. So strange was this obsession, that one of his techniques for memorizing difficult, because unconnected, material was "high-voiced repetition," the style of chanting learned in the seminary for morning prayer. "Of course this was a madness," he reflected, but he "yielded to the temptation" and pushed himself relentlessly, rising "several hours before dawn, to study hard even before going to mass. . . . But the obsession of my passion was so irrepressible and so dominated my spirit and excited my nerves that toward the end of summer, it no longer let me sleep." He recalled one time having gone to bed at 10 PM only to awake at 11 PM and immediately return to his Latin, "as though I had slept six or more hours." At the time, Luis seems not to have realized that he was in the grip of a compulsion, but he certainly realized it later, even if he did not use that psychological descriptor. "The demon," he said, "had determined to kill me." [62]

Where were his parents in all this? They showed concern, but Luis reflected that they were too proud of his academic honors to intervene very seriously. From time to time his mother chided him good-naturedly, and his father invited him for walks into the fields, but Luis brushed aside the admonitions and regarded the walks as distractions.

The upshot was, he said, that he made himself proficient in Latin grammar and style and developed his mind very powerfully in ordering his own ideas and expanding his powers of memory; but that the risk he ran of permanently damaging his health also risked his continuing in studies. "But God protected me . . . with that same loving providence" that saved him from "infinite miseries" in the past and enabled him to excel in his studies and learn "the elements of the life of perfection." And "now that my health was in so much danger, he granted me the grace of a religious vocation," and "placed me under the direction of prudent and wholly experienced fathers, who, making use of all my errors and absurdities, prevented me from falling into other more serious ones."[63] Thus he saw his vocation as God's saving him from his own death-dealing compulsions.

Vocation to the Society of Jesus

Martín believed that nothing in his early family or cultural background supported a vocation to the religious life, let alone to the Jesuits. The only priests with whom he had any direct contact early on were diocesan, which is why at first he did not consider any other option. Religious priests he knew only by the government-inspired propaganda against them—he had heard of monastery closings and confiscation of properties and of Jesuits vilified as "Carlist rebels or supporters."[64] In 1861, when he began to study theology at San Jerónimo, the Jesuits assumed the direction of his former College of San Carlos. From that point on, Luis began to hear more and more about them—nothing favorable at first, as his diocesan professors fomented the unfounded rumor that the Jesuits sought to gain control of San Jerónimo as well.[65]

Even Luis's favorite professor, Don Manuel, seemed to endorse the rumors, but they "disgusted" Luis, whose own experience of a former Jesuit, Don Manuel Fuidio y Moraza, now a diocesan priest teaching at San Carlos, threw them into question. To Luis and his fellow students, Don Fuidio stood out from his fellow diocesan professors by his dignified manner, polished rhetoric, and power as a teacher and preacher, all of which the students credited to his Jesuit formation.[66] Moreover, the regular reference to Jesuit authors in lectures led Luis to "conceive a grand idea of [the Society], considering its men to be of the soundest doctrine, the most profound thought, and greatest lovers of the Church and the pope, and at the same time the greatest haters of all heresies and enemies of the truth and of religion,"[67] sentiments clearly reflective of ultramontane ecclesiology. The regular sermons by Jesuit preachers, the articles translated from *La Civiltà Cattolica* in *El Pensamiento Español*, books by Jesuits read in the refectory, as well as the regular reading of Rodriguez and La Puenta in chapel confirmed his exalted image of the Society of Jesus and led him to desire membership in its august company.[68]

Following the events of his summer vacation 1864, Luis acted on that desire. That summer a young priest, Parmenio Ocampo, had been assigned to Melgar, his home town, as a "patrimonial" curate to let him catch up on studies missed in the seminary due to illness. He invited Luis to study with him. Flattered, Luis accepted. In fact, he adopted a regime of following Ocampo to the church in the morning—having arisen at 4 AM to study Latin for nearly three hours—serving his mass, returning home for breakfast, then going to Ocampo's house for three hours of study in the morning, three more in the afternoon, and a short walk and talk after sundown. One day when Luis was tidying Ocampo's small library, he came upon Jacques Crétineau-Joly's six-volume history of the Society of Jesus. Piqued by curiosity, he read it "with great avidity."

> This reading was for me completely providential, and the admiration excited in me by the description of so many admirable things—how the Society was born and constituted, its ministries, Saints, preachers, teachers, writers, apostolic men, etc., etc.—not only confirmed my previous ideas on this matter, but raised them to a point of decision and filled me with enthusiasm for so great a work. Blessed be the Lord who with his loving Providence had caused the parents of that good friend to buy such a history, which they perhaps had never read, and to preserve it among the dust of that room with its old clothes and furniture until that summer, so that I could read it! Thanks be to you, my Lord and my God, who, foreseeing my need to be comforted and strengthened in my vocation, prepared for me such a discovery!

Despite the consonance Luis experienced between his sense of himself and what he now knew about the Jesuit order, and despite his enthusiasm for it, he still "did not think about it, much less decide to enter it." That, he said, would take a strong blow to his pride. [69]

The blow struck toward the end of that summer vacation (1864) and caught Luis completely by surprise; it suggests a certain character flaw in him. He learned that two classmates had recently entered the Jesuits, José Zayas on 12 June and Matías Abad on 25 July. He could understand why Zayas would enter—he did not rank high in the class, so his ecclesiastical career was not very promising. But Abad ranked first and so could expect high office. That Abad had the freedom to squander his potential by joining the Jesuits completely confused Luis. Moreover, the realization that he himself had loftier pretensions than Abad despite a lower ranking in class humiliated him, and he began seriously to think of following Abad's lead.

Yet another event occurred that Luis saw as a final providential spur to his Jesuit vocation. Shortly before his return to Burgos for his final year of theology, Father Ramón Sureda y Bojadors, the Jesuit vice-rector of San Carlos, came to Melgar to preach on the feast of the Assumption. That a Jesuit would travel such a distance just to preach in his little hometown astonished Luis. It almost never happened. The coincidence of Abad's entrance and Sureda's visit had to have been providential: "God surely brought him here so that, without his knowing it, he might win me over for God and the Society."[70] Luis made it a point to see

Sureda on that occasion but oddly did not bring up his desire to enter the order.

In September, Luis left Melgar without a word to his parents or to any of his friends about his vocational musings. He would never again return to Melgar during the lifetimes of his parents. He took his secret with him to Burgos. Fifteen days after the beginning of the school year 1864, driven to distraction by the vocational question, Luis realized that he had to make a decision. He determined to present himself at once to the Jesuits at San Carlos for admission into the Society.

A visit to San Carlos, however, required leave from the vice-rector of San Jerónimo, as well as a companion. He selected García Melo to accompany him, the one he most trusted in this matter, and got the necessary permission, but not without having prevaricated when the vice-rector guessed Luis's motive. One wonders why Luis could trust no one with his secret. Perhaps such matters were regarded in that culture as too personal. At any rate, he seems not to have been by nature a very trusting person, as his vocational journey would soon indicate, and as English Jesuits would later learn.[71]

Luis visited Fr. Sureda at San Carlos on 2 October and announced his desire to enter the Society. After a brief interview, Sureda told Luis that, as Providence would have it, the provincial superior of Castile was at that very moment in the house and would be willing to interview him on the spot. That done, Luis heard from Sureda two days later that he had been accepted pending parental approval. Overjoyed, Luis wrote at once to his father, asking that he come to Burgos the following Monday to confer about a matter of great importance—he did not specify the matter. He gave the letter to an extern to mail, so as not to arouse the vice-rector's suspicions, but the extern forgot to mail it. Nevertheless, that following Monday, 10 October, Luis's father showed up at San Jerónimo with his brother León, "without having received my notice and, what is more, without having had any special reason to make this trip, as he told me later, but moved by an inner impulse, that he himself did not know how to explain."[72]

When Don Clemente and Uncle León arrived, Luis naturally assumed they came because of his letter. But not having received the letter, Don Clemente was there simply to visit. After an hour of small talk during which not a single allusion was made to the burning issue, father and uncle signaled their imminent departure. At this, Luis had to broach the subject. He asked his father if he had not come about the letter. "What letter?" his father asked, then sent his brother off to take care of private business while he and Luis got to the point. Upon hearing of Luis's plans, his father "complained lovingly" that Luis "had not trusted him enough to tell him" earlier. He counseled his son "to seriously weigh the matter before carrying out such a resolution." Then he broke down sobbing. Luis found this reaction excruciatingly painful as he "had always loved [his father] most intensely, and at that moment more than ever." He tried to explain that he had kept the matter secret because he had not been sure and did want to cause his parents needless pain. But now that he was sure, he "insisted on the serious obligation incumbent on him to follow God's call."[73]

Father and son decided to sleep on the matter, but they both had dreadful nights. "That was the most terrible meeting I have ever had in my entire life," Luis reflected, "and I do not believe that I shall ever be able to erase it from my memory." When his father returned the next morning, "he looked like a man exhausted by sorrow, who had spent the whole night weeping and wrestling with horrible nightmares." His father did not oppose Luis's entrance into the Society, but he begged him— "with a voice broken by sobs such as I had never heard from my father" —to come home to tell his mother, because he knew that she would be devastated and would never believe that Luis had made such a decision without first having spoken to his father, and he did not want Luis's vocation to be a source of discord in their marriage, on top of the terrible pain of separation. The argument, though forceful, Luis resisted, he said, as a temptation against his vocation, because he knew he was "incapable of withstanding the tears of my mother." He argued that facing his mother would place his vocation in serious jeopardy, and that God would help his mother accept the facts as they really were and not to think falsely about her husband. His father countered that they must seek the counsel of a wise and prudent priest like Don Manuel who knew and loved Luis. This they did. Don Manuel heard both sides but declined to come down on either, thus father and son departed with the question unresolved.[74]

Once again Luis dissembled with his father, telling him that they now had to visit Father Sureda "to give an account of things," but Luis did not mention the parental consent requirement for fear that his father would refuse. At San Carlos, Sureda spoke consolingly, praising the grace of vocation and informing Don Clemente that his son had been admitted into the Society by Father Provincial, assuming his parents agreed. Sureda then asked Don Clemente point blank for his consent. As Luis told it, his father seemed caught off guard by the question and dared not refuse, given his "fear of God" and reverence for priests, particularly one like Father Sureda.[75] Consent given, Sureda consoled

Don Clemente and spoke gently to his fears about his son's seemingly precipitous decision and not seeking his mother's dismissal. Finally, to Luis he promised letters of introduction to the rector of Loyola.

The two left San Carlos, the father with a broken heart and Luis in anguish at his father's pain. After walking some distance in silence, Luis told his father gently that, "to end this cruel suffering, it would be better if he returned to Melgar that day." Years later, in reflecting on that moment, Luis realized that this advice came from an egoistic desire not so much to spare his father as to spare himself further pain. But the advice only wounded his father more deeply. "He stopped in the middle of the street, looked at me like a crazed person, and shouted with a heart-rending voice, 'Go on, my son, go!'" and then retreated into the doorway of a shop, where he wailed and sobbed, while Luis in total confusion ran into the cathedral nearby to pray. His prayer calmed him, and he said he was able to see his father's reaction as the last effort of the evil spirit to turn him aside from his vocation.[76]

Luis hurried back to San Jerónimo, gathered his belongings, said goodbye to his closest friends, and spent the next day at the home of Don Calixto, who was almost as hard on him as was his father. On 12 October, Don Calixto saw Luis off on the train for Aspeitzia, where Luis would catch a coach to Loyola. Relieved finally to be alone with his thoughts, he found himself disturbed by a new temptation. At the Miranda stop, his attention was captured by an attractive man who entered his compartment—"a young person of refined manners and noble bearing," whose accent

> seemed Andalusian by its sweetness and affect. But, whether that was the devil using him to do battle with me, or whether in that state of mind I felt naturally moved to seek some comfort in worldly pleasure, it is certain that I began to feel bad temptations within me, putting me in danger of yielding my renunciation to God and religious life to enjoy the world and its pleasures. The Most Holy Virgin, however, who had assisted me until then, did not abandon me in such a critical situation.[77]

Luis entered the novitiate at Loyola on 13 October 1864, a young man who had just endured the most painful experience of his life, but also a young man who was not unacquainted with finding his own way, having lived away from is family now for most of six years.

Years of Jesuit Formation

One month after Luis's arrival at Loyola, his father visited him to let him know that he and his wife were now reconciled to his vocation. Luis for his part, never one for half measures, threw himself completely into the novitiate discipline. He suffered through the many exercises of humility—sweeping floors, washing dishes, cleaning toilets, etc.—but the weekly "exercise of modesty," in which the novice's external faults were pointed out in public forum, was particularly painful for him; and to avoid the humiliation, he became extremely guarded in exterior comportment. He "loathed" as "childish" the banter between his companions and the assistant to the novice master, as well as having to display his ineptitude at singing, public reading, and serving in liturgical ceremonies. Nevertheless, Luis found that the new environment, the daily rhythms and good food, agreed with him and lifted him out of the compulsions and anxieties of his previous life, at least for a time. An eye infection that lasted several months and prevented his reading—always a singular pleasure for him, but particularly now in that dour environment—reawakened fears that he would not be good enough, that he could not measure up morally, that he might lose his vocation. In time his eyes recovered, but the fears lingered beneath the surface.[78]

On 20 April 1865 Luis's class entered the month of the Spiritual Exercises. True to pattern, he was designated the "manuductor" for this period, a position given to a particularly edifying novice, who would serve as a liaison between the retreatants and the master or his assistant and assign household chores. Luis made the *Exercises* perfunctorily, that is, he experienced little or no movement of spirit—not unusual in one so young in the spiritual life—and when he came to assess the retreat with the master, particularly on the matter of his choice of vocation, he could only report that he felt called "through no extraordinary and supernatural illuminations but . . . strictly by the light of reason." And when he showed Father Master his scribal effort to delineate his defects and his root sin (not specified in the *Memorias*), the master astutely corrected him by writing in the margin, "impatience and vainglory" and subsequently exhorted him "vehemently" and "persistently" to "humility and scorn of honors." Oddly, the next month the master honored Luis by appointing him manuductor of all the novices.[79]

In his assessment of his first year in the Jesuits, Luis recalled two mutually opposing experiences: The first was of dubious value—the scrutiny of external faults which he found so mortifying, as it played into his perfectionism. The second was decidedly positive—the experience of living with men from virtually every province of central Spain and one from Ireland. "It is beyond words how much it changed my way of judging things and people, clearing or beginning to clear out the corners of my exclusivist and very provincial character." This expansion of character and thought, however, would have been enhanced and secured, Luis believed, had he been allowed to participate in the several out-of-house "probations" normally assigned to novices: a "pilgrimage" to some shrine by begging for food and shelter on the way, working as an orderly in a hospital, and teaching catechism to children. Why was he not sent on these probations? "Reasons of prudence," Luis explained cryptically. Perhaps his master figured that Luis's eye infection, which forced him to endure endless hours with nothing but prayer to help pass the time, had already sufficiently tried him. More likely, he knew that Luis's shyness would have made the probations too difficult for him. In any case, he passed through the novitiate without having benefited, he thought, from *Exercises* that would have tempered his pride and strengthened him against those disordered sexual desires that became the bane of his later life.[80]

Concerning these troubles, Luis recorded that he was freer of them during the novitiate than at any other time in his life. Sequestered from the occasion of sin, "I neither heard nor saw anything that excited my former passion. . . . No impure desire or movement disturbed my heart. . . . Even when sleeping and dreaming I recall having felt nothing against this angelic virtue, and so I scarcely had anything on this matter of which to accuse myself, except, after July, some internal and particular affection for one of my fellow novices." At the time, "the fear of such temptations never [bothered] me, because I considered them improbable, if not impossible." On after-reflection, however, Luis judged that this period of amnesty was "perhaps Satan's scheme by which he tried to lull my passion to sleep and blind the eyes of my soul to the dangers to which I would later be exposed."[81] What Luis feared most was that he would be found unfit for Jesuit life, thus he focused, perhaps obsessively, on excelling in virtue and academic performance.

Juniorate Years, 1866–1868

On 14 October 1866, Luis pronounced his fist vows, witnessed by his parents, Clemente and Francisca; his brother Hermenegildo; and a cousin. It was a moment of great consolation and reconciliation for everyone, but particularly for Francisca, who had not seen her son in over two years and never had the chance to bid him farewell. Upon their departure, Luis donned his biretta and "crossed the bridge" to the juniorate wing, leaving behind the peace of the novitiate for a two-year study of classical languages and rhetoric.[82] The transition from the highly secluded and regimented life of the novice to the more liberal life of the junior is typically difficult, but for Luis the juniorate marked the beginning of personal struggles under the vows that would end only with his death.

An undifferentiated sense of "malaise" characterized his whole first year of juniorate. It began with ill health—feeling "very weak in the chest"—and was followed by some "barbaric" tooth-pulling and an analogous assault by his rhetoric teacher on his literary gorgonism, which proved quite intractable for one "inclined by character to everything extreme and grandiose"; then the unnerving experience of witnessing Father Prefect upbraid the rhetoric teacher in front of his whole class, a "scandal that I had never believed possible . . . in a classroom of the Society."[83]

Finally, Luis's sexual troubles reasserted themselves, stimulated, he believed, by his teacher's encouragement to cultivate a vivid imagination—which, we have seen, Luis already had in excess but was able to suppress during the novitiate—and by the subject matter of certain assigned readings ("profane things and love-making"). He began to experience "great spiritual aridity," grave distractions during prayer, "bad thoughts and concupiscence at night," all of which he frequently took to his spiritual director who made light of them and so proved of little help. So agitated had Luis become that others began to notice and inquire after his health, an unwelcome attention that scared him and induced even more anxiety. Particularly troubling was "a natural affection" he experienced, first for a fellow junior, then for a novice who joined the juniorate prior to taking vows. To counter these temptations he redoubled his spiritual exercises and mortifications, and these, at least for a time, "broke down the passions and subdued the reluctant body."[84]

From his first year in the Society, superiors designated Luis Martín for leadership. This mark perhaps would not have troubled him, had not his obscure sexual problems returned in full force in the juniorate, where he had been appointed "beadle" in his second year, an office of peer leadership given to one regarded as exceptionally exemplary. The discrepancy between his sexual attractions, which he regarded as shameful, and the charge of leadership resulted in a tension that he could scarcely endure. A year later, during the next stage of seminary training (philosophy), Martín came down with a pulmonary ailment, which he saw as the beginning of chronic ill health stemming directly from his carnal struggles.

Not unconnected, in my view, with Luis's conflicted sense of discrepancy between his interior and exterior self is an incident occurring toward the end of his juniorate years that tellingly demonstrates how inculturated into an elitist society he had become. Luis's father had come to Loyola at his son's invitation for an eight-day experience of the Spiritual Exercises. Having his father there, however, left Luis with mixed feelings:

> The crudeness of his manners for lack of a more polished education and his manner of dress, conversation, and interaction with people were a clear indication of his humble circumstances and, therefore, also of mine. This naturally humiliated me somewhat before my brothers, who, although religious, always felt themselves more drawn, by the misery of our culture, to appreciate what the world esteems.

Still, Luis allowed, he was "very glad to have procured for my good father this spiritual help at the end of that year" in return "for all that he had sacrificed for me throughout all my life." Moreover, the timing "was very providential, because shortly thereafter the revolution broke out, making it impossible for us to remain there."[85]

At the outbreak of the revolution in late September, 1868, the Jesuits were expelled from Spain. A philosophate was established at Poyanne in southern France. There Martín finished philosophy and went on to regency, a period of training when the Jesuit scholastic typically is assigned to teach in a secondary school. Once again Luis was set apart by being assigned to teach rhetoric to younger Jesuits at Poyanne. He recalled how during this time he began to read sexually suggestive materials, a practice that soon became compulsive. He would search out "nearly all of the indelicate passages of Vergil, Horace, Catullus, Tibulo, Ovide [sic], Juvenal, Martial, Plautus, Aristophanes, Theocritus, Anecreonte, and some other writers of the Roman and Greek decay." This adventurism led to the reading of other Italian, Spanish, and Latin works "dealing with scientific subjects." Here, writing in English, Martín concluded that

> such a curiosity was unsound and hurtful to me yet my passion was so strong that I did not succeed neither [sic] that year nor the following ones to get rid of it. . . . I fell again and again without finding out the way to get rid of it. . . . It was a shame for me to find myself so poor and unable to control my fierce passion and I should not have drawn up any idea of the human weakness if I had not felt such an impotence to overcome a little difficulty like that. I think it was something providential and healthy for me to have been so weak that

I should know, first, how powerful is the passion, excited by the occasion, to drag worldly men to the abyss of sin, and keep them there years and years.[86]

When Martín went on to study theology (1873–77), his compulsive curiosity for sexually suggestive reading materials continued. Nor was it helped by his study of moral theology. He used to sneak books from the professors' library, books stored in a hallway to make room in the stacks for new books, and he would read them, especially Aristophanes, at times when he should have been at common recreation or doing other things. The trouble increased into his third year of theology, when he suffered a series of ailments, the last one, an infection that nearly cost him the loss of his index finger. That would have precipitated a major crisis, because the index fingers, along with the thumbs, are the so-called "canonicals" anointed in ordination for the celebration of the Eucharist. Without one of them, he would need papal dispensation to be ordained. But, Luis said,

> when God saw that these diseases and pains were not enough . . . to turn me from the sad path I was on, many subsequent afflictions, one after the other . . . fell upon me like a severe atonement.
> I am not going to speak of the Carlist defeats, that I mentioned last year. I want to add only that the catastrophe took place finally with so sad circumstances, that the hand of God manifested itself by pressing down on us in punishment for our miseries and faults.[87]

He was referring to news received by letter that his father had suffered a "cerebral attack" and was not expected to live. This news threw Luis into a state of anxiety more terrible than any he had experienced before, not only because of the possible loss of his father whom he loved more than life itself, and who would then not realize his—and Luis's—dream of seeing his son ordained and receiving communion from his hand, but also because his mother would be left alone with no means of support. This "catastrophe" totally distracted Luis from his sexual self-involvement and sent him into a mode of anxious prayer and sacrifice that God might spare his father. Which indeed God did, as Luis thought, in answer to his prayers.

After theology and ordination, Luis went on to his final year of formation called "tertianship," an experience, as the name suggests, much like a third year of novitiate. Once again superiors set him apart from his classmates by assigning him to do his tertianship privately while acting as assistant to the master of novices at Poyanne. Consequently the exercises of humility that he missed in the novitiate he again missed during tertianship—caring for the sick, serving in the kitchen, and cleaning floors. As a result, he concluded, "I did not tame at all my passions and they went on so unbridled as they had been up to then and perhaps much more." Because of his sexual struggles, he reproached himself with the judgment that his work with the novices was hypocritical and that he had done nothing that year but "interfere with the work of the Master of novices."[88]

In fact, during that year Luis had become so enamored of one of the novices that the following year his new assignment—to teach in the theologate—was "a mortification for me," because the rule of division prevented contact with the novices. During that year, while he never tried to speak with the novice in question, he did seek every opportunity to catch a glimpse of him—for example, when the novice served mass in the theologians' chapel or was out for a walk in the evening. This "passionate love," Martín confessed, "was forever fixed in my heart," although he knew that it "was not pleasing to God." Try as he might "to end it," he could not. But what he could not do, "God did" for him, as in late December, 1878, the revolution over, most of the novices moved back to Spain, "one of them . . . the Brother of whom I had become so fond."[89]

Another incident, not unlike the one which his father mentioned above, suggests how conflicted Luis felt about his humble origins. In September, 1878, when he returned to Melgar to settle his family's estate, he arranged to arrive at night in secret. He could not depart in secrecy, however, because he had to visit all of his relatives who had some claim on the estate. The negotiations completed, he departed, leaving behind a very bad impression: "1. because I preached without preparation; 2. because I did not compensate, as I should have, my father's relatives who cared for him in his infirmity; and 3. for not having provided for my cousins on my mother's side, the children of Eusebia, already dead." Then, almost as an afterthought he added, "Besides that, I forgot to go to the cemetery to pray at the tomb of my parents, which was noticed and displeased not a few in the town."[90] Given Luis's complete lack of experience, not knowing the protocol surrounding claims on estates is understandable. Less understandable is how he could have listed in first place his having preached without preparation, unless one recalls that he was now living in a different culture by different rules that would have made giving a shoddy sermon a *brutta figura*. Even less understandable is how he could have "forgot" to visit his parents' grave, particularly when his absence from Melgar for their deaths and burials caused him such grievous pain.

Post-Formation Years

Two years later, in 1880, Martín was appointed superior of the Jesuit community and professor in the diocesan seminary at Salamanca. In March, 1881 the bishop designated him rector of the seminary. Martin's tenure as rector ordinarily would have lasted six years, but ill health forced him to resign after five years. In fact, he had tried to resign two years earlier for other reasons, but the Jesuit General Peter Beckx rejected his request. This episode is particularly important for understanding Martín's interior life, so I will spend some time on it here.

The loss of all his siblings—most recently his sole surviving brother in 1869, his father in 1877, and his mother in 1878, all while he was still in exile and could not return for their funerals—devastated Martín. Thus his return to Spain in 1880 was a most bittersweet experience. In that state of mind—lone survivor of his family, burdened with feelings surrounding his return from exile to rebuild a life, emotionally bereft of close friendships—the burdens of high office at such a young age seem to have intensified Martín's sexual struggles. As his obsession grew, so did his interior turmoil, due especially to the dissonance he felt between his private and public personae, between his sexual compulsions and his position as rector and role model. In fact, during this period he became what the American Psychiatric Association's *Diagnostic and Statistical Manual of Mental Disorders* would classify as a voyeur with attendant somatoform disorders.[91] Martín devoted seven folios, front and back, to a description of his disorder at this point in his life. He went into considerable, albeit nongraphic, detail, so that, he said, "one might see how insatiable was that miserable itch and how much trouble it gave me."[92] Thus we see again the self-conscious confessionary agendum of Martín's *Memorias*. Without going into all the details, some description is necessary, because the problem, which plagued him throughout his life, was for him a central personal issue.

He detailed the location of his voyeurism (the Seminary cortiles), the times, and methods (binoculars) year by year, describing how it progressed and caused him such anxiety that he was unable to pray or make his annual retreat without constant distraction. He was not explicit, however, either about the precise object of his voyeurism—other than to say that a common station for him was opposite the windows of the infirmary—or about what kind of sexual acting out it led to. But his behavior was so disturbing to him that it seems to have led to somatoform disorders involving intestinal problems, certain food-odor intolerance, migraines, etc.[93] Sometime during his third year in Salamanca, his voyeurism caused him such distress that he "threw the binoculars into the well." But he soon repented of that act and got a new set, "much better and more expensive than those I destroyed," and so he carried on as before.[94]

That first-step effort to avoid the occasion of his compulsion by destroying the binoculars having failed, he determined on the next step —resigning his post:

> On 21 September [1883] I wrote to Fr. General, laying bare my spiritual weakness, my innumerable and pitiful faults, the danger to which I was being exposed and, consequently, the impossibility of my governing such a house. Thus I humbly requested him to relieve me of such a burden and send me to another house where there might not be danger to my soul. I did not explain in detail the faults of which I was guilty at that time, and perhaps that was why Fr. General did not accede to my request.[95]

Because Martín had not been specific, the general interpreted the letter as an expression of humility; and because the seminary was prospering under Martín's direction, Beckx refused the request and simply encouraged Martín to "give no hearing at all to the enemy when he suggests difficulties and dangers, rather, supported by the grace of God, prepare yourself for even greater works and tougher battles."[96]

Little did General Beckx know how much tougher the battles would get. The next July 1884, Martín was invited to Loyola to deliver the panegyric for the feast of St. Ignatius. With his provincial's permission, he stayed on to make his annual retreat, during which he resolved to bare his soul to his provincial, but under the seal of confession. This he did, having "shed many tears" and "offering to God many prayers that I might be pardoned and strengthened"—an act that was "a great sacrifice of my vanity and pride, given that Fr. Provincial did not know very well my miseries and incredible weakness." While that confession may have been an act of abject humility, however, it in fact tied his provincial's hands, because, having received information under the seal of con-session, the provincial could not act on it; he could not remove Martín from his rectorship at Salamanca.[97]

Martín had hoped that this confession would have been the occasion for God "to cure me." Indeed he experienced "a great tranquility and peace of conscience which I had never felt in recent years," but when he returned to Salamanca, he suffered a discouraging relapse: "Absolutely nothing, neither my recent retreat, nor the fear of cholera that was . . . daily sending many victims to the grave, was able to check my uncontrollable passion."[98]

The cholera plague in Salamanca did, however, frighten him. One evening, "after having spent—as usual—quite a long time in the Gallery of Ireland looking around with the binoculars, the dinner hour called me to the refectory. . . . Halfway through the meal, I felt sick, left the refectory and vomited." Under the circumstances, Martín thought he had contracted cholera, went to bed, confessed to his confessor, heard the doctor confirm his own fears, and prepared for death. However, "after a short time, I felt completely well and, forgetting my past fears, I returned to my former habit and continued this way until the end . . . of my stay in Salamanca."[99]

This incident is important because it triggered Martín's first recorded reflection of the connection he drew between his sexual compulsion and the chronic illnesses he suffered over many years: "I think that that sudden attack came from my sinful conduct much more than from the cholera." Then, having recapitulated the history of his illnesses, earlier covered in some detail, he concluded: "The disease that I suffered in Poyanne (and even before in Vals and in Loyola) [1865–1880] was continually aggravated by my careless and disordered conduct in the Seminary." He gave three reasons for this aggravation: (1) Whereas he rationalized his extended visits to the various galleries as taking fresh air to ease his headaches, in fact, he said, "the north wind did not alleviate my migraine, but only made it worse." (2) During these visits, he often leaned "against a parapet, forcing me into a completely unnatural position, in order to see with the binoculars what was otherwise difficult to see. . . . In effect," he observed, "the pressure on my stomach irritated it, and the effort to see was drawing blood to my head, thus harming both parts of my body—the high [migraine] and the low [upset stomach]." (3) Many times he stalked the galleries late at night in his stocking feet to avoid detection. Standing on the cold flagstones, however, "in addition to my anxiety [over being detected] . . . and which coincided with the digestion problem from the dinner, did much damage to my health, and that, I believe, was the seed of the disease which later on afflicted me for many years. Perhaps that seed was even now in my body, but, at the very least, it is possible to say that my lamentable behavior developed and aggravated it very seriously."[100]

What Martín meant by "the seed of the disease which later on afflicted me for many years" is uncertain. Possibly he was conflating "the disease" with a chronic lung ailment that first appeared in 1875 in Poyanne, from which he nearly died, and which troubled him off and on thereafter. On 31 March 1906 during the last stage of his fatal cancer, he is reported to have told the brother infirmarian that "the old trouble had returned and was attacking his lungs. . . . The left lung, in which he suffered long ago when studying theology, was especially affected." Martín's physician subsequently confirmed that cancer had indeed invaded that lung.[101] Thus it appears that Martín had come to settle on that pulmonary ailment of 1875 as, in his imagination, "the old trouble," with which all his other ailments were somehow associated. Of primary significance, however, is that he himself seemed to have connected "the disease" with his sexual disorder, alleging that the latter "developed it and aggravated it very seriously."

Martín's resignation having been refused, he carried on unabated for nearly two more years, when deteriorating health forced him out of office. In autumn 1885, he left the seminary to become director of the *Messenger of the Sacred Heart* in Bilbao. In this new assignment, Martín's sexual preoccupations diminished, due perhaps to the altered environment and change of office, but they did not disappear. He recalled a particularly disturbing experience of September 1886, when, as elected representative of his province to a congregation of Jesuits at the general curia in Fiesole, he took the opportunity to see the sights along the way. At Nice and Monaco, he found his senses and imagination assaulted by the sumptuousness of the cities and—to him —unaccustomed but not unappreciated nudity of the bathers. Then, following the meeting at Fiesole, he toured the churches and monuments of Florence. Again he found his imagination besieged by disturbing images of the unclad subjects of painting and sculpture. Years later he recalled this experience with sadness.[102]

Concluding Evaluation:
The Private and Public Personae
and Anti-Modernism

Luis Martín's sexual revelations are hardly his whole story. They tell us intimate details about the man that one could never get from other sources. But they beg the question why he revealed these details and not only revealed them but kept returning to them at regular, self-reflective and self-evaluative moments. The dominant clue to his most self-conscious motive is supplied by his epigraph: "I want . . . to make a general examination of conscience for my entire life, to confess many sorrows, and to bless God who has shown himself to be so full of forgiveness and so infinitely merciful."[103] Martín carried out this desire. He regularly confessed "many sorrows" and just as regularly concluded with expostulations of blessing, praise, and wonderment that God should have gratuitously saved such an abject sinner.

An epigraph intends to capture the central truth of an auto-biographer's "mythic tale." So one must conclude that Martín's epigraph gives us the key to the central message he wanted to convey about what was for him the fundamental truth around which all the other words swirled, that he was a sinner gratuitously saved by God. Why did he supply such concrete evidence and detail? Because, I think, he wanted to set the record straight. He was keenly aware of, at least in some sense, living a lie. There was a reality about him that virtually no one knew, and living in the darkness as he did was deadly. He wanted finally to come clean.

One can sympathize and empathize with Martín's motives and perhaps even admire him for his desire to set the record straight. One wonders, however, about the historical significance of these revelations. Certainly they help us understand the man in an aspect that he himself considered to be of overriding personal significance. After all, he himself confessed that these revelations arose out of one of his principal motives for writing his *Memorias*—at least this motive was paramount at the outset. And, while the sexual revelations constitute only a fraction of the total physical dimension of the *Memorias*, the fact that he regularly returned to this subject, even as he was considering other globally important public issues—for example, "The War of Cuba and the Philippines" which I have treated at length elsewhere[104]—indicates that the trouble was never far from his mind.

The casual reader might object that only one such revelation appears in the entire second half of the *Memorias* covering the period of Martín's generalate, and that, therefore, the evidence does not warrant my conclusion that "the trouble was never far from his mind." I would rejoin that the absence of other such passages could suggest that Martín had lost sight of his confessionary goal in the face of grave, daily problems of governance. However, I believe it more plausible that the relative absence of confessionary passages was due to the grave illness that prevented Martín from carrying out the same kind of methodology that he had employed for the earlier years.

The latter part of the *Memorias* was left in folders of working documents on discrete topics, which Martín no doubt intended to refine and incorporate into the whole body, providing connecting narratives and summaries, consistent with the method of the earlier part. Had he lived to complete these sections, I believe he would have carried out his confessional intention to the end. Why? He wanted people to know him as he saw himself before God and, thus knowing him, to appreciate more profoundly God's mercy and fidelity. It is puzzling, however, that we do not find him confessing other areas of sinfulness—unkind thoughts, for example, or pride. But perhaps such sins did not awaken in him the depth of shame, confusion, and dissonance he felt from his sexual disorder and, therefore, did not awaken the same depth of gratitude for and wonderment over God's mercy toward him.

That having been said, we must still consider the question of the historical significance of these revelations. Would his story as an actor on the stage of history have been essentially the same had he simply left out these confessionary passages? We have his curial records: we have the letters he wrote and the proceedings of his meetings with his advisers, we know the decisions he made, and we know much of his role in the English bishops' condemnation of liberalism and in the modernist crisis. Would Luis Martín have made the same decisions, written the same letters, made the same appointments had he not been burdened by sexual compulsion? Such a question, while intriguing, is unanswerable. The record of what he wrote, said, and decided is that of a man burdened with a sexual disorder, of a man who *knew* he was so burdened, although he seems to have interpreted it rather as a moral than a psychological disorder. What we can legitimately wonder about is what difference this burden made in how he perceived himself and in the self-image that he projected in his interactions with others. We can then legitimately wonder about what impact that self-image had on his decisions and how he communicated them.

The people who knew Luis Martín, knew, in a sense, *all* of him. His sexual struggles, though secret, were part of him, so those who encountered him, encountered—without explicitly knowing it—a man who was one with his silent shame. His sexual struggles, assuming he was not schizoid, had to have affected his persona, his comportment with people, how he projected himself. Those who knew him well experienced him as shy, yet deeply affectionate. I am guessing that his sexual debasements humbled him before the world, softened him, made him compassionate in his dealings with others, even when he felt duty bound to dismiss a man from the Society.

Evidence shows that Martín agonized over his dismissal of Tyrrell, that he personally wrote him long letters in his own hand. Clearly he did not understand Tyrrell. Had he understood him, perhaps he would have taken other courses of action. But just as clearly he cared deeply for Tyrrell and tried his best to avoid dismissing him—which was scarcely avoidable since the Vatican had mandated it, and disloyalty to the pope was virtually unthinkable for a Jesuit superior general. With great sorrow and regret Martín carried out his mandate. Would he have agonized over this decision and felt such deep sorrow and regret had he not himself been so keenly aware of his own fragile humanity? No one can say for certain, but I doubt it.

There was another whole side of Luis Martín which I have so far remarked on only incidentally but which his friend and biographer Peter Chandlery covered extensively, namely, his public persona, how he dealt with and came across to others. We know that his considerable gifts of character and intelligence consistently earned him scholastic honors and positions of leadership. That persona, growing in stature and importance from the moment of his conversion in Burgos to his years as superior general, conflicted profoundly with his private persona in ways known to him alone. That conflict, along with his whole history of sexual struggles and deception, showed itself most evidently—but only to those who read his *Memorias*—in his first programmatic letter to the whole Society of Jesus, "On Some Dangers of Our Times" (4 October 1896). As I have treated that matter at length elsewhere,[105] I will here simply summarize.

That letter was indeed programmatic. It warned all Jesuits of the dangers of liberalism and, as such, served as subtext to and harbinger both of the English bishops' pastoral of 29 December 1900 condemning liberal Catholicism and of Pius X's encyclical *Pascendi Dominici Gregis* of 8 September 1907 condemning modernism.[106] Given what we have seen of Martín's autobiographical account, we can scarcely escape the inference that behind the rhetoric of "On Some Dangers of Our Times" lies the author's own struggles with sexuality and deception surrounding his own illicit readings. In the second part of the letter, for example, where he analyzed liberalism's infiltration into the Society of Jesus and proposed counter-strategies, he argued that liberalism's entrance is facilitated by "a natural levity of mind and character" which develops into a "habit" that in turn leads to a constant "craving for fresh excitement, ever bent upon seeing and reading something new," so that "in place of God and the laws of our Institute" one takes "the natural impulse of the senses as his rule of action."[107] How well he knew that! Martín credited liberalism's success in penetrating the Society of Jesus not to the intrinsic strength of outsiders but to the intrinsic weakness of insiders. He argued that the Jesuit order could well have dealt with the enemy had its membership not been weak. But it was weak. Why? Effeminate breeding and rearing:

This levity of mind is fostered and encouraged from early days by that delicacy of body which, in the opinion of men of experience, growing apace and bearing a punier offspring, renders the nervous system more and more excitable. And thus it comes to pass that our youth are becoming indolent, hare-brained and unfit for the battle of life; and far from seeking vigorous mental exertion they shrink from all serious effort of body and mind and are ever looking for relaxation and comfort. Small wonder that this evil propensity of nature brings forth in our day the most lamentable results, since the home-training, which is of paramount influence for good as well as for evil, seeing that it is for the most part soft, inconsistent, mainly bent on satisfying and pleasing the child's whims and flattering his passions that grow apace with the body's growth, only develops levity of mind while debilitating and enervating the will.

The subsequent college discipline and literary education are altogether incapable of remedying the many faults committed in this effeminate domestic training.[108]

After excoriating the system of education which, Martín said, merely excites curiosity and produces nothing of substance, he went on to describe the primary danger to religious life that arises from the failure to observe strictly all of the rules of the Institute, namely, that one is easily led from intellectual levity to moral levity. But, Martín charged, there were also the more subtle and therefore more pernicious snares of the enemy, who induces many to set aside their total dedication to God by amusing themselves with "foolish trifles" and "frittering away the time that belongs to God, in reading periodicals, newspapers and novels." These practices, while not in themselves violations of the rule, became dangerous under changed circumstances—"the flood of newspapers and periodicals that are being poured into town and country alike, so that they can scarcely be kept from invading even the cloister be it ever so closely guarded."[109]

Martín was not referring merely to "bad newspapers or periodicals" but to newspapers and periodicals of whatever stripe, even Catholic papers, because reading them, he argued, takes Jesuits away from "all serious application to those studies which are for us a necessity, and, in a special sense, peculiarly our own." The problem, he asserted, was twofold. On the personal level such reading opens the door to vain and ridiculous notions that are "utterly foreign to and inconsistent with our religious life," such that "the soul will grow weak, and the imagination, aroused and agitated by so many phantasms, will often obtrude upon the mind" and "violently" withdraw one from heavenly things. Then "all that is spiritual and divine will no longer possess any relish" or "afford solace and help, but will become irksome and produce only disgust and torment. From these beginnings will flow all those consequences which have been already described at length."[110]

It is difficult to escape the judgement that this letter is poignantly, if silently, autobiographical, that its rhetoric is clearly a projection out of Martín's own experience.

Up to this point in his life, Luis Martín cannot be considered an anti-modernist, but rather an anti-liberal, because "Modernism," described by von Hügel after *Pascendi* as a "strictly circumscribed" phenomenon, had not yet been invented.[111] Nor does the fact that Martín was the Vatican's hit man for Tyrrell make him an anti-modernist.

Why, then, include Martín in a collection of essays on modernists and anti-modernists? For at least two good reasons. First, because he was associated with the mounting Vatican effort to rein in those like Loisy whom they regarded as doctrinally dangerous if not heretical. Second, because, had he lived another couple of years, he probably would have become a card-carrying anti-modernist, not so much because he would have been intellectually aligned with the anti-modernists, but because he would have with unquestioning loyalty enforced the anti-modernist prescriptions of Pius X and Merry del Val—just as he faithfully carried out the Pope's *mot d'ordre* to dismiss Tyrrell from the Jesuits in 1906. Moreover, he would have done so not simply out of blind obedience to the Pope, but because he would have, as head of an order bound to the pope by a special vow of availability for mission, bent his intellect to conform to his will. That vow, it must be noted, was not a vow to the pope; nor was it about special obedience to the pope's wishes, except in the matter of sending Jesuits where they could best serve the church; and therefore, as such, it was never intended to stifle critical thinking, as the example of Ignatius amply demonstrates.[112] However, in the warming ultramontane climate of the nineteenth century, that vow gradually came to be construed as a vow of special obedience to pope.[113]

More technically accurate, Martín was anti-liberal, and this in the more political than theological sense but certainly also in the latter sense. He was predisposed by background, upbringing, and formation in the Spanish Jesuit order to be anti liberal. And, yes, just as the Vatican saw modernism cut from the same cloth as liberalism—as I have argued elsewhere[114]—so anti-liberalism can be seen as a precursor to anti-modernism.

When Martín wrote his first encyclical to the whole Society of Jesus, "On Some Dangers of Our Times," he had in mind first of all political liberalism. But he saw in it the seeds of a liberal caste of mind which could infect everyone's way of thinking and behaving. Indeed, he saw the liberal virus in the writings of certain English Jesuits, not first of all Tyrrell, but eventually especially Tyrrell, even though he found it difficult to say precisely what he objected to in his writings, other than his style. Both by personality and educational and political background, Martín was keenly sensitive to style.

In fact, style was the main issue in Martín's censure of the Bollandists, whose writings were delated to him toward the end of 1900 by powerful figures in Rome. Now, Martín supported the Bollandists' project. He had, after all, quite a sophisticated historical sense; it was he who assembled a team of Jesuits to write the history of the various Jesuit assistancies and who personally schooled his writers on modern historical method.[115] His problem was not so much with the Bollandists' findings—for example, on the questionable historicality of the translation of the House of Loreto, certain stories in the Roman Martyrology, the Coliseum as the primary site for the execution of Christians. Rather, his problem was with how and where they reported their findings. He insisted that Jesuit historians exercise extreme care and modesty and not cast doubt on venerable traditions with findings that are not utterly unassailable. In this, he was echoing the pope's sentiments, who "was very hurt by the audacity with which more than one pious tradition was rejected on the basis of slight arguments."[116]

Although intemperate style was, at least overtly, Martín's principal objection to the Bollandists and to Tyrrell, the furor unleashed in England and Rome by St. George Jackson Mivart's essays impugning the Catholic doctrine on hell and the controversy over Americanism quickly propelled Martín to press the connection between political and theological liberalism.[117] As we have seen him repeatedly assert in his *Memorias*, reading illicit materials can insinuate dangerous ideas into the reader without his even suspecting it. He reiterated this theme both in his 1896 letter to the whole Society of Jesus and in his reflections on the exaggerated "higher criticism" of the Bollandists. He mentioned it again when reflecting on his conflict with the English Jesuits over Herbert Lucas's essays on Isaac Hecker and Heckerism and over the Dreyfus affair. On 16 May 1899, he complained sharply to John Gerard, the English provincial superior, that an American newspaper had linked the Lucas articles, Americanism, and liberalism. Martín had by this date firmly established the connection between political and theological liberalism.[118]

Tyrrell suffered the misfortune of bad timing. At the peak of Martín's alarm over this malignant connection and over the Bollandist controversy, Tyrrell had published his two "defining" essays, "The Relation of Theology to Devotion" (November, 1899) and "A Perverted Devotion" (December, 1899). Both were delated to Rome in January, 1900. Three months later, Richard F. Clarke, superior of "Clarke's Hall," Oxford, sent Tyrrell's Preface and Epilogue to *The Testament of Ignatius Loyola* to Rudolf Meyer, Martín's Assistant for the English-speaking provinces, as evidence that "there is a sort of clique of quasi-Liberals among the present House of writers" in London and that "something [is] very wrong with our system of Censorship." Tyrrell, linked by censors to the infamous Mivart, found himself tarred with the same judgment imposed on the Bollandists—overly natural explanations for supernatural events.[119]

The upshot of the Mivart affair was the English bishops' condemnation of "Catholic liberalism" in a joint pastoral published on 5 and 12 January 1900, which, as I have shown elsewhere, Luis Martín and his appointees secretly wrote at the behest of Monsignor Merry del Val, Vatican confidant of Cardinal Maughan and consultor for the Index.[120]

Because of the nexus Martín now saw between political and theological liberalism, he was poised for the role of anti-modernist. Had he lived long enough for that, however, I believe he would have been a moderate anti-modernist—for two reasons: (1) He appreciated historical criticism and so was sympathetic at least in principle to part of the "modernist" agenda; (2) His *Memorias* show that he was not keen on enforcing the neo-Thomism requirement of Leo XIII. In fact, he attempted to moderate this influence in the Gregorian University much to the displeasure of the Jesuit Cardinal Camilo Mazzella.[121]

Thus, if Martín had become an anti-modernist—and I think we can so classify him both because of the political-theological liberalism connection he came to see and because he willingly cooperated with the same forces that set out to indict Loisy—it would have been grounded not so much in intellectual conviction as in his cultural and spiritual conviction, namely, his duty of fidelity to the Holy See.

The driving energy for this latter arises from Martín's cultural background and upbringing. From both experiences, he deeply imbibed the value of belonging and its concomitant value of unity. We saw how he was reared in a deeply divided Spain and suffered the horrors of revolution and exile, during which he was separated from his family and missed the deaths and funerals of his mother and father and his last surviving sibling. I believe that the experience of growing up in a family that suffered the catastrophic loss of six of seven children exaggerated Martín's culturally-induced need to belong. When he left his family of origin to join his fictive family, the Society of Jesus, his exaggerated need to belong accompanied him. Thus he became an exceptionally loyal "Company man," a quality intensified by his role as superior general of a religious order bound to the papacy by a special vow.

That need to belong served Martín well when, as provincial of Castile, he had to deal with the divisions in his communities, particularly between extreme and moderate Carlists. While Martín himself sympathized with Carlism and fiercely opposed liberal government, to preserve some measure of harmony in his communities, he mandated that all Jesuits strictly avoid political partisanship in public and at home maintain strict silence on political issues. This tactic, although seemingly harsh, saved the Society of Jesus in Spain during this very troubled period.[122]

The other factor that Martín brought to his public persona and that played into his style first as a seminarian and later as a leader was perfectionism. I have argued that Luis, as a child, suffered emotional neglect from parents whose time and energy were consumed in caring for their sick and dying children. I would further argue that this neglect impacted Martín in a number of ways: It very likely induced him to try to establish his self-worth by excelling in school, turning a normal perfectionist into an obsessive-compulsive one, a trait that Martín recognized in himself, albeit not in those terms. It also led him to seek admission into the most elite corps he could find, the Society of Jesus; and, once there, it occasioned in him a need to excel among his peers in the ways of spiritual perfection and learning. And excel he did, but at enormous personal cost.

Obsessive perfectionism won Martín honor and esteem through his academic accomplishments. It should also have made him a poor superior, but he was not. What accounts for his success in that role, I believe, was his life-long struggle with sexual compulsions. As an obsessive perfectionist and a man of iron will, had he not suffered the humiliations of sexual deviance and the dissonance this created with his public persona, he would probably have been an insufferable tyrant—as people hate most in others what is most embarrassing in themselves, Martín's secret deviance could have made him intolerably aggressive in rooting out the flaws he saw in others. As it was, he was shy and awkward in his comportment toward others, he never felt personally self-assured, he intimately understood human weakness, and so he came across as humble both before God and men. His personal struggles, consistently brought to prayer, humanized him and converted a pathological perfectionist into a compassionate and holy man. When, for the sake of unity and fidelity to his office, he felt constrained to come down on men like Tyrrell, he did so only with the greatest care and at the greatest personal cost.

What finally, then, is Luis Martín's "mythic tale"? As a child, he could never have imagined that he would rise from the lower middle class Martín García family of the village of Melgar de Fernamental, Spain, to become the superior general of the Society of Jesus. But the folk piety in which he was raised led him to interpret every event in his life providentially, as though it were somehow directed by God in every detail for some salvific purpose. This faith vision, sophisticated by his later Jesuit spirituality, was the interpretive envelope of Luis Martín's life. It enabled him to grow through and out of what had to have been a terrible childhood into a productive adult. It also enabled him to draw his character defects—products of personality and family influences: his perfectionism, compulsions for completeness and detail, iron will—as well as his somatizations and life-long, humiliating sexual struggles into a meaningful sense of himself as first and finally a loved sinner. Martín might have grown up with this conviction, but it was enhanced and confirmed by his experience of what Jesuits know as the fruit of the "first week" of the Spiritual Exercises of St. Ignatius. Martín seems never to have gone beyond that "first week" experience of knowing himself as an abject sinner loved by God. This conviction motivated the prominent, confessionary aspect of his *Memorias*. It was this aspect of himself, first and last, that he wanted the world to recognize as the burden of his "mythic tale."

NOTES

[1] Georges Gusdorf, "Conditions and Limits of Autobiography," trans. James Olney, in *Autobiography: Essays Theoretical and Critical*, ed. James Olney (Princeton, NJ: Princeton University Press, 1980), 48.

[2] Alerted to the existence of this source by Ignacio Echarte, a Basque Jesuit I met in 1984 in the Jesuit archives in Rome, I traveled to Loyola castle, the ancestral home of St. Ignatius, the founder of the Jesuits, at Azpeitia in the Basque province of Guipuzcoa, and there discovered this exceptionally rich resource for turn of the century European history in general and for modernist studies in particular. Since my first encounter with Martín's *Memorias*, a large portion has been rendered entirely in Spanish and published in two large volumes of more than a thousand pages each, under the title, *Memorias del P. Luis Martín, General de la Compañía de Jesús*, vol. 1 (1846–1891), vol. 2 (1892–1906) (Rome: Historical Institute of the Society of Jesus; Madrid: Pontifical University of Comillas; Bilbao: University of Deusto and Ediciones Mensajero, 1988); edited by three Jesuits: Manuel Revuelta González and Ravael Maria Sanz de Diego,

professors of the University of Comillas (Madrid), and José Ramón Eguillar, archivist of the Loyola province. About the end date of vol. 2 (1906), it should be noted that the *Memorias* themselves go only up to the end of 1901. Illness between 1902 and 1904 forced Martín to suspend work on them almost entirely. On 9 April 1905, Martín's right arm was amputated to try to prevent the spread of cancer. Twenty-one days later he began writing with his left hand in an amazingly clear and well-proportioned script an account of his last infirmity, *Cuadernos de la última enfermedad.* The editors included this work of 32 pp. (21 x 16 cm.) as the final chapter of the *Memorias,* but it does not, strictly speaking, belong to it. In fact the *Cuadernos* are kept in the Roman archives of the Society of Jesus (hereafter, ARSJ). A note about my own use of the *Memorias*: I made photocopies of those sections of the original manuscripts that directly concerned England and Tyrrell, and many folios concerning France. I also took notes on other sections. So in what follows, I will sometimes be working from the original manuscripts, sometimes from my notes, and sometimes (more often than not) from the published text, the latter because it is now the only source available to me for the vast majority of the *Memorias* that I could not photocopy. In what follows, unless noted otherwise, I will be working with the published text.

[3] Gerald Brenan, *The Spanish Labyrinth: A Account of the Social and Political Background of the Civil War* (Cambridge: At the University Press, 1943, 1950).

[4] For what follows, I depend on José Mariano Sánchez, *Reform and Reaction: The Politico-Religious Background of the Spanish Civil War* (Chapel Hill, NC: University of North Carolina Press, 1964), 13ff.

[5] See Alejandro Lerroux, *La pequeña historia: Apuntes para la historia grande vivido y redactados por el autor* (Buenos Aires: Editorial Cimera, 1945) and Sánchez, 17.

[6] William V. Bangert, S.J., *A History of the Society of Jesus* (St. Louis, MO: Institute of Jesuit Sources, 1972), 449–452. Sánchez says that about 100 Jesuits were killed (22). Bangert, arguing from Jesuit archival sources, says fifteen.

[7] In 1900 the archbishop of Toledo reported that only four per cent of the population of Madrid made their Easter duty and only five per cent received the last sacraments. The rural areas show a similar pattern. See E. Vargas Zúñiga, S.J., "El problema religoso de España," *Razón y Fe,* 462–463 (July–August 1935) 302; and Francisco Pieró, *El problema religioso-social de España,* 2d ed. (Madrid, 1936), 13–14, quoted in Sánchez, 50–51.

[8] See William V. Bangert, S.J., *A History of the Society of Jesus* (St. Louis: Institute of Jesuit Sources, 1972), 450–451.

[9] Peter J. Chandlery, "The Very Rev. Father General Luis Martín, S.J.: A Biographical Sketch," *Letters and Notices of the English Province of the Society of Jesus* [hereafter, LN] 28 (July, October 1906) 433–450, 510–517; LN 29 (January, April, July, October 1907; January, April, July, October 1908) 1–13, 73–84, 145–157, 217–230, 296–307, 361–375, 442–457, 535–547; LN 30 (January, April, July, October 1909; January 1910) 21–36, 119–130, 191–198, 256–263, 291–297.

[10] *Memorias,* Fr. Martín quickly reverted to writing in Spanish and added other languages as he went along.

[11] The history of literature indicates that biography became increasingly popular in the modern period. Autobiography arrived relatively late as a common genre, making increasingly frequent appearances from the Renaissance onward. Recent interest in the nature and motives of biography and autobiography has spawned a large bibliography. See, e.g., James Olney, ed., *Autobiography: Essays Theoretical and Critical* (Princeton, NJ: Princeton University Press, 1980), esp. essays by Olney, "Autobiography and the Cultural Moment: A Thematic, Historical, and Bibliographical Introduction," 3–27, and "Some Versions of Memory/Some Versions of *Bios:* The Ontology of Autobiography,"

236–267; and the seminal essay by Georges Gusdorf, "Conditions and Limits of Autobiography," 28–48.

[12] On 1 June 1894 Martín disseminated a decree to the whole Society of Jesus on the writing of a complete history of the Society according to proposition 21 of the twenty-fourth general congregation (1892). Copy of the *Decreta XXIV Congregationis* in the archives of the English Province of the Society of Jesus, BT[1]. The *Decreta* are available in English translation with helpful historical notes: John W. Padberg, Martin D. O'Keefe, John L. McCarthy, eds., *For Matters of Greater Moment: The First Thirty Jesuit General Congregations: A Brief History and a Translation of the Decrees* (St. Louis, MO: Institute of Jesuit Sources, 1994).

[13] On Bismarck, the Jesuits, and Exaeten, see Count Paul von Hönsbröch, *Fourteen Years A Jesuit: A Record of Personal Experience and a Criticism*, trans. Alice Zimmern, 2 vols. (London: Cassell & Co., 1911), 2:369–98; Michael J. King, S.J., "The German Fathers at Ditton and Portico," *Letters and Notices* 28 (July 1905) 190–193. Martín went beyond the mandate to the general congregation and instigated the production of critical editions of documents on Jesuit origins and history. To date, this enterprise has resulted in the publication of 131 tomes of the *Monumenta Historica Societatis Jesu*. See Chandlery, "A Biographical Sketch," LN 29 (April 1908) 367.

[14] The Jesuit curia at that time was housed in temporary quarters on the upper floor of the Collegium Germanicum-Hungaricum in the Via S. Nicolo da Tolentino, the lower floors being occupied by the students and faculty of the Collegium.

[15] Eduardo Gallo (1846–1912) was born the same year as Martín, but he entered the Jesuit order four years earlier, at the age of 14 (!). He was considered a *"cabeza,"* that is, very bright, and was teaching rhetoric to the "junior" Jesuit scholastics in exile in Poyanne, France, in 1869 when Martín was studying philosophy in the same house. He loaned reading materials to Martín from the faculty library. When Gallo completed his term as professor of rhetoric, Martín replaced him. After ordination, Gallo and Martín both occupied positions of governance that threw them together on a regular and sympathetic basis. See *Memorias* 1:305, 316, 369–370, 376, plus numerous other citations in the Index.

[16] See Revuelta, Introduction to *Memorias*, 1:xxvii–xlvii, esp. xxviii–xxix.

[17] The onset of Martín's final illness was marked by an attack of influenza—thus it was called—on 28 November 1904 and a fever that stayed with him off and on to end. The first sarcoma appeared on his right forearm on 14 or 15 January 1905 and was surgically removed on 20 January. On 14 February a second sarcoma erupted higher up the arm and was removed on 17 February. In both surgeries Martín refused anaesthesia. Only when his arm had finally to be removed, on 9 April 1906, did he consent to anaesthesia. Chandlery chronicled the course of Martín's battle against cancer and sent the following reports to LN: "Father General's Illness," LN 28 (April 1905) 73–82; "Father General's Recent Illness," LN 28 (July 1905) 169–170; "Father General's Convalescence," LN 28 (October 1905) 217–219; "Fatal Termination to Very Rev. Father General's Long Illness," LN 28 (April 1906) 361–369.

[18] For a full, if incomplete, annotated bibliography of materials available in Jesuit curial archives in Rome see David G. Schultenover, S.J., "George Tyrrell: Caught in the Roman Archives of the Society of Jesus," in *Three Discussions: Biblical Exegesis, George Tyrrell, Jesuit Archives*. Proceedings of the Working Group on Roman Catholic Modernism of the American Academy of Religion, ed. Ronald Burke and George Gilmore (Mobile, AL: Spring Hill College, 1981), 85–114. See my *A View from Rome: On the Eve of the Modernist Crisis* (New York: Fordham University Press, 1993).

[19] The curia moved to Fiesole in 1873 after Piedmontese troups had entered Rome, seized Jesuit properties, and expelled the Jesuits. See Bangert, 438–439. The special relationship of the Jesuits to the pope stems from the so-called "fourth vow," on which see "The Formula of the Institute of the Society of Jesus," in Ignatius of Loyola, *The Constitutions of the Society of Jesus*, trans. with introduction and commentary by George E. Ganss, S.J. (St. Louis: Institute of Jesuit Sources, 1970), 68. On Leo XIII's and Pius X's relationship to Martín and the Jesuits, see Schultenover, *A View from Rome*, 164–168, 217 n. 3, 218 nn. 7, 8.

[20] Antonio Pérez, "Semblanza del M. R. P. Luis Martín," *Razón y fe* 15 (1906) 141. This past summer I visited Melgar and was hosted by several of Martín's relatives. I was dismayed to see that his family home, of adobe construction and crumbling beyond restoration, had been demolished. A suitable monument is planned for that site.

[21] Chandlery, "Biographical Sketch," LN 28 (July 1906) 437 is mistaken about the year of Francisca's death. He has 1877. The editors of *Memorias* confirmed that she died on 3 February 1878 of "congestión cerebral." *Memorias* 1:439, n. 10.

[22] *Memorias*, 10.

[23] Letter of 23 October 1892 to a certain Señor Alcalde of the village of Melgar. See Pérez, "Semblanza," 142. *Memorias*, 31ff.

[24] A document in the archives of the Seminary of San Jerónimo in Borgos from Don Lorenzo attests to these facts. Other documents from the mayor of Melgar, Don Julián Martín, and the pastor, Don Domingo Pablos, testify that Luis had "in all that time exhibited irreprehensible conduct" such that he earned "the esteem and appreciation of the public." See Pérez, "Semblanza," 142–143.

[25] Ibid, 144.

[26] Ibid.

[27] The Society of Jesus is governed primarily through the practice of the "manifestation of conscience," whereby each member at least once a year has a conference with his major superior in which he reveals every significant detail about himself. In addition, when a man is being considered for a position of leadership, his provincial superior or his superior general confidentially solicits letters of evaluation (called *informationes*) from fellow Jesuits who know the man well. Obviously this system depends on self-knowledge, candor, and trust. When the system works as designed, the unfit are not ordained, and the ordained unfit for leadership are not appointed superiors.

[28] Arthur Kleinman, M.D., *Social Origins of Distress and Disease: Depression, Neurasthenia, and Pain in Modern China* (New Haven: Yale University Press, 1986), 2. Although many of Kleinman's clinical studies are of Chinese patients, his general treatment is applicable to any ethnic group. See also Kleinman and Byron J. Good, eds., *Culture and Depression: Studies in the Anthropology and Cross-Cultural Psychiatry of Affect and Disorder*, Comparative Studies of Health Systems and Medical Care (Berkeley: University of California Press, 1985).

[29] Martín's symptoms accord with the description of somatization in the authoritative *Diagnostic and Statistical Manual of Mental Disorders* (Washington, D.C.: American Psychiatric Association, 1994), see also Kleinman and Good, eds., *Culture and Depression;* Byron J. Good, *Medicine, Rationality, and Experience: An Anthropological Perspective*, The Lewis Henry Morgan Lectures, 1990 (Cambridge; New York: Cambridge University Press, 1994); Wayne Katon, et al., "Depression and Somatization: A Review, Parts 1 and 2," *American Journal of Medicine* 72 (1982) 127–135, 241–247; "The Prevalence of Somatization in Primary Care," *Comprehensive Psychiatry* 25.2 (1984) 208–215; Atwood D. Gaines, ed., *Ethnopsychiatry: The Cultural Construction of Professional and Folk Psychiatries* (Albany, NY: State University of New York Press, 1992); Antonio Seva-Diaz, et al, "Sociocultural Studies of Mental Disorders in

the Iberian Peninsula," *Transcultural Psychiatric Research Review* 22.4 (1985) 225–236; L. Riddick Lynch, ed., *The Cross-Cultural Approach to Health Behavior* (Rutherford, NJ: Fairleigh Dickinson University Press,, 1969); Monica McGoldrick, John K. Pearce, and Joseph Giordano, eds., *Ethnicity and Family Therapy* (New York/London: The Guilford Press, 1981).

[30] *Memorias* 1:439, n. 10.

[31] Walter Lowrie, *A Short Life of Kierkegaard* (Princeton, NY: Princeton University Press, 1970), 71, 67.

[32] Here I am following the analysis of Dennis P. McNeilly, S.J., Psy.D., Assistant Professor of Psychiatry in the combined Creighton University and University of Nebraska Department of Psychiatry. See also Jean Piaget, *The Child's Conception of the World*, trans. Joan and Andrew Tomlinson (Totowa, NJ: Littlefield, Adams & Co., 1979); Piaget, *The Child's Conception of Physical Causality*, trans. Marjorie Gabain (London: Routledge & Kegan Paul, 1969); Piaget and Barbel Inhelder, *The Psychology of the Child*, trans. Helen Weaver (New York: Basic Books, 1969); Richard Lonetto, *Children's Conceptions of Death* (New York: Springer Publishing Co., 1980); ed. Hannelore Wass and Charles A. Corr, *Childhood and Death* (Washington, DC: Hemisphere Publishing Corp., 1984).

[33] Lawrence Kohlberg, *Kohlberg's Original Study of Moral Development*, ed. and intro. Bill Puka (New York: Garland, 1994); Kohlberg, *The Psychology of Moral Development: The Nature and Validity of Moral Stages* (San Francisco: Harper & Row, 1984); Kohlberg with Rheta DeVries et al., *Child Psychology and Childhood Development: A Cognitive-Developmental View* (New York: Longman, 1987).

[34] Erna Furman, "Children's Patterns in Mourning the Death of a Loved One," in Wass and Corr, 185–203, here 200–201.

[35] Oddly, Martín never gives the man's full name. He refers to him several times as "Don Calixto." Chandlery gave his name as Don Callisto Martinez ["Bibliographical Sketch," 28 (July 1906) 441]; the editors of *Memorias* name him Don Calixto Melo (*Memorias*, 57, n. 7). I trust the latter.

[36] See *Memorias*, fols. 47r, 57v, 58t, 68v.

[37] *Memorias*, fols. 47r, 41v.

[38] *Memorias*, fol. 47r, Martín's own English words.

[39] See, e.g., *Memorias*, fols. 181v, 279a&v, 296a–297a, 306a&v, 347a, 492a–493a, 498v–499a, 519–550 passim.

[40] *Memorias*, fol. 62v.

[41] *Memorias*, fol. 65r.

[42] *Memorias* 1:88–89, n. 59.

[43] *Memorias*, fols. 65r–v, 33r.

[44] *Memorias*, fol. 66v.

[45] *Memorias*, fol. 67v.

[46] See Søren Aabye Kierkegaard, *Concluding Unscientific Postscript*, trans. David F. Swenson and Walter Lowrie (Princeton, NJ: Princeton University Press, 1941), esp. 280–281. See also Merold Westphal, *Becoming a Self : A Reading of Kierkegaard's Concluding Unscientific Postscript* (West Lafayette, Ind.: Purdue University Press, 1996).

[47] *Memorias*, fol. 68r.

[48] *Memorias*, fols. 68v–69r.

[49] *Memorias* 1:117, n. 20.

[50] *Memorias*, fols. 74r, 82r, 84v, 99v.

[51] *Memorias*, fol. 77r.

[52] *Memorias*, fols. 79r–v.

[53] *Memorias*, fols. 83r–v.

[54] *Memorias*, fol. 90r.

[55] *Memorias* 1:124, n. 27.

[56] De Maistre espoused *ultramontanism*. *Ultramontanism*, meaning literally "beyond the mountains," refers to the centralization of church authority and influence in the Roman curia *and the extension of this authority and influence in its fullness beyond the Alps and into all countries of the world*. While the name dates to the 11th century, the movement steadily gained adherents from the 17th century on, as ecclesiastics reacted to Gallicanism, Jansenism, Josephinism, and most especially to the secularizing effects of the French Revolution.

[57] *Memorias*, fol. 94v.

[58] "I Principii dell-Ottantanove esposti ed esaminati," serialized in *Civiltà Cattolica*, ser. 5, vol. 7, 513ff, vol. 8, 19ff, 291ff, 438ff, a critical exposition of the rights of man promulgated by the French Revolution.

[59] *Memorias*, fols. 101r–v.

[60] *Memorias*, fol. 101v.

[61] *Memorias*, for. 103v.

[62] *Memorias*, for. 104r.

[63] *Memorias*, fol. 105r.

[64] *Memorias*, fol. 106v.

[65] See *Memorias* 1:139, n. 6. In fact, the Jesuits reluctantly agreed to take on San Carlos only after repeated requests from Cardinal La Puente, Archbishop of Salamanca, from whom they had received great favors.

[66] *Memorias*, fols. 49v–50r, 57v, 107v.

[67] *Memorias*, fol. 107v.

[68] *Memorias*, fols. 107v–108r.

[69] *Memorias*, fols. 108v–109r. Jacques Crétineau-Joly 1803–1875), French historian and journalist. His most important work, *Histoire religieuse, politique et litteraire dela Compagnie de Jésus, composée sur les documents inedits et authentiques*, 6 vols. (Paris: P. Mellier, 1844–1846), was translated into Spanish as *Historia religiosa, politica, y literaria de la Compañia de Jésus*, 7 vols., trans. José González Hebrero (Madrid: T. Aguado, 1845–1848); another edition was published in Barcelona: J. Oliveres, 1845, and in Paris: Rosa, Douret, y Cu, 4 vols., 1845). Martín had no doubt read the Spanish version.

[70] *Memorias*, fols. 109v–110r.

[71] Schultenover, *A View from Rome*, 65–130, esp. 66–67.

[72] *Memorias*, fol. 113v.

[73] *Memorias*, fol. 114v.

[74] *Memorias*, fols. 115r–v.

[75] *Memorias*, fols. 117r–v.

[76] *Memorias*, fols. 118v–119r. Students of Mediterranean anthropology would find the extreme reaction of Luis's father not unexpected on two counts: (1) In Mediterranean culture, life makes sense so long as men and women, dominated by group consciousness and strict male/female roles, play their familiar roles; but get them outside their roles—alone, as here with Luis's father—and all seems chaotic. (2) Luis's father and mother had already buried five of their seven children. Remaining were Luis and Hermenegildo, the latter now twelve and not as promising as Luis—he was not sent on for higher studies. Luis's entrance into religious life would probably have seemed to his father an incalculable loss, the virtual death of the one on whom the family's honor rested.

[77] *Memorias*, fol. 120r.

[78] *Memorias*, fols. 125r–133v.

[79] *Memorias*, fols. 133v, 136r–v.

[80] *Memorias*, fols. 144v–145v.

[81] *Memorias*, fols. 144r–v.

[82] Jesuit houses of first formation in the post-restoration period were typically designed to keep the juniors physically separated from the novices. On vow day, the newly vowed juniors "crossed the bridge" from the novitiate to the juniorate.

[83] *Memorias*, fols. 164r–167v.

[84] *Memorias*, fols. 172v–173v, 181v (Martín's own English words).

[85] *Memorias*, fol. 187v.

[86] *Memorias*, fols. 279r&v, Martín's own English words.

[87] *Memorias*, fols. 306r&v, Martín's own English words.

[88] *Memorias*, fols. 327r–330v, Martín's own English words.

[89] *Memorias*, fol. 347r.

[90] *Memorias*, fols. 338v–339r.

[91] *Diagnostic and Statistical Manual of Mental Disorders*, 4th ed. [DSM–IV] (Washington, D.C.: American Psychiatric Association, 1994), 532, 445–450.

[92] *Memorias*, fols. 492r–499r.

[93] Martín's descriptions of his health problems throughout his *Memorias* conform with remarkable correspondence to the descriptions and diagnostic criteria for "Somatization Disorder" given in DSM–IV, loc. cit. Descriptions of health problems continue episodically throughout the *Memorias*, as would be expected for an author suffering from somatization disorder.

[94] *Memorias*, fol. 494r.

[95] Martín to Beckx, 21 September 1883, reported in *Memorias*, fol. 494v.

[96] Beckx to Martín, 1 November 1883, quoted in *Memorias*, fol. 495r.

[97] *Memorias*, fols. 496r–v.

[98] *Memorias*, fols. 496r–v.

[99] *Memorias*, fols. 496v–497r.

[100] *Memorias*, fols. 498r–499r; see also fols. 492r–499r. The "Gallery of Ireland" was so-named because Irish seminarians were housed on that corridor.

[101] Letter of Dennis J. Kavanaugh, S.J., to *Woodstock Letters* 35 (1906) 100–106, here, 101. Kavanaugh apparently worked in the General Curia. It is interesting that he should have known about the chronic lung ailment. It must have been common knowledge among Martín's household.

[102] *Memorias*, fols. 539r&v.

[103] *Memorias*, fol. 1r.

[104] *Memorias*, chap. 53, fols. 2435r–2471'v. See my treatment in *A View from Rome*, 199–203, 213–214.

[105] *A View from Rome*, 68–4, 193–8.

[106] Cardinal Herbert Vaughan and the Bishops of the Province of Westminster, "The Church and Liberal Catholicism: A Joint Pastoral Letter," 29 December 1900, the *Tablet* 97 (5, 12 January 1901) 8–12, 50–52. Pius X, *Pascendi Dominici Gregis, Acta Sanctae Sedis*, 40:593–650; official English trans, *Tablet* 110 (28 September 1907) 501–515; in *The Papal Encyclicals*, Vol. 3, 1903–1939, ed. Claudia Carlen (Salem, NH: McGrath Publishing Co., 1981), 71–97. The meaning of "liberalism" is seldom clear from its context. The word gained prominence in the political sphere following the American and French revolutions, which called into question the divine right of kings. It was soon applied to the divine right of popes and other church authorities over against the theologian. In its broadest advocacy, from the Hebrew prophets on up, liberalism has sought to protect the individual from the arbitrary external restraints of higher authorities. It seeks a world order based first on the dignity of the person, second on the

social contract. Such an emphasis does not set well with traditional authorities who, for the most part, hold that group rights come before individual rights. When Martín used the word, he almost always had in mind the democratizing political movements that fueled the revolutions in Spain. For him, this liberalism has infected the church and the church's "liberal" theologians who opposed top-down thinking (for example, the imposition on the church of neo-scholasticism and its ultramontane ecclesiology).

[107] Luis Martín, "On Some Dangers of Our Times," in *Select Letters of Our Very Reverend Fathers General to the Fathers and Brothers of the Society of Jesus* (Woodstock, MD: Woodstock College, 1900), 501–46, here pars. 7–8.

[108] Ibid., par. 10.

[109] Ibid., par. 21.

[110] Ibid., pars. 24, 25.

[111] Friedrich von Hügel, *Selected Letters, 1896–1924*, ed. with memoir by Bernard Holland (London: J. M. Dent & Sons, 1927), 247–249.

[112] See John W. O'Malley, *The First Jesuits* (Cambridge, MA: Harvard University Press, 1993), 6, 32, 35, 73, 298–301, 353–355.

[113] See Schultenover, *A View from Rome*, 165–66, 217 n. 3, 218 nn. 7, 8.

[114] Schultenover, *A View from Rome*, 17–61.

[115] *Memorias*, fols. 2656r–2670v.

[116] *Memorias*, fols. 2691r.

[117] See John D. Root, "The Final Apostasy of St. George Jackson Mivart," *Catholic Historical Reivew* 71 (January, 1985): 1–25.

[118] See Schultenover, *A View from Rome*, 74–83.

[119] Schultenover, *A View from Rome*, 83–158; 154, n. 48. On Martín's problems with the Bollandists, see *Memorias*, fols. 2671r–2692v. On Tyrrell, Martín, and the Mivart affair, see Schultenover, *George Tyrrell*, 48–112, esp. 99–108, and *A View from Rome*, 131–158.

[120] Schultenover, *A View from Rome*, 133–158.

[121] See Sanz, "Introduction," *Memorias* 2:xlviii–xlix, 548 ff.

[122] Martín covers this matter at great length in *Memorias* 2:521–674.

Index